Baden

BADENS
IN AMERICA

Compiled by

Betty J. Carson
DAR Member #832584

HERITAGE BOOKS
2014

HERITAGE BOOKS

AN IMPRINT OF HERITAGE BOOKS, INC.

Books, CDs, and more—Worldwide

For our listing of thousands of titles see our website
at
www.HeritageBooks.com

Published 2014 by
HERITAGE BOOKS, INC.
Publishing Division
5810 Ruatan Street
Berwyn Heights, Md. 20740

Copyright © 2014 Betty Jewell Durbin Carson

Heritage Books by the author:

Durbin and Logsdon Genealogy with Related Families, 1626–1991

The Durbin and Logsdon Genealogy with Related Families, 1626–1991, Volume 2

Durbin and Logsdon Genealogy with Related Families, 1626–1994

Durbin and Logsdon Genealogy with Related Families, 1626–1998

Durbin-Logsdon Genealogy and Related Families from Maryland to Kentucky, Volumes 1–2

CD: The Durbin and Logsdon Genealogy with Related Families, 1626–2000, 3rd Revised Edition

Our Ewing Heritage, with Related Families, Part One and Two, Revised Edition
Betty Jewell Durbin Carson and Doris M. Durbin Wooley

CD: Our Ewing Heritage, with Related Families, Revised Edition
Betty Jewell Durbin Carson and Doris M. Durbin Wooley

International Standard Book Numbers
Paperbound: 978-0-7884-5578-0
Clothbound: 978-0-7884-6028-9

Baden

Baden Coat of Arms

The Baden Coat of Arms displayed here is the English version. Spelling variations of this family name include: Batten, Batlin, Battyne, Batin, Batton, and many more.

It was first found in Somerset, England, where they had been granted lands after the Norman Conquest in 1066, by William the Conqueror, for their assistance at the Battle of Hastings.

The Norman people became established in England after the Norman Conquest of 1066. The Normans, or Northmen, were descendants of the Vikings. The Vikings, under Chief Stirgud the Stout, invaded the Orkneys and Northern Scotland in the 9th century.

The Britons, who were one of the ancient races that inhabited medieval England, were subject to Roman invasions since the 1st century BC, when Julius Caesar sent expeditions to the island. Under Claudius, in 43 AD, the Romans invaded England once again and established the Roman province of Britannia. The Romans occupied England for approximately four centuries. They used the Britons in their military enterprises abroad and most of those who remained in Britain were reduced to slavery.

The Cornish people, who inhabited the southwest of England, have a rich Celtic heritage. Cornwall (pronounced /ˈkɔrnwɔːl/, Cornish: *Kernow* [ˈkɛrnɔʊ]) is a county of England in the United Kingdom, forming the tip of the south-western peninsula of Great Britain. It is bordered to the north and west by the Atlantic Ocean, to the south by the English Channel, and to the east by the county of Devon, over the River Tamar. Taken with the Isles of Scilly Cornwall has a population of 534,300, and covers an area of 3,563 km^2 (1,376 sq mi). The administrative centre and only city is Truro.

The area now known as Cornwall was first inhabited in the Palaeolithic and Mesolithic periods. It continued to be occupied by Neolithic and then Bronze Age peoples, and later (in the Iron Age) by Celts. There is little evidence that Roman rule was effective west of Exeter and few Roman remains have been found. Cornwall was afterwards part of the Brythonic (Celtic) area of Dumnonia, separated from Wales after the Battle of Deorham, often coming into conflict with the expanding English kingdom of Wessex before King Athelstan in 936 AD set the boundary between English and Cornish people at the Tamar. Today, Cornwall's economy struggles after the decline of the mining and fishing industries, and has become more dependent on tourism: however some decline in this has also occurred. The area is noted for its wild moorland landscapes, its extensive and varied coastline and its mild climate.

Cornwall is recognized as one of the "Celtic nations" by many Cornish people, residents and organizations. It retains a distinct cultural identity, reflecting its history, and modern use of the formerly extinct Cornish language is increasing.

HISTORY OF MARYLAND

Maryland was so called in honor of Henrietta Maria, Queen of Charles I, in his patent to Lord Baltimore, on June 30, 1632.

Maryland, one of the eastern states of the United States. Maryland is bordered by Pennsylvania on the north, Delaware and the Atlantic Ocean on the east, Virginia on the south, and West Virginia on the southwest and west. Washington, D.C., the national capital, is an enclave along the Virginia border. The Potomac River forms most of Maryland's western boundary and the Chesapeake Bay deeply indents the eastern part of the state. Annapolis is the state capital and Baltimore is the largest city.

The Maryland colony was founded in 1634 and was named for the wife of English King Charles I, Queen Henrietta Maria. Colonial Maryland attracted many settlers and, as its economy prospered, so did its social, political, and cultural life. Maryland entered the Union on April 28, 1788, as the 7th of the original 13 states.

In 1629, George Calvert, 1st Lord Baltimore in the Irish House of Lords, fresh from his failure further north with Newfoundland's Avalon colony, applied to Charles I for a new royal charter for what was to become the Province of Maryland. Calvert's interest in creating a colony derived from his Catholicism and his desire for the creation of a haven for Catholics in the new world. In addition, he was familiar with the fortunes that had been made in tobacco in Virginia, and hoped to recoup some of the financial losses he had sustained in his earlier colonial venture in Newfoundland. George Calvert died in April 1632, but a charter for "Maryland Colony" (in Latin, "Terra Maria") was granted to his son, Cæcilius Calvert, 2nd Lord Baltimore, on June 20, 1632. The new colony was named in honor of Henrietta Maria, Queen Consort of Charles I. The specific name given in the charter was phrased "Terra Mariae, *anglice*, Maryland". The English name was preferred over the Latin due in part to the undesired association of "Mariae" with the Spanish Jesuit Juan de Mariana. Leonard, Cæcilius' younger brother, was put in charge of the expedition because Cæcilius did not want to go.

To try to gain settlers, Maryland used what is known as the headright system, which originated in Jamestown. The government awarded land to people who transported colonists to Maryland.

On March 25, 1634, Lord Baltimore sent the first settlers into this area. Although most of the settlers were Protestants, Maryland soon became one of the few regions in the British Empire where Catholics held the highest positions of political authority. Maryland was also one of the key destinations of tens of thousands of British convicts. The Maryland Toleration Act of 1649 was one of the first laws that explicitly dictated religious tolerance, though toleration was limited to Trinitarian Christians.

The royal charter granted Maryland the land north of the entire length of the Potomac River up to the 40th parallel. A problem arose when Charles II granted a charter for Pennsylvania. The grant defined Pennsylvania's southern border as identical to Maryland's northern border, the 40th parallel. But the terms of the grant clearly indicate that Charles II and William Penn assumed the 40th parallel would pass close to New Castle, Delaware when in fact it falls north of Philadelphia, the site of which Penn had already selected for his colony's capital city. Negotiations ensued after the problem was discovered in 1681. A compromise proposed by Charles II in 1682, which might have resolved the issue, was undermined by Penn receiving the additional grant of what is now Delaware—which previously had been part of Maryland.[39] The dispute remained unresolved for nearly a century, carried on by the descendants of William Penn and Lord Baltimore—the Calvert family, which controlled Maryland, and the Penn family, which controlled Pennsylvania. The conflict led to the Cresap's War (also known as the Conojocular War), a border conflict between Pennsylvania and Maryland, fought in the 1730s. Hostilities erupted in 1730 with a series of violent incidents prompted by disputes over property rights and law enforcement, and escalated through the first half of the decade, culminating in the deployment of military forces by Maryland in 1736 and by Pennsylvania in 1737. The armed phase of the conflict ended in May 1738 with the intervention of King George II, who compelled the negotiation of a cease-fire. A provisional agreement had been established in 1732. Negotiations continuing until a final agreement was signed in 1760. The agreement defined Maryland's border with what is now Delaware as well as Pennsylvania. The border between Maryland and Pennsylvania was defined as the line of latitude fifteen miles south of the southernmost house of Philadelphia, a line now known as the Mason-Dixon Line. Maryland's border with Delaware was based on a Transpeninsular Line and the Twelve-Mile Circle around New Castle. After Virginia made the practice of Anglicanism mandatory, a large number of Puritans migrated from Virginia to Maryland, and were given land for a settlement called Providence (now Annapolis). In 1650, the Puritans revolted against the proprietary government and set up a new government that outlawed both Catholicism and Anglicanism. In March 1654, the 2nd Lord Baltimore sent an army under the command of Governor William Stone to put down the revolt. His Roman Catholic army was decisively defeated by a Puritan army near Annapolis in what was to be known as the "Battle of the Severn".

The Puritan revolt lasted until 1658. In that year the Calvert family regained control of the colony and re-enacted the Toleration Act. However, after England's "Glorious Revolution" of 1688, when William of Orange and his wife Mary came to the throne and firmly established the Protestant faith in England, Catholicism was again outlawed in Maryland, until after the American Revolutionary War. Many wealthy plantation owners built chapels on their land so they could practice their Catholicism in relative secrecy. During the persecution of Maryland Catholics by the Puritan revolutionary government, all of the original Catholic churches of southern Maryland were burned down.

St. Mary's City was the largest site of the original Maryland colony, and was the seat of the colonial government until 1708. St. Mary's is now a historical site, with a small tourist center. In 1708, the seat of government was moved to Providence, which had been renamed Annapolis. The city was renamed in honor of Queen Anne in 1694.

Most of the English colonists arrived in Maryland as indentured servants, hiring themselves out as laborers for a fixed period to pay for their passage. In the early years the line between indentured servants and African slaves or laborers was fluid. Some Africans were allowed to earn their freedom before slavery became a lifelong status. Most of the free colored families formed in Maryland before the Revolution were descended from relationships or marriages between servant or free white women and enslaved, servant or free African or African-American men. Many such families migrated to Delaware, where land was cheaper. As the flow of indentured laborers to the colony decreased with improving economic conditions in England, more slaves were imported. The economy's growth and prosperity was based on slave labor, devoted first to the production of tobacco.

An artist's rendering of the bombardment of Fort McHenry in Baltimore, which inspired the composition of the Star Spangled Banner.

Maryland was one of the thirteen colonies that revolted against British rule in the American Revolution. On February 2, 1781, Maryland became the 13th state to approve the ratification of the Articles of Confederation which brought into being the United States as a united, sovereign and national state. It also became the seventh state admitted to the U.S. after ratifying the new Constitution. The following year, in December 1790, Maryland ceded land selected by President George Washington to the federal government for the creation of Washington, D.C. The land was provided from Montgomery and Prince George's Counties, as well as from Fairfax County and Alexandria in Virginia (though the lands from Virginia were later returned through retrocession). The land provided to Washington, D.C. is actually "sitting" inside the state of Maryland (land that is now defunct in theory).

During the War of 1812, the British military attempted to capture the port of Baltimore, which was protected by Fort McHenry. It was during this bombardment that the Star Spangled Banner was written by Francis Scott Key.

As in Virginia and Delaware, numerous planters in Maryland had freed their slaves in the twenty years after the Revolutionary War. By 1860 Maryland's free black population comprised 49.1% of the total of African Americans in the state. In addition, Governor Thomas Holliday Hicks temporarily suspended the legislature, and President Abraham Lincoln had many of its fire eaters arrested prior to its reconvening. Many historians contend that there would never have been sufficient votes for secession.

Of the 115,000 men who joined the militaries during the Civil War, 85,000, or 77%, joined the Union army. To help ensure Maryland's inclusion in the Union, President Lincoln suspended several civil liberties, including the writ of *habeas corpus*, an act deemed illegal by Maryland native Chief Justice Roger Taney. Lincoln ordered U.S. troops to place artillery on Federal Hill to threaten the city of Baltimore, and helped ensure the election of a new pro-union governor and legislature. Lincoln went so far as to jail certain pro-South members of the state legislature at Fort McHenry, including the Mayor of Baltimore, George William Brown. The grandson of Francis Scott Key was included in those jailed. The constitutionality of these actions is still debated.

Because Maryland remained in the Union, it was exempted from the anti-slavery provisions of the Emancipation Proclamation (The Emancipation Proclamation only applied to states in rebellion). In 1864 the state held a constitutional convention that culminated in the passage of a new state constitution. Article 24 of that document outlawed the practice of slavery. In 1867 the state extended suffrage to non-white males.

Maryland has no official nickname. However, the most commonly accepted name, and also one of the oldest, is the Old Line State. This nickname honors the memory of Maryland's regiments of the line, which fought with distinction in the American Revolution (1775-1783). The official state website is **http://www.maryland.gov/**.

A significant point in Maryland's history was the passage of the Act of Toleration in 1649, which encouraged settlement by many non-conformists, not only Catholics (in Calvert, Charles, and St. Mary's Counties) but also dissenters from Virginia (in Anne Arundel County) and Friends (Quakers). The Protestant Revolution in England, however, spread unrest to Maryland, and the proprietary government was overthrown by the Crown in 1689. The Anglican church was established as the state church of Maryland, and the capital moved to a more central location at Annapolis. With the conversion of the young Lord Baltimore to Protestantism, the proprietorship was restored in 1715. In 1781 Catholics were disfranchised and barred from public office, but Jesuit Fathers continued to quietly serve a growing Catholic populace despite laws forbidding them to celebrate the Mass or perform the sacraments. A number of early Maryland gentry unions occurred through Catholic-Protestant marriages.

The earliest settlements congregated in southern Maryland, on the Western Shore, in Anne Arundel, Calvert, Charles, and St. Mary's Counties. By 1695, this included Prince George's

County, which until 1748 stretched from Pennsylvania to Virginia. Virginia fur traders had settled at Kent Island prior to Calvert's immigrants' arrival in 1634. On Maryland's Eastern Shore, Somerset County bordered Virginia, from which colony came the first settlers, soon joined by emigrants from St. Mary's and new arrivals from Britain. By the 1680s Baltimore County, along the waterways of the Patapsco and Gunpowder rivers, was seated. Because of an uncertain border, evidence of many settlers in western Kent and southern and western Sussex Counties in Delaware are found in Maryland records until the time of the Revolutionary War.

In the eighteenth century settlers left the Chesapeake region and began building homes among the hills and valleys of western Maryland. Beginning in the 1730s, Germans from bordering Pennsylvania counties poured into what were then Baltimore and Frederick Counties; some Quaker groups came about this time from New Jersey. In the mid-1700s many settlers came from Pennsylvania, and servants, felons, and Jacobite rebels numbered heavily among the eighteenth-century emigrants from Britain, with the Jacobites sold as laborers. Migrations out of Maryland in the eighteenth century included Catholics from St. Mary's into Kentucky, and Moravians, most of whom went to Winston-Salem, North Carolina, in the 1760s to obtain free land. Other Germans, Ulster-Scots, and Quakers went south to Virginia and the Carolinas. With the completion of the National Road in 1818, migration westward through and out of Maryland was greatly increased. The building of the country's first railroad, the Baltimore and Ohio, as well as a canal system along the Potomac River, also increased mobility within and out of the state.

Although British warships visited the Chesapeake in 1777, and there was a sizable number of Loyalists among the populace, no major battles were fought in Maryland during the American Revolution. The state was, however, the site for much action during the War of 1812. Although loyal to the Union during the Civil War, there was much sympathy for the South in southern Western Shore counties and among the upper classes, and many fought for the Confederacy. After the war, many black Southerners fled to Maryland from their devastated homes. About this same time began a large influx of Germans and eastern Europeans through Baltimore, one of the major eastern ports.

Slavery in Maryland

Slaves were different from indentured servants because they had to work for life. They were considered property by the people who owned them. They could be bought or sold, and had no control over their lives. Many slaves were Africans, but not all people of color in the colony were enslaved. Some came to Maryland as indentured servants and worked under exactly the same conditions as white indentured servants.

There is evidence of slavery in Maryland as early as 1638. In 1642, Leonard Calvert offered to sell some land for "fourteene negro men slaves & three women slaves, of betweene 16 and 26 yeare old." We don't know if those people ever really came to Maryland. There were also several court cases in the 17th century that involved slavery in St. Mary's County. In one case in 1658, a plantation owner, Simon Overzee, was accused of killing one of his slaves. The slave, Antonio, had refused to work or learn English. Overzee punished him. Slave masters had the right under the law to punish slaves who would not work. Antonio was punished then left alone. When Overzee came back, Antonio was dead. Master Overzee was brought to court for murder, but was found innocent. No one could prove that he had punished Antonio more than he was allowed.

In another case, in 1676, a black indentured servant named Thomas Hagleton brought a case to court against his master, Major Thomas Truman. Major Truman was trying to hold him as a slave. He refused to let his servant go when his indenture was finished. Hagleton brought witnesses to court that proved he had come to Maryland as an indentured servant. He won his case and was set free by his master.

For most of the 17th century, few people owned slaves. Slaves were expensive to import. Most planters did not have enough money to spend so much on a worker. Only the wealthiest men could afford slaves. By the end of the century, many people had begun turning to slave labor because they could not get indentured servants to come from England. By the end of the 17th century, most people bound to work on plantations in St. Mary's County were enslaved.

The first enslaved people to Maryland did not arrive directly from Africa. Instead, they came from the Caribbean Islands where some of them had worked for many years. Sometimes this meant that they were already used to the climate in the New World. There was less chance that they would get sick in Maryland and die. Many of these slaves also spoke English, which made it easier to communicate with them. Some had experience working in fields and growing crops.

Eventually, planters needed more workers than what they could get from the Caribbean. Maryland planters began to bring laborers directly from Africa. These people were stolen from their homes and sold into slavery. They were forced to come to a land that they knew nothing about. Their first challenge was to survive the journey to the New World. The trip became known as the "middle passage." Hundreds of people did not survive it. Sometimes hundreds of people were crowded aboard ships and chained below deck for the entire journey. There was little light or fresh air. The conditions were very bad.

Adapting to the New World

In the village that Wannas spoke of lived a tribe of Indians called the Yaocomaco. The Yaocomaco were a peaceful tribe of farmers and hunters. They were living on both sides of a river that the English named the St. George's River (now known as the St. Mary's River). The natives on one side of the river were moving to be closer to the rest of their tribe. It is possible that they were being attacked by another tribe of Indians called the Susquehannocks. These natives were a war-like tribe that attacked other people in the area.

Whatever the Yaocomaco's reason for leaving, it was lucky for the English colonists. They were allowed to move into some of the Indian houses and live there until they could build their own homes. Some Yaocomaco stayed in the village, but they agreed that they would move within the first year. The colonists built a fort for protection. The Yaocomaco seemed to be very friendly, but they did not know whom else they might find in this new area. They were afraid of the Spanish, as well as other Indian tribes. The colonists soon learned that they were safe in their new home and moved out of the fort.

What did the colonists need to learn about planting in Maryland?
The colonists were also very lucky because they could use fields that the natives had been planting. This made it possible to grow food crops in time for their first winter in the New World. The natives taught the English how to farm and what sort of plants to grow in the new colony. The English learned about corn, which would become their most important food crop. The colonists had never seen a crop that could grow so much food from so few plants. They were used to growing plants like wheat and barley, but they learned that these were not good crops to grow in Maryland.

To grow this new type of food, the colonists had to learn a new way to plant their crops. In England, farmers used plows pulled by oxen or horses to get fields ready for planting. The colonists quickly learned, though, that plows would not work well in Maryland. There were too many large trees with huge roots under the ground. The plow blades would break when they hit the roots. It would have taken a very long time to cut down the trees and pull out the roots. Instead, the natives taught the colonists to plant around the trees. They taught the colonists to girdle the trees by cutting a strip of bark off around the trunk of the tree. The tree's leaves would fall off and the tree would die. As soon as the leaves were gone, the sun could reach anything planted around the tree. The natives taught the colonists to pile up dirt into small hills and plant seeds in those hills. That way, the corn's roots were above any large roots left by the trees. This also made it much easier to weed around the plants. The colonists learned to grow their corn in this way, but also learned about another very important plant – tobacco.

When Lord Baltimore sent the first colonists to Maryland, he thought that they might make their livings trapping animals for their furs. He hoped that his colonists would send beaver furs back to England. Beaver was very popular because the fur was perfect for making warm, waterproof hats. The colonists could not make enough money in this fur trade. Instead, the Maryland colonists started growing tobacco.

The first person to bring tobacco back to Europe was Christopher Columbus. He discovered the Indians in South America growing and smoking a plant that he had never seen before. He took this plant back to Europe and it became very popular. Many things from the New World like coffee and chocolate were popular, but none more so than tobacco. In fact, people in the 17th century used tobacco as a medicine. They believed that it was good for treating coughs and colds and toothaches. It would be a long time before people learned how dangerous tobacco smoke could be.

The colonists had many difficult problems to deal with in the New World. They had moved to a brand new environment. There were many diseases in the New World that they had never had before. Many colonists got sick with what they called the seasoning. The seasoning was a combination of many diseases including malaria. Malaria was especially difficult because it made people very weak and tired. Many settlers, perhaps one out of every three people in the first year, died in the colony from the seasoning. Life would prove to be very difficult for the settlers to Maryland.

The Founding of a Colony

The history of Maryland actually began in England over 350 years ago. England in the 1600s could be a terrible place to live. Many people lived in large cities like London, which could be very dangerous. Cities were overcrowded and many people could not find jobs. These cities were often very dirty and disease spread very quickly. Poor people had very little chance of making a better life for themselves. Wealthier people owned land in the country. For the most part, if your family did not own land when you were born, you would probably never own land, either.

Even some people who did not live in the cities had a difficult life in England in the 17th century. According to the law, all people in England had to be members of the King's church, called the Church of England. The laws said that people who did not belong to this church could be fined, could not vote, and could not hold any position in the government. Because of the poor conditions and unfair laws, many people were looking for a better way of life. Some eventually decided to look for it across the Atlantic Ocean in the New World.

Who was George Calvert?

George Calvert was born in 1580 to a wealthy family in Yorkshire, England. He attended Oxford University and became an important member of the English government. Calvert was a Secretary of State for King James I, which meant that he helped the King to make some of his most important decisions. He was very good at his job. In appreciation, the King gave him a large amount of land in Ireland and named him the Baron of Baltimore, or Lord Baltimore. Then, in 1625, Calvert announced that he was becoming a Catholic. By deciding to attend the Catholic Church, he could no longer be a member of the government. Instead, like many others, he decided to try to make a better life for himself in the New World.

Avalon

". . . from the middest of October to the middest of May there is a sad face of winter upon all this land."

- George Calvert to the King of England, 1628. Avalon was the colony founded by George Calvert in 1621. It was on the coast of Newfoundland in what is now Canada. He sent twelve settlers with Governor Edward Wynne in 1621. Calvert hoped that his colonists would make a good living catching fish from the Atlantic Ocean. He thought that they could trade these fish with other colonies and with England.

Governor Wynne wrote to Lord Baltimore to tell him how much progress they had made in their new land. When Lord Baltimore moved there with his family in 1628, he was surprised at the severe weather. It was cold and dark for much of the year. Many people got very sick at Avalon. Lord Baltimore wrote the King about living at Avalon. The quote above comes from a letter that Lord Baltimore wrote to the King. It was in this letter that Lord Baltimore asked for land further south to start another colony. That colony eventually became Maryland.

Archaeologists are working now to learn more about the settlement at Avalon. They have found the remains of the house that George Calvert and his family lived in when they moved to Avalon.

They have also found a cobblestone road from the 17th century and a blacksmith's shop where metal items were made. There is now a museum called The Colony of Avalon that is dedicated to teaching people about Newfoundland's history and the story of Lord Baltimore's first colony.

George Calvert had been interested in starting a colony in the New World for some time. He had invested money in the colonies of Virginia and Massachusetts. Calvert had also asked the King for permission to start a colony in Newfoundland, which is now in Canada. He purchased land there and in 1621, sent a group of settlers to the colony he called Avalon. Several years later, he and his family moved there. Calvert found that it was very cold in Avalon and decided that it was not a good place for his new colony. Instead, he sailed back to England to ask the King for land further south. On the way, he stopped in the colony of Virginia. He decided that the area around the Chesapeake Bay would be the best place for his new colony.

On March 27, 1625, King Charles I became the new king of England after his father, King James, died. In 1632, Lord Baltimore presented the new king with a charter. This document said that Lord Baltimore would become the owner of a large piece of land next to the colony of Virginia. He would be called the proprietor of this new colony, which meant that he would own all of the land. The charter also said that he would be allowed to make the laws in his new colony as long as the colonists agreed. The charter gave him permission to give land to anyone he chose and to raise an army to defend his colony.

Many people in England did not want to see Calvert get the land he was asking for because he was a Catholic. They tried to convince the King not to grant Calvert his request, but after a time, the King did grant the charter for the colony. Unfortunately, by the time the King made his decision, George Calvert had died. Instead, the charter was granted to his son. In 1632, George Calvert's oldest son, Cecilius, became the second Lord Baltimore and the first proprietor of Maryland.

How do you prepare for a new colony?
Cecilius began to make plans to settle his new colony. He decided to call the land Terra Maria, or Maryland, after the King's Catholic wife, Henrietta Maria. He knew he needed to find investors, or people to help him pay for the expense of starting the new colony. He found seventeen men who were interested in helping him start Maryland. Most of these men were Catholic, like Cecilius. Many of them went on the first voyage to Maryland and hoped to find riches there.

Cecilius also found members of a group of Catholic priests, called the Society of Jesus, or Jesuits, who were interested in going to Maryland. These priests hoped to convince more people, including the Indians in Maryland, to join the Catholic Church.

Cecilius also needed someone to be the leader of the new colony. He had realized that he would not be able to leave England and go to Maryland, himself. The people who did not want Lord Baltimore to receive his charter were still causing problems for him in England. Instead, Cecilius sent his younger brother, Leonard, to be the leader of the first journey and the first governor of Maryland.

What was the voyage to Maryland like?

In November 1633, about one hundred and forty passengers boarded a ship called the *Ark* at Cowes, England, and set sail for the New World. Of the colonists, seventeen were the gentlemen investors, four were with the Jesuits, and almost all of the rest were servants. These servants worked for the others.

Almost all of the servants were Protestants and members of the King's Church of England. There were very few women on the voyage and no families. There was at least one young boy. A ten year old boy named William Browne was a servant on the voyage.

Leonard Calvert and the other Catholic gentlemen had to be very careful on the voyage. They had to make sure that there were no problems about religion between themselves and their Protestant servants. To avoid any arguments, Lord Baltimore instructed the gentlemen to worship quietly and let the servants worship in any way that they wanted. This idea is called religious toleration.

The *Ark* was accompanied by a smaller ship called the *Dove* that was owned by the Calvert family and several of the investors. The smaller ship carried all of the supplies that the settlers would need when they got to their new home. Lord Baltimore wrote a list of supplies that he thought people would need to bring to the new colony. Once the settlers got to Maryland, the *Dove* would be used to explore the rivers in the area.

Not long after the ships left England, they sailed into a bad storm. The Ark became separated from the *Dove*. People on the *Ark* were afraid that the *Dove* had sunk with all of their supplies. The *Ark* had to go on with its journey and hope for the best. The journey took the ship down the coast of Africa then across the Atlantic Ocean to the Caribbean Islands. Once the *Ark* landed on the island of Barbados, the passengers had a great surprise. The *Dove* had survived the storm and come across the ocean with the supplies that they would need to start their new colony.

Although they were happy to find the *Dove* again, the passengers on the *Ark* had a very difficult journey from England to the New World. Along with the storms, there were long periods at sea with no wind to move the ship along. The passengers were always nervous about pirates that might try to take the ship. They also had to live in very cramped spaces and eat bad food. The settlers and sailors on board the *Ark* had to heat pots over wood fires to cook their food. If the ship was in rough weather, they could not cook because the fire from the hearth might get out of hand and burn the entire wooden ship. The passengers might go days without any hot food. The passengers also had to make sure that the food that they brought on board would last for the entire journey. Most food was dried or salted to ensure that it did not spoil.

The bread was baked for a long time until it was very, very hard. This kept the bread from getting moldy and also kept insects and mice from eating it. The bread would have to be soaked in soup or beer before it could be eaten. Passengers and sailors were always anxious for any opportunity to get fresh food.

Maryland: Catholic Colony?

Many people think of Maryland as a "Catholic colony," but only about twenty of the first 140 settlers to Maryland were Catholic. There were always more Protestants in Maryland than Catholics.

Why then is Maryland called a Catholic colony?
In the 17th century, people who belonged to the Catholic Church in England were not treated fairly. They had to pay fines for not attending the King's Church of England. They also could not vote or hold any positions in the government. It was against the law to be a Catholic in England. When George Calvert announced that he was becoming a Catholic, he decided to start a colony where Catholics would have the same rights as Protestants. He knew that he would not be able to convince the King to give him a colony where only Catholics would be allowed to live. It would also have been difficult to find enough people to settle a colony like that. Calvert needed to think of a way to protect Catholics in a place where people of different religions could live. He decided to build his new colony on the idea of religious toleration.

What is religious toleration?
Religious toleration is an idea that we still live by today in this country. It means that people of different religions can live in the United States and worship in whatever way they chose. No one can be punished for what they believe. Also, all people, no matter what their religion, can vote or can run for political office. Another important idea that is related to religious toleration is the separation of the church and the government. In England in the 17th century, the King said that he was the head of the government and of the church. People who were Catholic believed that the Pope was the head of their church. The King called this idea treason because he was afraid that it might take away from his power.

George Calvert knew that he had to be very careful about how he protected Catholics in his new colony. His son Cecilius also knew how important this was. When Cecilius sent the first colonists to Maryland in 1634, he gave the leaders instructions about religion. He told them that they should not try to convince any of the Protestants on board to join the Catholic Church. He also told them to worship very quietly on the voyage so that they did not upset the other passengers. They followed his instructions on the voyage and after they arrived in Maryland.

This idea of letting everyone worship quietly as they chose is the basis of the idea of religious toleration.

For a number of years, the people in Maryland lived by the instructions that Cecilius Calvert gave the first settlers. Unfortunately, this did not last for very long. After the colony was attacked by Protestants in 1645, Cecilius decided that Catholics who lived in Maryland needed more protection. He wrote a law that was passed by the Assembly in Maryland. The law, passed on April 21, 1649, was called "An Act concerning Religion." It said that any Christian could worship in Maryland. The law protected Catholics and Protestants, but did not include everyone. For example, people who are Jewish are not Christians, so they were not protected by the Act. In fact, the law said that people who did not believe certain things about God could be punished. A Jewish man named Jacob Lambruzo was brought to court because of that law.

Even though the Act did not apply to everyone, it helped people of different religions to live and work together peacefully. While there were wars being fought over religion in Europe, Catholics and Protestants were making laws, trading, and building a colony together in Maryland. The policy of religious toleration only lasted in Maryland for about sixty years. Nevertheless, it was a great accomplishment for Lord Baltimore and the colonists of Maryland.

Tobacco: The Stinking Sotweed

Almost everyone in the colony of Maryland in the 17th century lived on a plantation and raised tobacco. Any farm that raised tobacco was called a plantation. It could be very large, sometimes thousands of acres, or perhaps as small as fifty acres. There were very few people who did not make their living growing what the colonists called the "stinking sotweed" on their own or someone else's plantation. In fact, people in the 17th century thought that tobacco was good for their health. They used many herbs that they grew as medicines and considered tobacco just one more. Tobacco was used as a cure for coughs and colds. Also, fresh leaves were put on sore teeth to help stop the pain. Men, women, and even children used tobacco as a cure. There were a few people in the 17th century who did not like tobacco, including King James I, but most people paid little attention to their arguments.

Tobacco became the cash crop for Maryland. A cash crop is one that is grown to be sold. In fact, tobacco became so important in Maryland that it was used as money. Anything that was bought or sold in the colony was priced in pounds of tobacco. For instance, if you wanted to buy a cow, it might cost four hundred pounds of tobacco. You might have to pay about twenty pounds of tobacco for a new hat.

Tobacco took a lot of time and energy to grow. In fact, almost everyone might help with the tobacco crop, especially on a small plantation. Plantation owners who could afford help would bring indentured servants from England. An indentured servant was someone who worked for a plantation owner in Maryland in return for passage to the New World. The servant would have to work for about four years. During that time, he would get food, clothing, and a place to live, but he would have to do whatever his master asked of him. He could not marry or start a life of his own. After his indenture was finished, the servant received his freedom dues – one ax, two hoes, three barrels of corn, a new suit of clothes, and the rights to fifty acres of land. Although this land was free, the new owner could not start a plantation without money. He would have to pay to have the land mapped out and registered with the government. Coming to Maryland as an indentured servant was often the best opportunity to own land for many people who could not in England.

How do you grow tobacco?
Most servants coming to Maryland, especially men, were brought to help with the long, hard task of growing tobacco. The growing season started in February or March when the tiny tobacco seeds were planted in a small patch of ground called a seed bed. As the seeds began to grow, they would have to be watched very carefully. If it got too cold at night, the plants might die, so they had to be covered with pine branches to protect them. While the plants grew in seed beds, the fields were prepared. To clear new fields, large trees were girdled so that tobacco could be planted around them without having to cut them down. After the field was cleared, planters piled up the soil into small hills with a hoe. When the tobacco plants were large enough, they were transplanted into these hills. The plants would take the rest of the summer to grow.

As the tobacco grew in the fields, it would have to be checked quite often. Weeds that grew around the plants had to be pulled and sometimes plants might have to be watered if there was little rain. Most importantly, farmers had to make sure that tobacco worms did not eat their tobacco plants.

These worms fed on the leaves of the tobacco as it grew. The only way that farmers found to get rid of the worms was to go through the fields and pick them off the leaves, one at a time. With hundreds or even thousands of tobacco plants to check, this would take a great deal of time. If it was not done, the worms might eat all of the leaves, leaving the farmer with no money. A servant was expected to pick off every worm. If he missed a single one, the planter might make him bite off its head. The servant would surely try harder after that! Plants had to be watched all summer in the hot Chesapeake sun until they were ready to be harvested.

Late summer or fall was harvest time for the tobacco crop. The entire stalk of each tobacco plant was cut at the bottom and allowed to wilt in the fields for a few hours. Then, a hole was cut in each stalk so that it could be threaded onto a long stick, called a tobacco stake. Perhaps as many as six or eight stalks could be put on each stake. These stakes were then hung in tobacco barns to dry for six to ten weeks. Once they were dry, the plants were taken down and the leaves were stripped from the stalks. Planters made sure to do this on a rainy day so the leaves were not so dry that they would crumble and break. The leaves were bundled into "hands." A hand was a bunch of ten to twenty leaves wrapped together. These hands were packed into very large casks called hogsheads and readied for shipping. These hogsheads could hold between 300 and 500 pounds of tobacco, depending on how well they were packed.

Once the crop was grown and harvested, the only thing left to do was to trade it to England. Most plantations were located next to rivers or other waterways. These waterways were the easiest way to travel and to transport goods in the 17th century. Large ships coming from England anchored in the river and sent small boats to plantations up and down the coast. These boats delivered the goods that the plantation owners had ordered from England and picked up hogsheads of tobacco to be carried back to London. Planters would simply roll the hogsheads to the water's edge and onto the boats. Almost all of the goods that colonists bought with their tobacco were made in England and delivered on these ships.

What good was tobacco anyway?
Things made of metal, glass, and pottery, and finished pieces of furniture would be imported from England. Most people in the colonies did not have the skill to make all of these goods. Even if they did know how to make these items, they did not want to take the time. Tobacco was a very difficult crop to grow and took a great deal of time and energy, as we have seen. Tradesmen who came to Maryland usually discovered that they could make more money raising tobacco than practicing their trade. They often found that they would not have time to do both, so they gave up their trade and grew tobacco, instead.

The ships from England only came to Maryland once each year. They arrived in the fall as the tobacco crop was being harvested and stayed through the winter to finish all of their trading. In the spring, they sailed back to England with a load of tobacco. That meant that colonists in Maryland often had just one chance each year to get supplies from England. News of the rest of the world, or from family and friends back in England came on those ships, too. It also meant that anything that a planter ordered in the spring before the ships sailed for England might not be delivered until the next fall. There were some merchants, or shopkeepers, who might have supplies for sale if a family was in need of something, but planters would probably pay a very high price for these items. More likely, the family would simply do without until the fall.

Since tobacco was only harvested from the fields once a year, colonists could only pay for goods at that time. The rest of the year they had to work on credit. Credit means buy now, pay later, and is similar to our modern-day credit cards. A farmer would buy the things that he needed and then promise to pay for them when his tobacco crop was harvested for the year. He might even sign something called a promissory note to prove that he would pay his debt. If there was a drought or the tobacco crop was ruined one year, the farmer could have a very difficult time paying all the people that he owed. Colonists were quite often in court trying to get the tobacco that they were owed by their neighbors.

Life on a 17th-Century Plantation

Let's imagine that suddenly you were transported back to the year 1661. Colonists have been in Maryland for almost 30 years. What would your life have been like if you lived in Maryland 350 years ago? It probably would have been very difficult. Let's imagine your typical day: You wake up with the sunrise, for there is much to do today. You sleep upstairs in the loft of your father's house with all of your brothers and sisters. You also share the space with the indentured servants that are working for your father. One servant has only a few months left on his indenture. He will leave the plantation soon. He hopes to start his own farm. Your father will surely want to bring another indentured servant from England to replace him. Your parents want to have as many people as possible on the plantation to help with all the work there is to be done.

Your house is like many others in the area. The frame is made of large wooden posts sunk into the ground. The outside is covered with long split pieces of wood called clapboard. Inside, there is only one room on the main floor. This is where your parents and youngest brothers and sisters sleep. It is also where the cooking is done and where your family eats. The girls of the house often do their chores here, as well. Upstairs, there are two large rooms, one for the girls and female servants and the other for the boys and male servants. There is almost no furniture in these rooms and not a great deal downstairs, either. Father says that you are lucky for all that you have because most of the furniture had to be imported from England at great expense. He also points out the glass windows and wooden floor that many of your poorer neighbors can not afford. You hope that someday your own home will be so nice.

You have slept in your shift, or long shirt, as usual, and put on your outer clothes before going downstairs. Your first chore every day is to beat out the bed tick that you use as a mattress. The straw and cornhusks on the inside get very dusty and provide the perfect place for unwanted bugs to live. You will have to ask your mother to put more herbs in the tick to keep away the bed bugs. She says that she has several plants in her garden that will do the trick. Mother then shoos everyone away to their morning chores before breakfast. She has to start the fire and begin the cooking for the day. Father takes the boys and male servants out to clean out the cow barn and then bring in firewood for the day's cooking. The youngest boys can't bring in the heaviest wood, but they can still collect kindling, or small sticks, for starting fires. They also take wooden buckets down to the nearby stream to fetch fresh water.

Meanwhile, the girls head out to let the chickens out of their coop and collect the eggs that were laid overnight. After that, they go to milk the cows and cool the milk for use later. The cows are nearby, but not in fences. They are allowed to roam freely through the woods so that they can search for food. There are fences around all the fields and the garden so that the cows and pigs do not go where they do not belong.

Father explains that by letting the animals run wild, food does not have to be grown for them. That land, instead, can be used to grow more tobacco. That is just one of the things that father had to get used to in this New World.

Soon, it is time for the morning meal. Mother has made cold corn mush again this morning. You are thankful that your family can afford a bit of sugar and cream to sweeten the mush. Mother reminds those who complain that many families can not afford such luxuries. You have corn with almost every meal. Father says that Englishmen did not even know what corn was before they came to Maryland. In England, he grew wheat, barley, and other grains in his fields. Once he arrived in Maryland, though, he had to learn to grow corn instead. The old grains do not grow nearly so well in his new home. Your whole family and all your father's servants eat together. Everyone hurries to finish their meal to get to the rest of the chores for the day.

Once the meal has been finished, mother and the girls wash the dishes and put them away. Then, they must begin to prepare for the next meal. It can take an entire morning to cook a large enough meal for your whole family. As the meal cooks, some of the girls churn the milk into butter. Others must grind corn into flour for cooking. Many say that corn grinding is the worst job on the plantation. Each person on the plantation eats between two and four cups of corn everyday and it can take up to ten minutes to grind each cup. On many plantations, there can be as many as ten people to feed. That means it takes hours to grind corn every day. You will probably have to take your turn at the grinding, as well.

As the women start their chores, father and the other men and boys go out to the fields to take care of the tobacco. At many times of the year, the men spend almost the whole day in the tobacco fields. It is very hard work, especially in the summertime. Even boys as young as five or six work with the men in the fields. These boys help with the chores, but also are taking this time to learn how to farm in Maryland. Father says that farmers here have learned much since arriving in the colony. Every generation makes improvements and grows more and more tobacco every year.

The youngest babies in the house do not have much work expected of them, but by the time you are two or three you have chores to do. The youngest children stay close to the house where mother and the older girls can look after them. They collect small pieces of kindling for the fire and collect eggs from the chickens. They also watch the chickens to make sure that they do not get into the garden or into any food that is being stored or dried. They may even help with weeding the garden or grinding the corn.

When the sun gets to be its highest in the sky, it is time for the mid-day meal. This is always the largest meal of the day. Mother and the other women have been cooking all morning. The meal today is a pottage, or thick stew, made of meat from animals on the plantation and vegetables grown in the garden. Mother says that the easiest way to feed all the people in the house is to cook what she calls a one-pot meal. She takes whatever vegetables are in season and whatever meat she happens to have on hand and puts them in one pot to cook slowly over the fire all day. She has also taken some herbs that she grows in the garden and has put them in the pot for flavor. Sometimes, when the meat on hand is starting to get old, this is especially important. With the pottage, the ladies have prepared a green sallet (salad). Often, mother will use any vegetables that do not go into the pottage to make something to eat with the stew. In the spring and summer, greens like spinach, kale, lettuce, and collards are often made into a simple salad. The final part of the meal is the same everyday – some type of bread made from corn. Today, mother has made corn cakes by mixing corn flour and water, making it into patties, and frying them in a long-legged skillet. Just when you think that is all that you have to eat, though, you discover that mother has a surprise for you. The apples have just begun to ripen, so she has made your favorite, apple tart. It is very similar to the pies that she makes of spinach and meat, but this one is very sweet and has imported spices like cinnamon and cloves. You know you will probably not have another treat like this for some time, so you enjoy every bit, spooning the last of it off your wooden trencher, or plate.

You can't sit and enjoy this meal for long, though, as there is still work to do before the sun goes down. Father and the men and boys head right back out into the tobacco fields where they were this morning. The only time that they do not spend their days in the fields is in the winter after the crop has been harvested. Even then there is much work to do. Repairs are made to the house and the fences and woodworking projects can be completed. There also may be some time for hunting and fishing in these months. Almost all of the meat that you eat is raised on the plantation, but there are plenty of deer in the woods that can be caught from time to time. Father says that he never had deer until he came to Maryland. In England, he says, all the deer belong to the King. Only royalty could eat deer in England. Even though there are many deer here, there is often very little time to hunt them. Time is much better spent in the fields growing tobacco.

After mother and the girls finish cleaning up the mid-day meal, they might spend the afternoon in the garden. When the sun begins to set, it is a bit cooler to work outside. It is very important that the garden is well cared for. Most of the vegetables that will feed your family are grown there. Perhaps even more important, so are your medicines. Mother is very good at using the herbs that she grows in her garden to make simples. She says that her mother taught her how to take care of her family with these herbs. She has had much practice lately with your brother being so sick. Sometimes mother's herbs are not enough to help. You remember the servant that died last winter very well.

The girls have the cows to milk again and more milk to skim. Young children collect more firewood and several more buckets of water from the nearby stream. As it gets toward winter, the women will do more work inside the house like sewing and knitting. The women are also responsible for butchering the cows and pigs so they can be eaten. Some of the meat is soaked in salt so that it can be preserved for later use.

There will be time for a small supper in the evening, but it is mostly just the food that has been left from the mid-day meal. Unfortunately, there is no apple tart to be found. As the sun begins to set, chores from earlier in the day are completed and everyone comes back to the house for the night. The youngest children are put to bed first, while everyone else listens to father lead prayers or read from the Bible. Eventually, it is dark enough that everyone goes to sleep for the day. You sleep very well after everything you have accomplished on this busy day, knowing that tomorrow will bring more of the same.

As you begin to drift off to sleep, you look forward to Sunday. There is a little less work to do on the Lord's day. Some things though, like the cooking and gathering firewood and water, can not be forgotten on any day, even on Sunday. Perhaps you and your brothers and sisters might have a bit of time for fun on Sunday. Maybe you can play nine pins where you try to knock down pins with a wooden ball, or maybe quoits, a game trying to throw a ring of rope around a short wooden stake. You are very good at these and would love a chance to beat your older brother again. You usually don't get very much time to play these games because there is just too much work to be done. As you sleep, you dream of what your life will be like as you get older. Perhaps when you get to be as old as your father, you will own a plantation as prosperous as his. Maybe you will even be able to go into St. Mary's City as your father does to take care of his business dealings. As it is, you hardly ever see anyone except your family and the servants on your plantation. Your closest neighbor lives several miles away. Father tells stories, though, after he has been in town about all the exciting events there. He tells of court cases and other government business and of the news from the ships' masters. Maybe someday you will be able to go into town, yourself. For now, you will have to make do with your father's stories and your imagination.

The Changing Face of Tobacco

How were 18th-century plantations different from plantations in the 17th century?
In the 18th century, more and more people living in Maryland had been born there. People born in Maryland did not have to live through the new diseases of the seasoning like the people coming from England did. They were healthier and lived longer. They did not have to work as indentured servants because they did not need passage to Maryland. They could marry at a younger age. They had the chance to have more children. The children were healthier, too. More of the children lived to become adults and inherit land from their fathers. Often in the 17th century, when men died they had no children who were old enough to take over their farm. The father's land was sold to pay money that was owed. These children would have to wait until they got older to buy land to start a whole new plantation. It was much more difficult to be successful when you had to start from scratch.

In the 18th century, boys were more often old enough to take over the plantation when their father died. These boys did not have to buy their own land. They could add on to what their fathers had already built. Men who could inherit property became richer. As they did, they bought more land, and needed more people to work on it. Soon, there were not enough indentured servants to do all the work.

In the 17th century, planters imported almost all of the supplies that they needed from England. Eighteenth-century planters made some of their own goods. They did not have to rely as much on the ships to bring things from England. Some plantations had outbuildings, or extra buildings, that had particular purposes. Plantations had blacksmith shops where metal tools were made and repaired. Dairy houses were built to store milk and cheese. Smokehouses were also built for preserving meats for the winter. Some plantations even had spinning houses where wool was spun and woven into cloth. These plantations also often had their kitchen in a separate building. It was much safer to keep large cooking fires away from the main house.

The owners of the largest plantations became very wealthy men. They did not have to work in their fields because they had people working for them. Many of these men were also merchants, or traders. Some held positions in the government. This group of men became very powerful in Maryland. As they became wealthier, they bought even more land. It became more difficult for smaller planters to make a good living. This also made it difficult for indentured servants to be successful once they were done with their time.

Marylanders had always relied on indentured servants from England to work in their fields. At the end of the 17th century, fewer Englishmen were willing to come to Maryland as indentured servants. There were many reasons for this. There was not as much opportunity in Maryland for indentured servants after they were freed as there was at the beginning of the colony. The first indentured servants who came to Maryland had a very good chance of owning land once they got out of their indenture. There was a lot of good land and very few people to work it. The biggest challenge for these servants was living long enough to start their own plantations. As more people came to Maryland, the good land was being taken. People looking for good land at the end of the century had to travel north or west to find it. Also, they might have to work for several years as tenant farmers or hired servants to earn enough money to start their own plantations. Suddenly, risking the voyage across the ocean and working for a master for four long years did not sound like such a bargain.

At the same time, conditions in England were getting better for poor people. There were more jobs and higher pay. There were also fewer people living in England and competing for jobs. People had a better chance of success in England. The combination of fewer things "pulling" people to Maryland and fewer things "pushing" people out of England meant fewer indentured servants for Maryland's planters.

Instead, farmers in Maryland had to find another way to make sure that their crops were taken care of. They had to find a new source of labor. They found it in enslaved people brought from Africa.

Life on an 18th-Century Plantation

If you lived in the 18th century in Maryland, you would probably want to be the son or daughter of a wealthy plantation owner. You would have had many privileges that other children might not have. You would live in a large plantation home with your brothers and sisters. You might also have some servants or slaves living in the house with you. These people would be responsible for cooking, cleaning, and taking care of the house. Other slaves would have different jobs on the plantation.

Your father would own a large amount of land. You couldn't imagine sometimes how far his land stretches. You would not go to the edges of the plantation very often. Those are the areas where the tobacco is grown. Slaves work in the tobacco fields. Those slaves live in cabins near the fields where they work. Slaves might also work to take care of animals, or work as blacksmiths or carpenters.

Your father would have to travel beyond the plantation quite often. He might be a member of the Assembly, the group that makes laws for the colony. He also might have to go to court to help to decide how to punish people who have broken the law. Your father might be away quite a lot of the time. Your mother would stay home, though, to watch after the plantation and the children.

What would children do on the plantation?

You don't have to work outside. You have other things to keep you busy in the house. Some of the day is taken up with lessons. You might have a tutor to teach you or you might go to a small school with other children in the area. Boys learn to do math and to read many different languages, including Latin. Boys might also learn about navigation and science and about geography. They are taught everything that they will need to know to run a successful plantation of their own some day. Eventually, the boys might be sent to college, like the College of William and Mary in Virginia, where George Plater III and other colonial leaders went to school. They also might have the opportunity to go to England for more education. When they finished their education, these boys were expected to become leaders in the colonies like their fathers.

One game that was very popular throughout the colonial period in Maryland was a board game called nine man's morris. This game was played by adults and children. It is similar to playing tic tac toe. It is a very easy game to learn. You can even play at home. All you need is to draw a board on a piece of paper. Then, you need two players and nine markers for each player. The markers can be beans or stones, but just make sure that you can tell the difference between the two players' pieces.

The object of the game is to try to get three of your pieces in a row as many times as possible. Play starts with one player putting a piece on the board at a spot where two lines cross. The players take turns putting one piece on the board at a time. Both players try to get three of their pieces in a row while blocking their opponent from doing the same thing.

Every time that a player does get a line of three pieces, he gets to take one of his opponent's pieces off the board. This piece is then out of play for the rest of the game. Once both players have all nine of their pieces on the board, the players take turns moving their pieces, one space at a time, still trying to get three in a row. The game is over when one player has only two pieces left. The other player is the winner!

Girls learned very different things in the 18th century. They would be taught to read and write and to do simple math. Other than that, they learned how to be ladies. They would be taught to dance and to play musical instruments. They would also spend hours practicing their fine sewing skills. They would learn to embroider on small pieces of cloth called samplers. They would sew letters or patterns into the sampler to practice what they had learned. Eventually, girls would marry, probably to the sons of other wealthy landowners, and become the mistresses of their own houses.

When not working on your lessons, you might have some time for play. You might play with board games in the house. Outside, you might enjoy a game of nine pins, a type of lawn bowling, or rolling a hoop with your sisters and brothers to see who could go the fastest. The clothes you wear would look very much like the clothes that your parents wear. Girls would wear something called stays under their dress. Stays were pieces of bone sewn into cloth and laced up under the jacket, or bodice, of a dress. They made certain that girls stood up straight and tall. Boys would wear pants called breeches and long, heavy coats. Babies would wear lose-fitting dresses called frocks. On their head they might wear something called a pudding cap. A pudding cap padded the baby's head like a helmet in case they fell while learning to walk.

You might have several different outfits. Some would be special clothes that you would wear when your parents were entertaining guests. People would come to stay at your plantation. Sometimes, they would stay for quite a long time. For very special guests, your father might have a party or a large dinner. Some of your neighbors might come for this occasion, as well. You would lead a very comfortable life. Not everyone in 18th-century Maryland was so lucky. Most children did not live on a large plantation with slaves to work for them. There were children on small plantations that probably had to help with chores around the house and in the fields. There were also enslaved children. These children would have to work the rest of their lives for someone else and would never have any control over their situation.

Slavery in Colonial Maryland

What might life have been like for enslaved people in colonial Maryland?
The Africans that did survive to see Maryland were only beginning their struggles. Just like Englishmen coming to the New World, Africans suffered a form of the seasoning. They got diseases to which they had no immunity. It was even more difficult to fight these diseases because they were weak from their difficult journey.

Africans coming to Maryland often came from different tribes and did not speak the same language. They may have had different traditions and ways of life in Africa. Once they reached Maryland, groups of slaves were often sold to many different owners. Some small planters could not afford many laborers, so sometimes there were only a few slaves on each plantation. A new slave could easily find himself on a plantation where he could not understand or speak to anyone else.

Even on larger farms, groups of slaves were often divided up and sent to work in different fields. Family was very important to Africans coming to the New World. It was very difficult for enslaved people to keep family ties. In the beginning, there were very few women being brought from Africa to America. Even after more women did arrive, masters did not often encourage slave marriages. Families were often split up and sometimes sold and separated for life. Eventually, masters allowed slaves to marry and sometimes even to have their own family houses, but some members of families were still sold to other owners. It was particularly difficult if a master died and he owed other people money. Slaves might be sent to many different plantations to settle these debts. Slaves were not allowed to travel without a pass, or written permission from their master.

Sometimes, slaves would risk punishment to see members of their family on other plantations. Those who left the plantation without permission were called runaways. Historians now believe that almost half the runaways in Maryland were people trying to visit family on other plantations.

Perhaps the most difficult part of slavery for families was the fact that it was passed from parent to child. Any child of an enslaved woman was also a slave for life. It was very difficult for slaves to change their situation. There are a few cases of slaves working for their freedom. Others ran away and started lives in other areas. These cases were rare. Most enslaved people had to live everyday knowing that their lives and the lives of their children probably would not change.

There was some resistance to slavery. Running away was a form of resistance, but there were others. Some slaves would purposefully work very slowly. Sometimes they stole things from the plantation. Other times they might pretend that they were sick. All of these things would cost the plantation owner time and money.

Most enslaved people lived in poor conditions even on the largest and wealthiest plantations. They were given some food by the master, but had to grow extra on their own time. They may have been able to get some food from fishing, as well. The work for this food had to be done after the master's crops were taken care of. Slave houses were often small with little furniture. They were usually wood houses with dirt floors. These houses were often only one room and gave people very little privacy. They had little in the way of luxury items. Their clothing was often poor. It was made from cheap fabric with very little decoration. House slaves might sometimes get hand-me-downs from the master and his family.

How would life have changed from Africa to Maryland?
It was very difficult under these conditions for enslaved people to have any control over their

lives. It was also difficult for them to remember traditions that they brought with them from Africa. Sometimes, elders were unable to teach traditions to the children. Some traditions and even languages died out as the elders died. If there was only one or two people on a plantation from the same tribe, it could be very difficult for them to keep traditions alive. Even with all of this pressure, Africans managed to hold on to some of the customs from their homeland. Many traditions were changed and adapted to their situation in the New World.

Africans brought music with them from their homeland. They made instruments that looked like the ones that they knew. Some also learned to play English instruments. Slaves worked usually six days a week. They had only a small amount of time for leisure activities. They would often spend Sundays playing music and dancing. They might also have ceremonies like weddings on Sundays.

Historians do not know much about the religion of Africans in Maryland. They do think, though, that they brought some religious traditions with them. There were medicine men and other religious leaders who helped to heal people with herbs and other remedies. Archaeologists have also found objects that they think were used by the slaves in their religion. Sometimes archaeologists find stones or other material that have been made into different shapes. These were probably used as symbols in religious ceremonies.

Archaeologists have found other examples of African culture in Maryland. On a plantation near Baltimore, archaeologists found pewter spoons with a very interesting decoration. There is a tribe in Africa today that makes spoons with a design that is very similar to the ones that the archaeologists found. It is possible that the slaves living on that plantation came from that tribe. They remembered the designs from Africa and used them in Maryland. There have also been pipes with African influences found on sites in Maryland.

Eventually, African traditions were adapted and changed in the New World and became part of a new African-American culture. There is still much to learn about the experience of Africans in Maryland during colonial times. Most slaves were not allowed to learn to read or write English, so there are few written records of their lives. Archaeologists and historians will continue to look for clues about the lives of the enslaved people in colonial Maryland.

As the Revolutionary War began, many people began to look closely at the institution of slavery in the colonies. Some of the leaders of the Revolution were slave owners. Some thought that it was unfair for Englishmen to fight for their independence while Africans were held as slaves. Even with this opposition, it would take another hundred years for slavery to change in America.

Prince George County was created in **1696** (Chapter 13, acts of 1695) and was formed from **Charles** and **Calvert** Counties. The county was named for **Prince George of Denmark**, husband to Queen Anne I of Great Britain. The County Seat is **Upper Marlboro**.

Prince George's County, located on the state's western shore. Like other southern Maryland counties, tobacco has always been an important crop in Prince George's County. Upper Marlboro, the county seat since 1721, has always been a tobacco marketing center. During the eighteenth century, shallow draft boats carried hogsheads of tobacco from the town down Western Branch to the Patuxent River, where ocean-going vessels anchored. From 1748 until about 1818, all locally grown tobacco was inspected here at a public warehouse before shipment overseas.

The history of Prince George's County is reflected in the numerous historic houses and sites located in the county. A few of the historic houses to be seen in the county are Belair Mansion, the home of Samuel Ogle, who served three terms as provincial of Maryland, and his son Benjamin Ogle, governor of Maryland from 1798-1801; Montpelier, one of the famous five part houses in Maryland; and the Surratt House, where in March of 1865 John Surratt and fellow conspirators hid guns and ammunition as part of a plot to kidnap Lincoln. The county is also the home of the University of Maryland College Park campus, Goddard Space Flight Center, and Andrews Air Force Base. **See also County History for more historical details.**

Counties adjacent to Prince George's County are **Anne Arundel County** (east), **Calvert County** (southeast), **Charles County** (south), **Howard County** (north), **Montgomery County** (northwest), **Fairfax County, Virginia** (southwest), Alexandria, VA (southwest), Washington, DC (west).

Prince George's County **cities include** Bowie, College Park, District Heights, Glenarden, Greenbelt, Hyattsville, Laurel, Mount Rainier, New Carrollton, Seat Pleasant. **Towns include** Berwyn Heights, Bladensburg, Brentwood, Capitol Heights, Cheverly, Colmar Manor, Cottage City, Eagle Harbor, Edmonston, Fairmount Heights, Forest Heights, Landover Hills, Morningside, North Brentwood, Riverdale Park, University Park, Upper Marlboro. **Communities include** Aquasco, Ardmore, Avondale, Berwyn, Carole Highlands, Cedar Heights, Cheltenham, Green Meadow, Lewisdale, Montpelier, North College Park, North Englewood, Rogers Heights, South Bowie, Tuxedo, West Bowie, West Hyattsville. **Localities include** Chapel Oaks, Muirkirk. *(Unincorporated areas are also considered as towns by many people and listed in many collections of towns, but they lack local government.)*

Various organizations, such as the United States Census Bureau, the United States Postal Service, and local chambers of commerce, define the communities they wish to recognize differently, and since they are not incorporated, their boundaries have no official status outside the organizations in question. The Census Bureau recognizes the following census-designated places in the county: Accokeek, Adelphi, Andrews Air Force Base, Beltsville, Brandywine, Calverton, Camp Springs, Carmody Hills-Pepper Mill Village, Chillum, Clinton, Collington, Coral Hills, East Riverdale, Forestville, Fort Washington, Friendly, Glenn Dale, Goddard, Greater Landover, Greater Upper Marlboro, Hillandale, Hillcrest Heights, Kettering, Lake Arbor, Langley Park, Lanham-Seabrook, Largo, Marlow Heights, Marlton, Mitchellville, Oxon Hill-Glassmanor, Rosaryville, South Laurel, Springdale, Suitland-Silver Hill, Temple Hills, Walker Mill, West Laurel, Woodlawn, Woodmore.

Sir George Calvert, whose title was Lord Baltimore, was a Roman Catholic nobleman. Finding the laws against the Roman Catholics in England severe, he resolved to immigrate to Virginia, in the hope of enjoying a liberty of conscience which was not permitted in England under the reign of James I. But he was disappointed, as the Virginians proved nearly as intolerant as those he had left; and he felt compelled to seek another asylum.

This he proposed to find, a territory on both sides of Chesapeake Bay, then inhabited only by natives; and which having sufficiently explored, he returned to England, for the purpose of procuring a patent of it, from Charles I, who succeeded James I. He readily received a grant of the territory; but he died before the patent was completed.

It was, however, subsequently made out, in 1632, in favor of Cecil Calvert, son of Sir George, who inherited his father's title, and who now came into possession of the country from the Potomac to the fortieth degree of north latitude. This grant covered the land which had long before been granted to Virginia, and what was now granted to Lord Baltimore was in part subsequently given to William Penn. In consequence of these arbitrary acts of the crown, long and obstinate contentions arose between the descendants of Penn and Lord Baltimore.

In 1633, Lord Baltimore appointed his brother, Leonard Calvert, governor of the province, who, with about two hundred planters, mostly Roman Catholics, left England near the close of this year, and arriving, in 1634, at the mouth of the river Potomac, purchased from the Indians Yoamaco, a considerable village, where they formed a settlement by the name of Saint Mary's.

Several circumstances contributed to the rapid growth and prosperity of Maryland. Her people were exempted from hostilities from the Indians, having satisfied them in the purchase of their land; the soil was fertile, and the seasons mild. But, more than all, their charter conferred on them more ample privileges than had been conferred in any other colony in America. It secured to emigrants equality in religious rights, and civil freedom; and it granted the privilege of passing laws, without any reservation on the part of the crown to revoke them. Even taxes could not be imposed upon the inhabitants without their consent.

At first, when few in number, the freemen assembled in person, and enacted the necessary laws; but, in 1639, it was found expedient to constitute a "house of assembly." This consisted of representatives chosen by the people, of others appointed by the proprietor, and, of the governor and secretary, who sat together. In 1650, the legislative body was divided into an upper and lower house; the members of the former being appointed by the proprietor, those of the latter by the people.

Few of the colonies escaped internal troubles, nor did Maryland form an exception. In 1635, a rebellion broke out, chiefly caused by one William Clayborne. This man, under license of the king to trade with the Indians, had farmed a settlement an the Island of Kent, nearly opposite Annapolis; and when the grant was made to Lord Baltimore, he refused to submit to his authority, and attempted to maintain his possession by force of arms. His followers, however, were taken prisoners, and he himself fled. The Maryland assembly confiscated his estate, and declared him guilty of treason.

Early in 1645, Clayborne once more returned to Maryland, and, heading a party of insurgents, overthrew the government. Calvert, the governor, was compelled to take refuge in Virginia. The revolt, however, was suppressed the following year, and Calvert resumed his office.

In 1649, the assembly of the colony reiterated in solemn form the original and fundamental principles of religious toleration of Lord Baltimore, in an act that no one professing faith in Jesus Christ should be molested on account of such belief, or in the free exercise of their religion; and, that anyone who should reproach another on account of his religious creed should pay a fine to the person thus abused. Thus religious toleration was established by law; and its benign influence was early perceived. Maryland presented an asylum for all who felt themselves religiously oppressed; and hither came Puritans from the south, and church men from the north, and found a welcome reception, and the largest liberty.

In 1651, Parliament, having triumphed over King Charles I, appointed commissioners, of whom Clayborne, the enemy of Maryland, was one, 'to reduce and govern the colonies within the Bay of Chesapeake.' This gave rise to a civil war in Maryland, between the Catholics, who adhered to the proprietor, and the Protestants, who sided with Parliament. At first, Stone, the lieutenant of the proprietor, was removed; but was soon restored, on his consenting to acknowledge the authority of Parliament. But in 1654, the commissioners again visited Maryland, and required him to surrender the government.

The next assembly that convened, which was entirely under the influence of the Protestant and now victorious party, ordained that no person professing the Catholic religion was entitled to the protection of the laws. Early the following year in 1655, civil war commenced. Having organized a military band, Stone assumed the government, intending to maintain his position by force; but the Protestant party resisted, and, at length, a battle ensued, in which the Catholics were defeated, with a loss of fifty killed. Stone was taken prisoner, and was executed, with four others, men of note from the province.

At the Restoration in 1660, Lord Baltimore was once more restored to his rights, and Philip Calvert appointed governor. A general pardon was extended to all political offenders, and the former mild and liberal principles of the proprietor once more held sway in Maryland.

Towards the close of the year 1675, Cecil Calvert, the Lord Baltimore, the founder of Maryland, died; and was succeeded by his son Charles, both in his honors and estates. For more than forty years, Cecil Calvert, in presiding over the province as its proprietor, had displayed the highest regard for the rights and happiness of others. He deserved well of posterity, and his name will be long honored and revered by the people of Maryland. In integrity, benevolence and practical wisdom, the son strongly resembled the father.

On the accession of William and Mary to the throne of England in 1689, the tranquility of Maryland was again interrupted. A rumor was fabricated, and industriously circulated, that the Catholics had combined with the Indians to cut off the Protestants of the colony. This roused the Catholics in their own defense, and to the assertion of the rights of the king and queen. The Protestants attempted to subdue the Catholics by force, and were compelled to relinquish the government into the hands of the former.

And in their hands it continued until 1691, when the king, in the exercise of sovereign power, wrested the province from Lord Baltimore, and erected it into a royal government. And in the further exercise of sovereignty, the following year, he sent Sir Lionel Copley as royal governor, 'to take charge of the province.' Under him religious toleration was disallowed, and the Church of England's forms of worship were established and supported by law.

But in 1716 this great wrong was rectified. The heir of Lord Baltimore, although an infant, was reestablished in his rights; the proprietary form of government was restored; and thus matters continued until the war of the Revolution, when the people formed a constitution for themselves, and no longer recognized the claims of the onetime proprietor to either jurisdiction or property. — *A History of the United States*, by Charles A. Goodrich, 1858 (edited)

Robert Baden married Mrs. Jane Holland, 16 Jan 1667, Amesbury, Wiltshire, England (England and Wales Marriages, 1538-1940).

Robert Baden, b. abt. 1670, christened 13 Feb 1670, Salisbury, Wiltshire, England (England and Wales Christening Records, 1530-1906).

Robert Baden married Anne Wenman, 10 Jan 1695 (marriage licenses issued by the Faculty Office, 1632-1714).

Robert Baden m. 7 Jul 1715 Jane Ray, Fisherton Anger, Wiltshire, England (England & Wales Marriages, 1538-1940).

It must be remembered that Maryland was originally a part of the Virginia Colony.

Badens of Maryland

In Prince George's County, Maryland Orphan's Courts, ". . . John Baden, aged 17 years old this past 9 December 1749 . . . Margaret Baden aged 15 years old this past 31st of July 1749, . . . made their choice of Thomas Baden to be their Guardian, who in his proper person in Court accepts the same." [LL 199] John Baden, Sr. left a will dated 7 July 1824, probated 25 October 1824. The *Maryland Gazette*, a newspaper, dated Baltimore, Maryland, 21 October 1824 published the following obituary: "Baden, John Sr. died at his residence near Nottingham, Prince George's County, Maryland 30 September last, aged 71 years, 9 months, 10 days, leaving an only son and a number of grandchildren, also several great grandchildren." But according to the date of birth in the Orphan's Court document, John, Sr. would have been 91 years, 9 months, and 2 days old when he died.

Thomas Baden, married by 1761, Eleanor, daughter of John Brightwell (Maryland Marriage References – B – Maryland State Archives PG Liber T#1:70).

Robert Baden, married by 1747 to Martha Lawson, daughter of Thomas and Elizabeth Lawson (Maryland Marriage References – B – Maryland State Archives; PGLR BB:661; PGWB 1:413).

Robert Baden Jr. served as an officer in the Maryland Militia during the Revolutionary War, under the direction of Capt. R. Bowie and Capt. J. Bean. At first, while serving as a 2nd Lt. his unnumbered Battalion was assigned to the Lower Prince Georges County, Maryland area. On his promotion from 2nd Lt to 1st Lt, he was assigned to the 11th Battalion. There is no mention in the historical documents that the 11th Battalion had any skirmishes with the British. Dates of service: 1 Sep 1777 (2nd Lt), 1 May 1778 (1st Lt promotion), 24 Mar 1779 on reassignment to new Captain. The 11th Battalion was dismantled in 1783 and the military men sent home.

In the Maryland Council, 1778-1779, on Monday 24 May 1779, a commission is issued to Robert Baden of Prince Georges County for 1st Lieutenant (C.B., *Journal and Correspondence*, pg. 414).

On page 62, commissions were issued to Thomas Baden, Ensign and Robert Baden 1st Lieutenant.

On Monday 3d July 1780, Commissions were issued to Thomas Baden 2d Lieutenant and to Benjamin Baden Ensign of Capt. Alexander Howard Magruder's Company belonging to the Lower Battalion of Militia in Prince Georges County. That said Treasurer pay to James Brice, Lieutenant of Ann Arundel County one hundred and ninety Pounds to pay Expresses sent by him under the Act for the New Enrollment of the Militia and to be by him Accounted for (the name Brice will appear in a generation much later).

In the *Records of Maryland Troops in the Continental Service,* Robert and Jeremiah Baden enlisted by Alexander Howard Magruder on July 3, 1776. Reviewed by Jos. Sim, Col. Of the 11th Battalion, Prince George's County, August 21st, 1776.

Raised by Alex. Trueman, Ensign, for Capt. Magruder's Company. Passed by Jos. Sim, Prince George's County, August 21st, 1776: Thomas Baden, July 3, 1776. Also listed is George Naylor (daughter Martha married George A. Baden 3/30/1832; and Samuel Grover whose daughter (Frances Gover) married Robert Baden, Jr. 11/10/1779.

In *Maryland Records, Vol. II,* published from Original Returns in the Archives of Maryland, and by Permission of the Historical Society of Maryland: Pages 25 to 36, *Revolutionary Records of Maryland*, Brumbaugh and Hodges, contain numerous references to individuals mentioned in the following "Returns" from Prince George's County, MD, and should be consulted.

Revolutionary Records of Maryland, page 30: "At a County Court held at Upper Marlborough Town, March 23, 1779 . . . Richard Henderson produces to the Court here his account against the County for an allowance for Administering the Oath of Fidelity and is allowed six pounds current money in the present County Levy for that purpose." (See Return No. 11) Fielder Bowie's Return:

____, John (probably Baden)

Baden, Robert

Baden Benj[n].

Naylor, Geo., [Jr].

Baden, John, Sen[r].

Baden, Jeremiah

Naylor, John Lawson

Roberts, Evan

Earley, William, J[r].

George Naylor enlisted on 4 July 1776 and his name is on the Muster Roll of Maryland Troops in the American Revolution. He served as a Private among the troops raised by Ensign Alex Trueman, for Captain Magruder's Company in Prince George's County, Maryland. As George Naylor, son of Batson Naylor, he is recorded on "A roll of the Guard kept at Magruder's

Warehouse that were from Captain Benjamin Wailes's Company of Militia of the Lower Battalion", in Revolutionary Papers recorded at Prince George's County, 27 May 1782. George Naylor, the son of Batson, also signed the Oath of Fidelity in said county where he was recorded on Fielder Bowie's Return of 30 March 1778.

JOHN BADEN

John Baden, Sr., b. 20 Sep 1732, d. 30 Sep 1824, married 12 Jan 1782, Willimina M. Maulden.[1] He was the son of Robert Baden and Martha Lawson and a brother to Thomas Baden.

John Baden, Jr. b.   , d. Jan. 1846, married 24 Mar 1814, Elizabeth Naylor.

John Thomas Baden, b. 1792, married 7 Dec 1813, Margaret Baden.[2]

Thomas George Baden, b. 1810, d. 1842, married 1853 Sarah Sabina b. 1811.

Jeremiah Smith Baden b. 1840, d. 30 Mar 1903 (Suwannee, FL); married Jul 1865 Angeline Lydia Barber b. 1843 Bryan Co., GA, d. 1823 Live Oak, Suwannee, FL.

Mary Harriet Baden b. 22 Oct 1885 (McAlpin/Suwannee, FL), d. 18 Nov 1962, married 25 Dec 1911 Marion Hampton Hicks b. 21 Nov 1889 New Bern/Suwannee, FL, d. May 1970 Clearwater/Pinellas, FL.

(aaa) Vivian Olive Hicks b. 27 Apr 1914 Live Oak/Suwannee, LD; d. 26 Oct 2008 Dunedin/Pinellas, married Joseph Lindsey Land 1 Jun 1942, Clearwater/Pinellas, FL.

(aaaa) Robert Brice Land b. 12 Jun 1843 Clearwater/Pinellas, FL, married Kathleen L. Wallace 29 Sep 1989 (Vol. 7061, Certificate 108176).

THE LAST WILL OF JOHN BADEN SENIOR

DATED 7 JULY 1824

Liber TT 1, folio 369-370

"In the name of God, Amen. I, **JOHN BADEN** Senr of Prince Georges County and State of Maryland, being weak in body but thanks be to God of a sound and disposing mind, memory & understanding do make and publish this my last will and . . . I give . . . to my son **JOHN BADEN** Jr. . . . in addition to what I have already given to him one Feather Bed and Bedding. Item. I give and bequeath to my Grand son **JOHN THOMAS BADEN** . . . all my part of two tracks of Land where on my son **ALEXANDER BADEN** decsd lived, called Mansfield and Cullings Comfort containing one hundred acres . . . . My will and desires that . . . **JOHN THOMAS BADEN** shall pay to my four grand children towit **GEORGE ADAM BADEN, BENJAMIN JOSIAS BADEN, HANNABLE AUSTIN BADEN** and **SARAH ANN BADEN** $300 to be equally divided among them share and share alike to be paid as they respectively arrive to the age of one and twenty years, it is my will and desire that my grand son **JOHN THOMAS BADEN** shall pay to my Grand son **ROBERT BADEN** three hundred dollars . . . to be clear of interest. Item. I give to my Grand children **ELIZABETH BADEN** and **JEREMIAH MAULDIN BADEN** . . . $75 to be equally divided . . . . Item. I give to my grand son **JOHN THOMAS BADEN** one negro man Harry and one negro woman Cate to be slaves during their lives and also give him one negro woman Harriot until the first day of January 1832 at which time my will and desire is that she be free from all services of any person or persons claiming any right under me. Item. I give to my grand daughter **ELIZABETH TERESA BADEN** the use of one negro woman Sylvia until the first day of January 1842 . . . to be free of all services . . . . Item. I give **JOHN THOMAS BADEN** . . . all the residue of my estate . . . I appoint . . . **JOHN THOMAS BADEN** . . sole Executor.

---

[1] Index to Marriages, Prince Georges County, Maryland.

[2] Margaret was a cousin.

Affixed my seal, 7 July 1824.

His

JOHN ><BADEN Senr.

Mark

Witness: THOMAS N. BADEN

LEONARD P. HARVEY

WILLIAM HARVEY

[Probated 25 October 1824]

JOHN BADEN, JR.

THE LAST WILL OF JOHN BADEN JR.

DATED 23 APRIL 1839

Liber PC 1, folio 305-308

In the name of God Amen. I, JOHN BADEN, Jr. of Prince George's County in the State of Maryland being in good health of body and of sound and disposing mind, memory & understanding considering the certainty of death and the uncertainty of the time there of and being desirous to settle my worldly affairs and thereby be the better prepared to leave this world when it shall please God to call me hence do therefore make and publish this my last will and testament in manner and form following: that is to say first and principally I commit my soul into the hands of Almighty God and my body to the earth to be decently buried at the discretion of the executor here in after named and after debts and funeral charges are paid I devise and request as follows –

Item. I give to my Grand son **ROBERT WM. GROVER BADEN** all the land within the following bounds – beginning at Spices Creek bridge <u>running</u> with the publick [sic] Road going toward the federal oak <u>until</u> it reaches the gate near the black peoples grave yard then with a straight line toward Sibspring branch <u>until</u> it intersects the old <u>Publick</u> Road then with said old <u>Roade</u> [sic] down the Ratherford's hill <u>until</u> it reaches **JOSEPH N. BADEN**'s Mill seat then with the line of said Mill seat and Reatherford's Branch to the cropway and then to the beginning at Spices Creek bridge – Reserving the use of said land to **MARGARET BADEN** the widow of my son **JOHN T. BADEN** during her single life.

Item. I give to my great grand son **JOHN BADEN** the son of my grand son **THOMAS GEORGE BADEN** all the <u>balance</u> [sic] of my plantation where on I now live Reserving the use of said plantation to my son **JAMES BADEN** during his life.

Item. I Give to my son **JAMES BADEN** one Negro woman named Betty, one Negro Woman named Beck one Man named Isaac & one named Sam. Item. I give to my Great Grand Son **JOHN BADEN** the son of Grand Son **THOS. GEORGE BADEN** one Negro boy named Sam and one Negro boy named David –

Item. I Give to my Great Grand son **JAMES THOMAS BADEN** the son of my grand son **THOS GEORGE BADEN** one Negro woman named Alley one negro girl <u>named</u> Margaret one boy named George and one Girl named Martha Anne –

Item. I Give to **MARGARET BADEN** my son **JOHN's** Widow one Negro Girl named Anne –

Item. I Give to my Grand Son **ROBERT WM. GROVER BADEN** one negro Girl named Maria –

Item. I Give to my Grand Son **JEREMIATH THOMAS BADEN** one Negro Girl named Mary –

Item. I Give to my Daughter **MARTHA NAYLOR** one Feather bed Bedstead and furniture and one cow and calf –

Item. I Give to my Negro Woman Alley one Feather Bed –

Item. I Give to my son **JAMES BADEN** all the residue of my property not herein mentioned.

And lastly I do hereby constitute and appoint my son **JAMES BADEN** to be sole executor of this my lastly Will and Testament revoking and annulling all former wills by me heretofore made ratifying this and <u>non</u> other to be my last will and testament – In testimony whereof I have here unto set my hand and affixed my seal this 23rd day of April 1839.

[signed] **JOHN BADEN**   <SEAL>

Signed, sealed, published and declared by **JOHN BADEN, Junr.** the above named Testator as and for his last will and testament in the presence of us who at request in his presence and in the presence of each other have subscribed our names as witnesses thereof.

THOS N. BADEN
JOSEPH A. TURNER
JOHN L. TURNER

Prince Georges County}
January 13th 1846   }

Then came JOSEPH A. TURNER one of the subscribing witnesses to the within Will & made oath on the Holy Evangelly of Almighty God that he did see **JOHN BADEN Jr.** Testator here in named Sign and seal this Will and heard him publish pronounce and declare the same to be his last Will and Testament that at the time of his so doing he was to the best of his appre-hension of sound and disposing mind memory and understanding and that he together with THOS B. BADEN & JOHN L. TURNER respectively subscribed their names to this Will in the presence of the Testator at his request and in the presence of each other.

Sworn before **JAMES HARPER** Regr of Wills for P. G. County

Prince Georges County}
January 23rd 1846   }

Then came JOHN L. TURNER one of the subscribing witnesses to the within Will & of **JOHN** BADEN Junr. Late of said County deceased, and made oath on the Holy Evangelly of Almighty God that he did see **JOHN BADEN Jr.** Testator here in named Sign and seal this Will and heard him publish pronounce and declare the same to be his last Will and Testament that at the time of his so doing he was to the best of his apprehension of sound and disposing mind memory and understanding and that he together with THOS B. BADEN & JOS. A. TURNER respectively subscribed their names to this Will in the presence of the Testator at his request and in the presence of each other.

Sworn before **JAMES HARPER** Regr of Wills for P. G. County

<u>Whereas</u> I **JOHN BADEN** of Prince Georges County have made and duly executed my last will and testament in writing bearing date the 23rd of April 1839 which said last will and testament and every clause bequest and devise there in contained I do hereby ratify and confirm and being desirous to make additions thereto do therefore hearby make this my codicil which I Will and direct shall be taken and held as a part of my said will and testament in manner and form following that is to say Item I give to my greate [sic] grand son **JOHN BADEN** son of my grand son **THOS GEORGE BADEN** one small boy named John the son of the negro girl Anne whom I gave her in my will and I also now give said **MARGARET BADEN** all her <u>future</u> increase – <u>Item</u> I give to my grand son **JORIMIAH** [sic] **THOMAS BADEN** one negro child named Julia the daughter of girl Mary I gave him in my will and I also give said **JEREYMIAH** [sic] **THOMAS BADEN** all the <u>future</u> increase of said girl Mary.

<u>Item</u> I direct that my son **JAMES BADEN** whom I appointed in my will my sole <u>Exetor</u> shall sell my crop of all descriptions and Horses Oxen and Cattle Vc immediately and apply the proceeds there of to the payment of all my just debs funeral charges & ect. And if thereby any <u>balance</u> remaining he <u>may</u> apply it to his own use – In testimony where of I have here to set my hand and affixed my seal this 1st day of January 1846.

Signed, sealed, published and declared by **JOHN BADEN** the above testator as and for a codicil to his last will and testament in the presence of us who at his request in the presence and in the presence of each other have subscribed our names as witnesses there to – Witnesses: **JOHN N. BADEN JOHN L. TOWNSHEND & THOS. N. BADEN.**

Prince Georges County jct}

January 24th 1846   }

Then came **JOSEPH N. BADEN** and **JOHN L. TOWNSHEND** two of the subscribing Witnesses to the afore going Codicil to the last Will and Testament of **JOHN BADEN Jr.** late of said county deceased & made oath on the Holy Evangely of Almighty God that they did see the said **JOHN BADEN** the Testator sign and seal, the said codicil and heard him publish pronounce and declare the same to be a codicil to his last Will and Testament that at the time of his so doing he was to the best of their apprehension of sound and disposing mind memory and understanding and that they respectively subscribed their names as Witnesses to the said Codicil in the presence of the Testator at his request and in the presence of each other.

                Sworn before **JAMES HARPER** Regr of Wills for P. G. County

Document 1: PRINCE GEORGE'S COUNTY REGISTER OF WILLS (Wills) John Baden Senr. will, dated 7 Jul 1824, prob. 25 Oct 1824, Liber TT 1, pp. 369-370, MSA CM816-3, Microfilm CR 34682-1; Maryland State Archives, Annapolis, Maryland.

In the name of God Amen, I John Baden Jr of Prince George's
County in the state of Maryland being in good health of body
and of sound and disposing mind, memory & understanding, considering
the certainty of death and the uncertainty of the time there of and
being desirous to settle my worldly affairs and thereby be the better
prepared to leave this world when it shall please God to call me
hence do therefore make and publish this my last will and testament
in manner and form following, that is to say, First and principally
I commit my soul into the hands of Almighty God and my body
to the earth to be decently buried at the discretion of the executor
here in after named and after debts and funeral charges are paid
I devise and bequeath as follows –

Item. I Give to my Grand Son Robert Wm Lemon Baden all the
land within the following bounds beginning at spice branch bridge
running with the publick Road going toward the ____ ____ until
it reaches the gate near the ____ poplar grain yard then with a
____ line towards ____ branch until it intersects the old
publick Road then with ____ Old Roads down the Heatherquits hill
until it reaches James N Baden's Mill seat then with the line
of said Mill seat and the Heatherquits branch to the ____ and
then to the beginning at spice branch bridge Reserving the use of
said land to Margaret Baden the widow of my son John S Baden
during her single life

Item. 2d Give to my great grand son John Baden the son of my great
son Thomas George Baden all the balance of my plantation whereon
I now live Reserving the use of said plantation to my son James
Baden during his life

Item. I Give to my son James Baden one Negro Woman named
Betty one Negro woman named Beck one Man named
Isaac & one named Sam Item. I Give to my great grand son
John Baden the ____ ____ ____ ____ ____ negro boy
named Sam and ____ ____ named ____ –

Item. I Give to my Great grand son James Thomas Baden the
son of my grand son George Baden one Negro woman named
Alley one negro girl named Margaret one boy named ____

Document 2: PRINCE GEORGE'S COUNTY REGISTER OF WILLS (Wills) John Baden Jr. will, dated 20 Apr 1839, prob. 15 Jan 1846, codicil dated 1 Jan 1846, prob. 24 Jan 1846, Liber PC 1, pp. 305-308, MSA MSA CM816-4, Microfilm CR 34682-2; Maryland State Archives, Annapolis, Maryland.

[Handwritten probate/will document, faded and largely illegible]

307

... Together to ... Tho ʃ Baden ... John L Turner ...
... that he respectfully subscribed their names to this will in their presence
... the Testator at his request and in the presence of each other

Sworn before James Harper Reg.
of Wills for P.G. County

Prince George's County ... Then came John L Turner on ... the ... instant
... January 23d 1846 ... witnesses to the within Will of John Baden Junr.
late of said county deceased and made oath on the Holy Evangely of
Almighty God that he did see ... John Baden ... Testator ... sign and seal and heard him pronounce publish and declare this
same to be his Last Will and Testament that at the time of his
so doing he was to the best of his apprehension ... of sound and disposing
mind, Memory and understanding and that he respectively subscribed
their name to this will in the presence of the Testator at his request
and in the presence of each ...

Sworn before James Harper Reg.
of Wills for P.G. County

Whereas I John Baden of Prince George County have made and duly
executed my Last Will and Testament in writing bearing date the 20th
day of April 1839 ... said last will and testament and every
clause ... and devise there in contained ... hereby ratify and con...
... and now declare ... make ... change ... making
this my codicil which I will and direct shall be taken and held as a part
of my said will and Testament in manner and form following that is to
say. Item I give to ... great grand son John Baden son of my grand son
... John ... will be ... John
Bowlett. — Item I give to Margaret Baden the widow of my son John S
Baden one small boy named John the son of the negro girl Susan
whom I gave her in my will and I also now give said Margaret
Baden all her future increase. — Item I give to my grand son Jeremiah
Thomas Baden one negro child named John the daughter of girl Mary
... I gave him in my will and I also give said Jeremiah Thomas Baden
all the future increase of said girl Mary. —
Item I direct that my son ... Baden whom I appointed
in my will my sole executor shall sell my crop of all description
and ... own ... cattle ... immediately and apply the proceeds

George and one Girl named Martha Anne —

Item I Give to Margaret Baden my son John's widow one Negro Girl named Anne —

Item I Give to my Grand Son Robert Wm Grover Baden one negro Girl named Maria —

Item I Give to my Grand son Jeremiah Thomas Baden one Negro Girl named Mary —

Item I Give to my Daughter Martha Naylor one Feather bed Bedstead and furniture and one cow & calf —

Item I Give to my negro Woman Lilly one Feather Bed

Item I Give to my son James Baden all the residue of my property not herein mentioned.

And lastly I do hereby constitute and appoint my son James Baden to be sole executor of this my last Will and Testament revoking and annulling all former wills by me heretofore made ratifying this and none other to be my last will and Testament. In Testimony whereof I have hereunto set my hand and affixed my seal this 20th day of April 1839 —

John Baden {Seal}

Signed sealed published and declared by John Baden Junr the above named Testator as and for his last will and testament in the presence of us who at his request in his presence and in the presence of each other have subscribed our names as witnesses thereto

Thos I. Baden
Joseph T. Ryon
Hen E. Turner.

Prince Georges County to wit[?] the same being at Page 18th ... Turner one of the ... witnesses to the within Will ... this ... of almighty God did he did see John Baden the Testator here in named sign and seal this will and heard him published pronounce and declare the same to be his last Will and Testament that at the time of his so doing he was to the best of his apprehension of sound and disposing mind memory and Understanding ...

Document 2: PRINCE GEORGE'S COUNTY REGISTER OF WILLS (Wills) John Baden Jr. will, dated 20 Apr 1839, prob. 15 Jan 1846, codicil dated 1 Jan 1846, prob. 24 Jan 1846, Liber PC 1, pp. 305-308, MSA MSA CM816-4, Microfilm CR 34682-2; Maryland State Archives, Annapolis, Maryland.

JOHN THOMAS BADEN

John Thomas Baden was the son of John Baden, Jr. and Elizabeth Naylor.

He was born in 1792 and married his cousin, Margaret Baden b. 1797, 7 Dec 1813, Prince Georges County, Maryland.[3]

Jeremiah Thomas Baden b. 1832, d. 1881, Prince George's County, Maryland, married his cousin, Susanna Isabella Rebecca Baden, born 26 Oct 1861, Prince George's County, d. 2 Feb 1919. Susanna Isabella Rebecca Baden was a daughter of Thomas George and Sarah Sabina Baden. She married Jeremiah Thomas Baden who is mentioned in his grandfather John Baden, Jr's. will. Both are buried in St. Paul's Cemetery, Baden, Maryland.

1.   William P. Baden, b. 4 Oct 1855, d. 4 Mar. 1937, married Ann Ellen Bean

2.   Sarah Margaret Baden, b. 26 Oct 1861, d. 2 Feb 1919, Baden, Prince George's County Maryland, married William Mortimer Baden 15 Dec 1885. They lived in Nottingham, Maryland in 1870 and in Brandywine, Maryland in 1920. The family is buried in St. Paul's Cemetery, Baden, Maryland.
    a.   Elmer La Roche Baden, b. 1887, d. 1965, Prince George's County, Maryland.
    b.   Mary Isabel Baden, b. 1891, d. 1967, Prince George's County, Maryland.
    c.   Mary T. Baden, b. 1891, Prince George's County, Maryland.
    d.   Joseph Ignatius Baden, b. 1893, Prince George's County, Maryland.
    e.   Elizabeth Grace Baden, b. 1895, d. 1982, Prince George's County, Maryland.

---

[3] Index to marriages, Prince Georges County, Maryland.

REGISTRATION CARD—(Men born on or after April 28, 1877 and on or before February 16, 1897)

SERIAL NUMBER | 1. NAME (Print) | ORDER NUMBER

U 990 Joseph Ignatius Baden

(First) (Middle) (Last)

2. PLACE OF RESIDENCE (Print)

Silver Hill Pr. Geo. Md

(Number and street) (Town, township, village, or city) (County) (State)

[THE PLACE OF RESIDENCE GIVEN ON THE LINE ABOVE WILL DETERMINE LOCAL BOARD
JURISDICTION; LINE 2 OF REGISTRATION CERTIFICATE WILL BE IDENTICAL]

3. MAILING ADDRESS

3330 Naylor Road S E Anacostia D C

[Mailing address if other than place indicated on line 2. If same insert word same]

4. TELEPHONE | 5. AGE IN YEARS | 6. PLACE OF BIRTH

49 Brandywine

Lincoln 9867 | DATE OF BIRTH | Maryland

(Exchange) (Number) | Mar 22 1893 | (Town) (County)

(Mo.) (Day) (Yr.) | (State or country)

7. NAME AND ADDRESS OF PERSON WHO WILL ALWAYS KNOW YOUR ADDRESS

James O Baden 4226 37th St N W Wash D C

8. EMPLOYER'S NAME AND ADDRESS

Self employed

9. PLACE OF EMPLOYMENT OR BUSINESS

(Number and street or R. F. D. number) (Town) (County) (State)

I AFFIRM THAT I HAVE VERIFIED ABOVE ANSWERS AND THAT THEY ARE TRUE.

D. S. S. Form 1
(Revised 4-1-42) (over) | 16—21630-2 | Joseph O Baden

(Registrant's signature)

14

f.   Desales A. Baden, b. 1904, Prince George's County, Maryland.

g.   Mary A. Baden, b. 1899, Prince George's County, Maryland.

3.   Ella Williams Baden, b. 11 Nov 1863, d. 24 Nov 1939.

4.   Mary Emma Baden b. 16 Feb 1865, d. 16 Jul 1942

5.   John Thomas Baden, b. 18 Sep 1867, d. 4 Feb 1938

6.   Jeremiah Millard Baden b. 1861, d. 24 Jan 1893; no stone found but listed in cemetery records.

JOHN HENRY BADEN

John Henry Baden was b. in 1839, d. 1905, the son of George Adams Baden, b. 1815, and Margaret Caroline Early, b. 1819, d. 1902, Baden, Prince George's County, Maryland. He m. 15 Dec 1885 Elizabeth Wright, b. 1840. Private, Civil War, 1st Maryland Confederate Cavalry.[4]

William Mortimer Baden, b. 21 Apr 1863, d. 27 Aug 1924, Baden, Prince George's County, Maryland, m. Sarah Margaret Baden, b. 26 Oct 1861, d. 2 Feb 1919, Baden, Prince George's County Maryland, 15 Dec 1885. They lived in Nottingham, Maryland in 1870 and in Brandywine, Maryland in 1920. The family is buried in St. Paul's Cemetery, Baden, Maryland.

Elmer La Roche Baden, b. 27 Nov 1887, d. Mar 1965, m. Verna Almira Duley b. 1887, d. 1937, Prince George's County, Maryland. (see World War I Registration Card).

Living Baden

James Elmer Baden, b. 1919, d. 1922.

William K. Baden, b. 1919, d. 1980, enlisted 11 Feb 1941,[5] Baltimore, Warrant Officer, Private; education – 4 years of high school, civil occupation – shipping & receiving clerk, single w/o dependents, height – 67 inches, weight – 142 lbs.

Mary Isabel Baden, b. 1891, d. 17 Nov 1967, 105 Highland, Arlington, VA. She m. Samuel Mudd Blandford.

Living Blandford

Living Blandford

William B. Blandford, b. 1917, d. 1917.

Evelyn Baden Blandford, b. 1919, d. 1989.

Mary T. Baden, b. 1891, Prince George's County, Maryland.

Joseph Ignatius Baden, b. 1893, Prince George's County, Maryland.

Elizabeth Grace Baden, b. 1895, d. 1982, Prince George's Co., MD; m. James Wilson

Rawlings, Jr. b. 1897, d. 1957; m. 2nd Harry C. Taylor, b. 1888, d. 1938.

Desales A. Baden, b. 1904, Prince George's County, Maryland.

Mary A. Baden, b. 1899, Prince George's County, Maryland.

George Henry Baden, b. ca 1860, Bryantown, Charles County, Maryland, d. 17 Jul 1907, Nottingham, MD, m. 1893 Bertie Baden, b. 1860, Baden, Prince George's County, Maryland.

Ruth E. Baden, b. 1896

---

[4] United States National Archives, *Civil War Records*, Provo, UT, HAS: The Generation Network, Inc., 1999.

[5] U.S. World War Army Enlistment Records, 1938-1946, National Archives & Records Administration, Record Group 64, National Archives at College Park, College Park, MD.

THOMAS EARLY, SR.

Thomas Early, Sr. was born in 1760, d. 1815, m. Willimina Slye, b. 1764, d. 1816.

Leonard Hollyday Early, b. 2 Nov 1791, d. 1876, age 85, Prince George's County, Maryland; m. Margaret Waters, b. 1792, d. 1847.

Dorinda Eleanor Early, b. 1817, d. 1851.

Margaret Caroline Early, b. 1819, d. 1902, m. George Adams Baden, b. 1815.
John Henry Baden was b. in 1839, d. 1905, the son of George Adams Baden, b. 1815, and Margaret Caroline Early, b. 1819, d. 1902, Baden, Prince George's County, Maryland. John Henry Baden m. 15 Dec 1885 Elizabeth Wright, b. 1840. He served in the 1st Maryland Confederate Cavalry, as a Private in the Civil War. Family buried in St. Paul's Cemetery, Baden, Maryland.

William Holliday Early b. 1820, d. 1902.

Thomas Ranelder Early b. 1823, d. 1855.

Melvina Josephine Early, b. 1824, d. 1860.

James Alfred Early, b. 1826, d. 1853.

Cornelia E. Early, b. 1826.

Joseph Edward Early, b. 1829, d. 1884.

JOHN B. BADEN

John B. Baden[6], born 7 Aug 1831, baptized 5 Apr 1832, died 17 Nov 1873 (Register of St. Paul's Church, Baden, Maryland), married 21 Jan 1857, Eleanor Ann Gantt Townshend.[7] He was murdered on the road to Washington, D.C.; interred 11 Jan 1874. No marker but is in the cemetery custodian's listing.

Thomas Baden, b. Dec 1868, d. 11 Jul 1869. No marker but is in the cemetery custodian's listing.

Richard Baden, 6 Jul 1869, d. 12 Jul 1869. No marker but is in the cemetery custodian's listing.

(Information from Stones and Bones: Cemetery Records of Prince George's County, Maryland).

---

[6] Information from a letter written by and for the widow of JAMES THOMAS BADEN, dated Washington, D.C., 21 Nov 1913.

[7] Index of Marriage Licenses, Prince Georges County, MD, 1777-1886 by Helen Brown, 1971.

Prince George's County, Sct } The First and Final
March 17th 1876 } Account of Francis
A. Ward, Administrator of John Baden late of said
County, deceased.

This Accountant charges himself with
this sum being amount collected from F.
Belt & Sons, in full of Draft in favor of
this decedent $ 250 00

And craves an allowance for the following
payments and disbursements, to wit
1 Of Current Money paid Wm. M. Ward & Bro in
full of Intestate's funeral expenses, as
per bill receipted $ 116 35
2 Of D° D° paid Thomas J. Turner in full
for publishing for Intestate's estate, as
per bill receipted 7 50
3 Of D° D° paid Hon A Jarboe Jr. Regr. of Wills
for stating this a/c, making distribution on
same, and in full of all fees due on this
administration to date, as per bill 17 00
4 Of D° D° paid C. C. & R. H. Hyatt in full
of judgment, and interest on same, against
Intestate, as per Copy of judgment 90 45
5 Of D° D° paid John G. Brownsherd in full
of judgment, and interest on same, against
Intestate, as per Copy of judgment 13 97
Of D° D° retained to pay this Accountant ten
per cent Commission on the assets accounted
for in this a/c Say on $250.00 25 00
$ 270 27
Balance due the Estate $ 42 73
Estate accounted for $ 250 00

Prince George's County, Set } Then came Francis Ward,
    March 17th 1876 } the aforegoing Accountant
and made oath on the Holy Evangels of Almighty
God that the aforegoing Account, as Stated, is just
and true, and that he has bona fide paid or secured
to be paid the several sums of money for which he
craves an allowance.

        Sworn before
          Wm A Jarboe Jr   Regr Wills

The aforegoing Account, after due examination, is passed
this 21st day of March A.D. 1876, by order of the
Orphans Court.
       Test,
          Wm A Jarboe Jr   Regr Wills

Upon the passage of the aforegoing Account there
appears a Balance due the Estate for distribution
among the unpreferred Creditors of said deceased,
amounting to

No					Dividend $ 149 73
1	To	M. J. Burke on open a/c for	$ 41.00		
		Int on same to date hereof	5.53		
			46.53	13 46	
2	"	J. B. B. Wilson on open a/c for	$ 30.00		
		Int on same to date hereof	2.25		
			32.25	9 67	
3	"	M. R. Latimer on medical a/c for	$ 20.00		
		Int on same	.50		
			21.50	6 45	
4	"	F. A. Ward on open a/c for	$ 6.73		
		Int on same	.90		
			2.63	2 29	
5	"	A. L. Osmer on note for	$ 39.94		
		Int on same	2.92		
			52.86	17 86	
		Amt of unpreferred claims	$ 165.77		
		Whole Amt distributed	$ 149 73		

    Test   Wm A Jarboe Jr. Regr of Wills

No. 956.

615

No. 1876 956.

John Baden's
First and Final
Account

Exhd March 17th

Recorded in Liber
W. A. J. Jr. No. 1 folio 1134
Paid

Fees for Stating in Offi[illegible] }
Making distribution Copy [illegible] } $9.55
Fees for 1875 7.45

Fees in Com $2.[illegible]

Chg'd Ent

No. 79

John G. Townshend
vs
John Baden

March 23d 1870

Judgment in favour of the plaintiff for Ten dollars and thirty seven cents current money Debt and 95 cents Costs with interest until paid

Witness my hand

Wm A Gate, J.P.

True Copy from the docket of Wm A. Gates, formerly a Justice of the peace of the 8 Election District of Prince Georges County now on file in my office

Henry Brooke
Apl. 14 1875

STATE OF MARYLAND---Prince George's County, Set:

On this 14th day of April in the year of our Lord 1875 before the subscriber, REGISTER OF WILLS for Prince George's County, personally appeared L. L. Orme (Constable)

and made oath on the Holy Evangely of Almighty God that the above Judgment is just and true, as it stands stated, and that he hath not, nor hath any other person for him, (to his knowledge,) received any part, parcel, security or other satisfaction for the same.

SWORN BEFORE

Wm A Fairbank (Register)

No. 79

John G. Townshend
vs
John Baden

March 23d 1870
Judgment in favour of
the plaintiff for Ten
dollars and thirty
seven cents current money Debt and
95 cents Costs with interest until paid
Witness my hand
Wm A Gate, J.P.
True Copy from the docket of Wm. A.
Gate, formerly a Justice of the peace
of the 8 Electn District of Prince Georges
County now on file in my office
Ic Henry Brooke
Ap 14 1875

STATE OF MARYLAND---Prince George's County, Sct;

On this 14 day of April in the year of our Lord 18
before the subscriber, REGISTER OF WILLS for Prince George's County, personally appeared

L L Orme (Constable)

and made oath on the Holy Evangely of Almighty God that the above Judgment
is just and true, as it stands stated, and that he hath not, nor hath any other person for
him, (to his knowledge,) received any part, parcel, security or other satisfaction for the
same.

SWORN BEFORE

Wm A Jarboe Jr Register

24

No 5.

The within Judgment will pass when

paid

Test. *Wm A Jarboe Jr* Reg of Wills

This is to Certify that I have given all my interest right and Claim to F. A. Ward to administer on the estate of my deceased husband John Baden.

Jan 15th 1875

E. A. G Baden,

Test

William Baden

1875 #936

Renunciation of
E. A. G. Baden

No 1 Ct Proceedings
of Jany. 19th

John Baden.

1873   Est of John Bade—   Dr
            To Wm M Ward & Bro

To 1 Coffin And Case
   and Mourning goods   45 00
      Interest for Error   1 35
                                          46 35

June 25 1875
Recd of F. A. Ward Admr of John
Baden the above amt in full
                 Wm M Ward & Bro
           Per S. J. Hewitt

No. 1.

This account will pass
when proved.
Test: Wm A Darborough
Reg of Wills

Francis A. Ward Admr of John Baker
1870   To Thomas J Farmer   Dr
January 22 To advertising notice to creditors — 3S New $ 7.5 0

28

State of Maryland
Prince George's County, Towet
I hereby certify that on this 29th day of
March, in the year eighteen hundred
and seventy-five before me, the subscriber a Justice of the peace in
and for the county and State a-
foresaid personally appeared
M. R. Latimer and made oath
on the Holy Evangely of Almighty God
that the above
stands stated is account or account is just and true
and that he has not, nor has any
person for him (to his knowledge)
received any payment for the same
Sworn before
James W. Richards J.P.

This a/c will pass when
paid.

Test. Wm. A. Jarboe
Reg. of Wills

No. 3 in
distribution

$20.00

John Baden
To M. R. Latimer Dr.

To medical services rendered
family from March 7th, 1872.
to Feb. 25th. 1873 $20.00

Mar. 2. 1873   Asm of Mrs E. A. Baden
                        M. R. Latimer

Horse Head, Md., *March 20th* 187*4*

Mr. John Baden

Bought of F. A. WARD & CO.

DEALERS IN

DRY GOODS, GROCERIES, BOOTS, SHOES, HATS, QUEENSWARE,

And all articles usually found in a Country Store.

Terms Cash or Produce.

1873

Sept	23	To amt of acct Rend			5	81
"	24	" 2 lb Sugar a 12½		25		
"	"	" 2 " Coffee a 30		6		
Oct	4	" Balance on goods		07	9	
					6	7

State of Maryland, Prince George's County, to wit:

On this 5th day of May 1875, before me, a justice of the peace of the State of Maryland, in and for said county, personally appeared F. A. Ward of the firm of F. A. Ward and Co. and made oath in due form of law that the above account is just and true, and that neither he, nor any other person, in the name of the firm, has received any part a parcel of the money charged as due, or any security or satisfaction for the same, to the best of his knowledge & belief.

Sworn before,

M. J. Rodenbach J. P.

Jno Baden

Inasmuch

J. A. Ward

The within A/o will (paid when paid)
Test. Jno. Fanberg? Reg of Wills

Entd & Chg.

E. C. & R. H. Hyatt } 1873. Oct. 25th. Judgment in favor of plaintiffs
                        for $726.00 debt, and $1.70 costs, with interest
No. 56 }

John Dorsey   Test. Wm. F. Birckhead C.C.
                                    True copy,

                        Reg. &c.   Test. Wm. F. Birckhead C.C.
                        Probat. 10c.

            State of Maryland,   Prince George's County, to wit:
On the 8th day of Apr. 1874, before me, a Justice of the Peace
in and for said county, personally appeared George &c., and deposes
and says that he has received no payment in satisfaction, and
made oath in due form of law that he had not, nor had
any other person to his knowledge, received any part of the
sum for which the above judgment was passed.
                        Sworn before
                            Wm. C. Roberts   J.P.

I By order of the Orphans' Court the
within judgment will pass when paid.
Test
    Wm. A. Jarboe   Reg. of Wills

£. L. & R. H. Hyatt
vs
John Dorsey

Judgment

JEREMIAH SMITH BADEN

Jeremiah Smith Baden was the son of Thomas George Baden and Sarah Sabina. He was born in 1840, Prince Georges County, Maryland. He died 30 Mar 1903, Suwannee County, FL. In Jul 1865 he married Angeline Lydia Barber, b. 1843, Bryan Co., Georgia. Angeline died 1923 in Live Oak/Suwannee County, FL.

In the St. Paul's Church records: [8]

20 May 1839: Baptized in the Church Chapel **Jeremiah Smith Baden**, son of Thomas George & Sarah Sabina Baden, born 8 December 4 1838 [B1, 40-41].

Brothers and Sisters of Jeremiah Smith Baden:

5 April 1832. Baptized in the home of Mrs. Naylor, John Baden, son of Thomas George & Sarah Sabina Baden, born 7 August 1831 – also a coloured child named Pheby. On this same evening I married George A. Baden to Martha Naylor, and received a $5 note for the same [B1, 2].

7 July 1833. Baptized in the home of Capt. James Baden, Susanna Isabella Rebecca Baden, daughter of Thomas George & Sarah Sabina Baden, born 16 December 1832 [B1, 18-19]. Married unknown: Children, Billy, Emma, John, Ellen, Sadie, an unnamed child.

23 June 1834. Baptized in the Church Chapel, Martha Ann Baden, daughter of Thomas George & Sarah Sabina Baden, born 6 February 1834 [BL, 22-23].

20 March 1836. Baptized in the Church Chapel, James Thomas Baden, son of Thomas George & Sarah Sabina Baden, born 12 December 1835 [B1, 32-33].

James Thomas Baden married Anna Maria Yates, 1 Jul 1836, Washington, D.C. She was born 6 Jan 1842, Alexandria, VA and died 25 Nov 1941, Washington, D.C. Both are buried in the Arlington Claim File XC2676.419.

1.   Flora Baden married Langley

2.   Harry E. Baden b. 1873, still living 18 Apr 1898 (sworn affadivit by father)

A letter dated 21 November 1913, Washington, D.C. and signed by Anna Maria Yates Baden, the widow of James Thomas Baden to Idella Jeanette Baden Frier is abstracted below:

---

[8]Helen W. Brown. Indexes of Protestant Episcopal (Angelican) Church Register of Prince George's County, Maryland, 1686-1885 (Vol. 2). St Paul's Parish at Baden (records begin 1831) and Prince George's Parish (known as Rock Creek Parish 1711-1798). Heritage Books, 2006.

". . . of course you know that the Baden family belonged to the old families of Maryland slave holders, and at one time they were considered "somebodies' in the county. Since the Civil War they have had to hustle. My husband James T. [Thomas] Baden was an Officer of the Regular Army when the War broke out and he remained in the Union Army. He was promptly dis-inherited by his Grandfather, Capt. John Baden, who characerically remarked 'that you stayed in the Union Army, now let the damn Yankees take care of you! . . ."

The Uncle John mentioned above married his cousin Nellie Townsend. He met a sad fate, being murdered on his way to Washington, by whom it was never discovered . . ." An entry in the Church Registrar of St. Paul's " . . . John Baden found dead on the road supposedly to have been murdered the 17th day of November 1873 . . . buried 11 January 1874, . . ." [B2, 159]

Further on in the letter she speaks of " . . . your Aunt Belle . . .." No doubt a corruption of the name of Susanna Isabella Rebecca Baden, sister of James Thomas and Jeremiah Smith Baden. Later on she speaks of "Mattie" which again is the accepted nickname for Martha, born prior to James Thomas Baden.

James Thomas Baden: "Enlisted 23 Oct. 1857 as a Private in the General Mounted Services in Baltimore, Maryland. He served as a private, Corpral, Sergeant and a First Sergeant in Troop "F", 5th Cavalry until 30 October 1862. Granted a commission of 2nd Lieut. 31 October 1862 in the Cavalry. He rejoined his Regiment at St. James, MD [about 5 miles from Sharpsburg, MD where he participated in that bloody battle as the 1st Sgt. of Troop "F", 5gh Cav. 17 Sept. 1862. The Yankees called this Antietam.]

Promoted to 1st Lt. 2 Nov. 1863.

Resigned 12 Sep 1864 due to an injury received in the "Seven Days Battle" when his horse fell from under him, during a Cavalry Charge by his Regt. Discharged 12 Sep 1864 at City Point, VA. 5' 8" tall, fair complexion, brown hair, grey eyes, date of birth 12 Sept 1835.

In his sworn affidavit to his pension application he states: name, J. Thos. Baden; residences, resided in Prince George's County from birth until May 1853 when I moved to Washington, D.C. He is buried in the present-day National Arlington Cemetery.

Arlington National Cemetery

Arlington House

On a Virginia hillside rising above the Potomac River and overlooking Washington, D.C., stands Arlington House. The 19th-century mansion seems out of place amid the more than 250,000 military grave sites that stretch out around it. Yet, when construction began in 1802, the estate was not intended to be a national cemetery.

Arlington House "Custis-Lee Mansion"

The mansion, which was intended as a living memorial to George Washington, was owned and constructed by the first president's adopted grandson, George Washington Parke Custis, son of John Parke Custis who himself was a child of Martha Washington by her first marriage and a ward of George Washington. Arlington won out as a name over Mount Washington, which is what George Washington Parke Custis first intended calling the 1,100-acre tract of land that he had inherited at the death of his father when he was three.

Arlington won out because it was the name of the Custis family ancestral estate in the Virginia tidewater area. Custis hired George Hadfield, an English architect who came to Washington in 1785 to help construct the U.S. Capitol, to design his estate. The Greek revival structure which Hadfield designed took Custis 16 years to complete.

The north wing was the first structure completed in 1802. It was in this building that Custis made his home, with a significant portion of it used to store George Washington memorabilia Custis was acquiring with regularity. Among the items purchased and stored in the north wing were portraits, Washington's personal papers and clothes, and the command tent which the president had used at Yorktown.

Even after the completion of the south wing in 1804, Arlington House was still only a set of detached buildings. With the completion of the central section in 1818, the house stretched 140 feet from the north to the south wing. The central section contained a formal dining room and sitting room, a large hall and a parlor. One of the most recognizable of the section's features are the eight columns of the exterior portico, each 5 feet in diameter at the base.

George Washington Parke Custis and his wife, Mary Lee Fitzhugh (whom he had married in 1804), lived in Arlington House for the rest of their lives and were buried together on the property after their deaths in 1857 and 853, respectively. They are buried in their original graves in Section 13, at map grid N-30. On June 30, 1831, Custis' only child, Mary Anna Randolph Custis, married her childhood friend and distant cousin, Robert E. Lee. Lee was the son of former three-term Virginia Governor Henry ("Light Horse Harry") Lee and was himself a graduate of West Point.

George Washington Parke Custis

Between 1841 and 1857, Lee was away from Arlington House for several extended periods. In 1846 he served in the Mexican war under Gen. Winfield Scott, and in 1852 he was appointed superintendent of the U.S. Military Academy at West Point, his alma mater. After his father-in-law died in 1857, Lee returned to Arlington to join his family and to serve as executor of the estate.

Under the terms of her father's will, Mary Anna Custis Lee was given the right to inhabit and control the house for the rest of her life. Custis' will also stipulated that upon Mary Anna's death, full title would pass to her eldest son, George Washington Custis Lee. Contrary to popular belief, Robert E. Lee never owned the Arlington estate. Lee did serve as custodian of the property, which had fallen into disrepair by the time he returned to execute his father-in-law's will. By 1859, Lee had returned the property and its holdings to profitability and good order.

Robert E. Lee and his wife, Mary Anna, lived at Arlington House until 1861, when Virginia ratified an alliance with the Confederacy and seceded from the Union. Lee, who had been named a major general for the Virginia military forces in April 1861, feared for his wife's safety and anticipated the loss of their family inheritance. In May 1861, Lee wrote to Mary Anna saying:
"War is inevitable, and there is not telling when it will burst around you . . . . You have to move and make arrangements to go to some point of safety which you must select. The Mount Vernon plate and pictures ought to be secured. Keep quiet while you remain, and in your preparations . . . May God keep and preserve you and have mercy on all our people."
Following the ratification of secession by Virginia, federal troops crossed the Potomac and, under Brig. Gen. Irvin McDowell, took up positions around Arlington. Following the occupation, military installations were erected at several locations around the 1,100-acre estate, including Fort Whipple (now Fort Myer) and Fort McPherson (now Section 11).

Lee deeply regretted the loss of his home at Arlington. During the early stages of the war, foreseeing the probable loss of his home and belongings, Lee wrote to his wife about Arlington:
"It is better to make up our minds to a general loss. They cannot take away the remembrance of the spot, and the memories of those that to us rendered it sacred. That will remain to us as long as life will last, and that we can preserve."

Lee continued to feel responsible for the estate and earnestly hoped that the slaves who were left behind would be educated and freed, according to the provisions of George Washington Parke Custis' will. The property was confiscated by the federal government when property taxes levied against Arlington estate were not paid in person by Mrs. Lee. The property was offered for public sale Jan. 11, 1864, and was purchased by a tax commissioner for "government use, for war, military, charitable and educational purposes."

Arlington National Cemetery was established by Brig. Gen. Montgomery C. Meigs, who commanded the garrison at Arlington House, appropriated the grounds June 15, 1864, for use as a military cemetery. His intention was to render the house uninhabitable should the Lee family ever attempt to return. A stone and masonry burial vault in the rose garden, 20 feet wide and 10 feet deep, and containing the remains of 1,800 Bull Run casualties, was among the first monuments to Union dead erected under Meigs' orders.

Meigs himself was later buried within 100 yards of Arlington House with his wife, father and son; the final statement to his original order. The federal government dedicated a model community for freed slaves, Freedman's Village, near the current Memorial Amphitheater, on Dec. 4, 1863. More than 1,100 freed slaves were given land by the government, where they farmed and lived during and after the Civil War.

Neither Robert E. Lee, nor his wife, as title holder, ever attempted to publicly recover control of Arlington House. They were buried at Washington University (later renamed Washington and Lee University) where Lee had served as president. The couple never returned to the home George Washington Parke Custis had built and treasured. After Gen. Lee's death in 1870, George Washington Custis Lee brought an action for ejectment in the Circuit Court of Alexandria (today Arlington) County, Va. Custis Lee, as eldest son of Gen. and Mrs. Lee, claimed that the land had been illegally confiscated and that, according to his grandfather's will, he was the legal owner. In December 1882, the U.S. Supreme Court, in a 5-4 decision, returned the property to Custis Lee, stating that it had been confiscated without due process. On March 3, 1883, the Congress purchased the property from Lee for $150,000. It became a military reservation, and Freedman's Village, but not the graves, was removed.

ARLINGTON NATIONAL CEMETERY
Arlington County, Virginia

ARLINGTON NATIONAL CEMETERY FACTS

Arlington Mansion and 200 acres of ground immediately surrounding it were designated officially as a military cemetery June 15, 1864, by Secretary of War Edwin M. Stanton.

More than 300,000 people are buried at Arlington Cemetery.

Veterans from all the nation's wars are buried in the cemetery, from the American Revolution through the Iraq and Afghanistan. Pre-Civil War dead were reinterred after 1900.

The federal government dedicated a model community for freed slaves, Freedman's Village, near the current Memorial Amphitheater, Dec. 4, 1863. More than 1,100 freed slaves were given land by the government, where they farmed and lived during and after the Civil War. They were turned out in 1890 when the estate was repurchased by the government and dedicated as a military installation.

In Section 27, are buried more than 3,800 former slaves, called "Contrabands" during the Civil War. Their headstones are designated with the word "Civilian" or "Citizen."

Arlington National Cemetery and Soldiers Home National Cemetery are administered by the Department of the Army. All other National Cemeteries are administered by the Department of Veterans Affairs, or the National Park Service.

Arlington House (Custis-Lee Mansion) and the grounds in its immediate vicinity are administered by the National Park Service.

The flags in Arlington National Cemetery are flown at half-staff from a half hour before the first funeral until a half hour after the last funeral each day. Funerals are normally conducted five days a week, excluding weekends.

Funerals, including interments and inurnments, average 28 a day.

With more than 300,000 people buried, Arlington National Cemetery has the second-largest number of people buried of any national cemetery in the United States. Arlington National Cemetery conducts approximately 6,400 burials each year. The largest of the 130 national cemeteries is the Calverton National Cemetery, on Long Island, near Riverhead, N.Y. That cemetery conducts more than 7,000 burials each year.

The Tomb of the Unknowns is one of the more-visited sites at Arlington National Cemetery. The Tomb is made from Yule marble quarried in Colorado. It consists of seven pieces, with a total weight of 79 tons. The Tomb was completed and opened to the public April 9, 1932, at a cost of $48,000.

Three unknown servicemen are buried at the Tomb of the Unknowns.

A joint-service casket team holds a U.S. flag outstretched above the casket bearing the remains of the Vietnam Unknown, while President Ronald Reagan places a wreath at the casket's head during entombment ceremonies at Arlington National Cemetery.

Unknown Soldier of World War I, interred Nov. 11, 1921. President Harding presided. Unknown Soldier of World War II, interred May 30, 1958. President Eisenhower presided. Unknown Soldier of the Korean Conflict, interred May 30, 1958. President Eisenhower presided, Vice President Nixon acted as next of kin. An Unknown Soldier of the Vietnam Conflict, interred May 28, 1984. President Reagan presided. The remains of the Vietnam Unknown were disinterred May 14, 1998, and were identified as those of Air Force 1st Lt. Michael J. Blassie, whose family has reinterred him near their home in St. Louis, Mo. It has been determined that the crypt at the Tomb of the Unknowns that contained the remains of the Vietnam Unknown will remain empty.) The Tomb of the Unknowns is guarded by the U.S. Army 24 hours a day, 365 days a year. The 3rd U.S. Infantry (The Old Guard) began guarding the Tomb April 6, 1948.

On July 24, 1998, U.S. Capitol Police Officers John Michael Gibson, 42, and Jacob Joseph Chestnut, 58, were killed in the line of duty. They are buried in Arlington National Cemetery. Special Agent Gibson is buried in Section 28. Officer Chestnut, a retired Air Force master sergeant, is buried in Section 4.

In addition to in-ground burial, Arlington National Cemetery also has one of the larger columbariums for cremated remains in the country. Seven courts are currently in use, with over 38,500 niches.

When construction is complete, there will be nine courts with a total of over 60,000 niches, capacity for more than 100,000 remains. Any honorably discharged veteran is eligible for inurnment in the columbarium.

40

National Weekly Tribune
WASHINGTON D.C.

#3932 Illinois Ave., N.W.
Friday, Nov. 21, 1913.

My dear Cousin,

Grandma and I have returned to Washington sometime ago, but as my health has been particularly poor since my return, neither she nor I have been able to correspond. I have not been able to be at office for over two months and Grandma has to "put it up" with my complaints.

My doctors say I suffer from nervous indigestion, and it truly is suffering, but I did not start this with the intention of telling you of my ailments. Suffice it to say, I am much better.

Day after day I have promised Grandma to write you a long letter, and today I said I positively would. She jotted down a few remarks concerning the older members of the family and I will embrace them in this communication.

Of course you know that the Baden family belonged to the old families of Maryland slaveholders, and at one time they were considered "Somebodies" in the County. Since the Civil War they have had to hustle. My husband does have had... Baden, was an officer of the

Regular Army when the War broke out, and he remained in the Union Army. He was promptly disinherited by his Grandfather, Capt. John Baden, who characteristically remarked that "you stayed in the Union Army, now let the d--- Yankees take care of you."

As all Badens are good spenders, it was quite a blow to my husband. He remained in the Union Army, nevertheless, and married me, Anna Maria Yates, also of the traditioned old families of Maryland and Virginia. We had three children, two of whom I raised, a daughter, Flora, and Harry, a son. My daughter was burned to death, an accident occurring in Chicago, and she left three children, Blanche, Jesse and Raymond. Blanche, (now Mrs. Clay G. Collette.) lives in New York and has two splendid children, Raynor and Alice Collette. Jesse is a bachelor, and Raymond married a Philadelphia girl, Mildred, and they have a daughter, Winnifred Langley.

No doubt you have heard your father speak of your Uncle John? He was the oldest boy and was a fine man. He married his Cousin, Nellie Townsend, and he met a sad fate, being murdered on his way to Washington, by whom it was never discovered. He left a number of children. Mattie (Mrs. O'Brien) Susie Yates, who married my brother and who lives in Virginia, Katie, also lives in Virginia, Lottie, who died a year or so ago, and Charlie Baden, who lives down in Maryland near the scenes of the Badens former home.

Your Aunt Belle had six children, five of whom are living. Billy Baden, Anna, John, Allen and Sadie. Billy has a son who promises to be an excellent musician. Sadie married her cousin and

lives in PrinceGeorges County, Md., and perpetuates the name there.

So you see we also have a large Baden family in this section of the Country, and we are very glad to hear of your large family, and also of your own little family.

If Mattie comes down to Florida I possible will come with her, as I have longed to visit the South, especially Florida."

We lead a busy life here in Washington and it is only between the duties we can write to those we care most for. Grandma is in office, 9 to 4:30, and has a large house in the suburbs to care for after office hours. Servants are very hard to keep, here in the suburbs, but now we have a good Indian girl from Wisconsin who has taken charge of the house and we hope to have more time for pleasure. We had a Chippewa Indian girl for a number of years but she went back West. This is a Menominee Indian girl and seems to do very nicely. Grandma belongs to a number of societies, besides, and it keeps her busy. She belongs to the Army and Navy Society, the Southern Society, the Woman's Relief Corps, she did belong to the Spanish War Auxiliary, etc., but it is too much for her to keep up with.

I have quoted the portion of the letter which Grandma, herself, included.

As I wish to get out today for a little fresh air, I must now close.

With best wishes to all our relatives to whom you might mention us, and especially you and your family,

Your Aunt and Cousin,
Anna

U.S. National Homes for Disabled Volunteer Soldiers, 1866-1938

Name:	**James T Baden**
Birth Year:	abt 1835
Keyed Birth Location:	Md
Birth State:	Maryland
Admitted Year:	1891
Age at Admission:	56
State:	Virginia
City:	Hampton
Branch:	Roseburg Branch

Source Information:
Ancestry.com. *U.S. National Homes for Disabled Volunteer Soldiers, 1866-1938* [database online]. Provo, UT, USA: Ancestry.com Operations Inc, 2007. Original data: Historical Register of National Homes for Disabled Volunteer Soldiers, 1866-1938. (National Archives Microfilm Publication M1749, 282 rolls); Records of the Department of Veterans Affairs, Record Group 15, National Archives, Washington, D.C.

Description:
This database contains records from twelve U.S. National Homes for Disabled Volunteer Soldiers. The majority of the records consist of historical registers, but other records included in this database are indexes to the historical registers, applications, admissions, deaths, burials and hospital records. Information available in these records includes: name of soldier, name of home or branch, date of admission, birthplace, rank, company and regiment, dates and places of enlistment and discharge, physical description, occupation, marital status, and religion. Learn more...

No.	NAME	Name and Address of Relatives or Friends	When Born	Company and Regiment	Date of Enlistment	Date of Discharge	DISABILITY	Date of Admission	By order of Manager	Age	Married or Single	REMARKS
8897	John Philbin alias Jno Hughes Latimer Cook		Ireland	Private E 105 Pa C 20 2100 Inf	Mar 18/63 Nov 24/66	July /66 Oct 23/69	Loss of Vision	Oct 1/91	Gen Sewell	46	S	1st ad. Pensioner No Discharged at own request Re Admitted 12-9-96
8898	James T. Burton Clerk Cook		Ala	Private F 5 US Cav 1st Lieut	Nov 30/69 Oct 3/62 Oct 0/66 Sep 17/66		Heart disease	Oct 1/91	Gen Sewell	56	M	1st ad. Pensioner Yes
8899	John Connery Latimer Cook	Philad Pa	Ireland	Private G 20 Pa	June 1/63	/65	G.S. Wound	Oct 2/91	Gen Sewell	52	M	Re Admitted 20-6-94
8900	Saml R. Phillips Cook		White	A 2nd Minn E 13 Keiser Inf	May 11/61 July 5/63	Dec 11/63 Aug 11/66	Wounds Heart disease	Oct 2/91		65		

U.S. National Homes for Disabled Volunteer Soldiers, 1866-1938

James T Baden

Birth Year: abt 1835
Keyed Birth Location: MD
Birth State: Maryland
Admitted Year: 1891
Age at Admission: 56
State: Virginia
City: Hampton
Branch: Roseburg Branch

In a book compiled by Maurice Walter Frier, March 1978, Honolulu, Hawaii a grandson on the maternal side "My oldest sister Hilory (Mrs. J. A. Bishop, Riverview, FL) was born in his log cabin in Suwannee County, FL. She said she remembered him well but knew little of any detail about him. In a later interview with Bessie she said he was from Maryland, he never spoke of his parents, no one ever heard him express a desire to visit his former home, those of his "far south" family knew nothing of his family in the "far north." Bessie and Hilory had been told he had taught school in Georgia before the War of the Rebellion, that he had met our Grandmother, Miss Angeline Lydia Barber, during the War and that he promised he would return and marry her when the war was over. He did just that for the license for the wedding was issued 14 Feb 1865. He was still fighting for the Yankee cause.

Jeremiah Smith Baden enlisted in Chatham County, Georgia, served as 4th Corporal, Company L, Georgia 25th Infantry Regiment on 9 Aug 1861. Mustered out on 16 Nov 1861, Camp Wilson, Savannah, Georgia. (Roster of Confederate Soldiers of Georgia, 1861-1865).

He served in Company "E", 47th Georgia Regiment of Infantry. He saw military service as a Sergeant at Chickamauga, Chattanooga, Atlanta Campaign, and throughout the Caroline Campaign. In the last campaign, his unit was under the command of General Joseph E. Johnson who surrendered 26 April 1865, 17 days after General Lee (Confederate Army Records).

It is recorded in his Confederate Army Records, the papers on file in the courthouse in Suwannee County, FL for the settlement of his estate, and it is the same on Grandmother Baden's Confederate Pension Application Records [3158].

No explanation has been found as to why Jeremiah Smith Baden was left out in the will of his great grandfather John Baden, Jr., while his two brothers reaped so much.
Jeremiah went south either on 8 December 1859, the day he became 21 or soon after. He has not been located on any census for 1860 either in Maryland, Washington, D.C. or Georgia nor on the 1870 census.
1.   Thomas Luther Baden b. 1868, Georgia, d.   , married Mary E. and was a woodsman.
2.   Susan Frances (Anna) Baden, b. 5 Sep 1871, Florida, d. 14 Jan 1960, married William Author Roberts, b. 31 Dec 1863, Florida, d. 30 Apr 1925.
3.   Idella Jeanette (Nettie) Baden, b. 12 Jun 1875, Florida, d. 15 May 1964, married 15 May 1896 Warren Walter "Mack" Frier, b. 23 Jan 1873, Florida,d. 5 Aug 1959.
4.   Isaac Barber Baden, b. Sept 1877, Florida, married Ola Sapp.
5.   James Edward Baden, b. Feb 1880, married Annie
6.   Will H. Baden, b. Oct 1881, Florida, married Willow Sapp
7.   Lily Belle Baden, b. 6 Oct 1883, Florida, d. 2 Feb 1919, married James Edard Vann, b. 22 Jan 1880, d. 23 Dec 1945.

8.	Mary Harriet Baden b. 22 Oct 1885, McAlpin/Suwannee Co., FL, d. 18 Nov 1962, Clearwater/Pinellas Co., FL. On 25 Dec 1911 she married Marion Hampton Hicks, b. 21 Nov 1889 New Bern/Suwannee Co., FL. He died May 1970 at Clearwater/Pinellas Co., FL.

    a.	George Olin Hicks, b. 25 Nov 1912, Live Oak, FL.

    b.	Vivian Olive Hicks, b. 27 Apr 1914, Live Oak, FL; d. She died 26 Oct 2008, Dunedin/ Pinellas County, FL. On 1 Jun 1942, she married Joseph Lindsey Land in Clearwater, FL.

    c.	Robert Brice Land is the son of Vivian Olive Hicks and Joseph Lindsey Land. He was born 12 Jun 1943, Clearwater/Pinellas County, Florida. He is a veteran of the Korean War.

3.	Elizabeth Inez Hicks, b. 10 Sep 1915, Live Oak, FL, married John Wilks, Jr. resided in Largo, FL.

4.	Hilda Videl Hicks, b. 30 Aug 1917, Live Oak, FL, married James Eubanks.

5.	James Lloyd Hicks, b. 10 Apr 1926, Largo, FL, married 10 Apr 1947, Janet Ruth Hancock.

Jeremiah and Angeline are buried in the Mt. Pisgah Church cemetery in Suwannee County, FL. His headstone announces he was born 8 December 1840, died 30 March 1903. This all tallies with his Army records and census records.

The application for Grandmother Baden's Confederate Pension Application had to be a sworn statement or it could not be accepted in Tallahassee, FL. It was a sworn statement and accepted.

Marriages

Angeline Barber and Jerry Baden Feb 16, 1865

William Roberts and Susana Baden Feb 14 1886

Thomas Luther Baden and W. E. Goff Alford Nov. 1890

Mack W. Frier and Janet Baden May 16, 1894

Isaac B Baden and Ola Sap Jan. 8 1902

James Edward Vann and Isabel Baden 26, 1904

William Horas Baden and Willa Sapp 24, 1906

James Edward Baden and Annie Lee Sept, 1910

Marion Hampton Hicks and Harriet Baden Dec 24, 1911

A. Edgar Baden   Deaths. July, 13. 1874.

W. Alma Baden   Aug. 10. 1874

Jerry Miah S. Baden   March 30. 1903

Pearl Roberts   Nov 1902

Jewel Angaline Baden   Nov Feb 21, 1908

Bell Vann   Feb. 2. 1919

William Angaline Baden   Nov, 17, 1923

William Horace Baden   March 29. 1946

Isaac Barber Baden May or June 1962

48

BIRTHS.

NAMES.

CERTIFICATE.

This Certifies

THAT THE RITE OF

HOLY MATRIMONY

WAS CELEBRATED BETWEEN

Marion Hampton Weeks of Falmouth, Fla.

and Hattie Baker of Pine Mount Fla.

on Dec 24, 1911 at C. M. Fielding's Home

by C. M. Fielding

Mrs. C. M. Fielding

Witness

51

51

SCHEDULE I.—Free Inhabitants in _The 17th Militia Dist_ in the County of _Lafayette_ Sta[te] of _Georgia_ enumerated by me, on the _30th_ day of _August_ 1850. _Bird_ Ass't Marsh[al]

		The Name of every Person whose usual place of abode on the first day of June, 1850, was in this family.	Age	Sex	Color	Profession, Occupation, or Trade of each Male Person over 15 years of age.	Value of Real Estate owned	Place of Birth, Naming the State, Territory, or Country.				Whether deaf dumb, blind, insane, idiotic, pauper, or convict.
1	2	3	4	5	6	7	8	9	10	11	12	13
61	61	Isaac Barber	48	M		Contractor & Wks	1000	Geo				
		Frances "	47	F				"				
		Susan "	27	F				"				
		Israel "	25	M		Farmer		"				
		Martha "	17	F				"				
		Mary Ann "	14	F				"	1			
		Caroline	12	F				"	1			
		Angeline	7	F				"	1			
62	62	Radick Curtis	30	M		Farmer	500	Geo				
		Susan "	30	F				"				
		Jordon "	6	M				"				
		Shepperd "	4	M				"				
		Alice C "	3	F				"				
		Cornelia "	2	F				"				
		Lucius G Wm "	9	M				"				
63	63	Obadiah Barber	25	M		"	500	Geo				
		Nancy "	20	F				"				
		Julia "	1/2	F				"				
		Martha Collins	11	F				"				
64	64	Thomas Connady	45	M		"	500	Geo				
		Sarah "	40	F				"				
		Jane "	18	F				"				
		John "	13	M				"	1			
		Henry "	12	M				"	1			
		William "	11	M				"	1			
		Elizabeth "	8	F				"	1			
		Sarah "	6	F				"	1			
		Mary "	1	F				"				
65	65	James Thompson	28	M		"	500	Geo				
		Rebecca "	27	F				"				
		Wm C "	7	M				"	1			
		Cornelia "	5	F				"				
66	66	John Rogers	60	M		"	600	N 3				
		Elizabeth "	30	F				Geo				
		Catharine Thompson	21	F				"				
		John Thompson	20	M		"		"	1			
67	67	Solomon Thompson	40	M		"	500	Geo			(?)	
		Susan Ann "	33	F				Geo			(?)	
		Joshua "	12	M							10	
		Elizabeth "	11	F								
		Julian "	9	F					1			
		Rebecca "	7	F				"				

52

Georgia
Bryan County
by W. H. Hayman Ordinary of Bryan Co.
to any Minister of the Gospel or Judge

Justice of the Inferior Court or Justice of the peace for said
County you are hereby authorized to Join in marriage Mr.
Jeremiah S. Baden and Miss Angeline Barber of said county
according to the Laws and constitution of this State for which
this Shall be your Sufficient License given under my hand and
private seal of office this Feby the 14th 1865

(LS) W. H. Hayman O.B.C.

I hereby certify that Jeremiah S. Baden & Miss Angeline Barber
were duly Joined in matrimony this day by me this Feby the 16th 1865

James Shuman J.P.

Recorded Feby the 20th 1865 By W. H. Hayman Ordinary B.C.

Georgia Bryan County By W. H. Hayman ordinary of said county
To any minister of the Gospel Judge Justice of the Inferior court or Justice
of the peace for said county you are hereby authorized to Join in marriage
Mr. A. J. Sapp and Miss Ann Brown of said county according to the constitution and Laws of said State for which this Shall be your Sufficient
License Given under my hand and private seal there being no Seal of office
the fourteenth day of April A.D. 1865

(LS) W. H. Hayman O.B.C.

The above Joined was duly Married by W. B. McHan upon
the 16th day of April 1865

Recorded this April the 17th 1865

53   W. H. Hayman Ordinary B.C.

CONFEDERATE PENSION RECORD ABSTRACT

VETERAN'S NAME (LAST, FIRST, MIDDLE):				FILE NO.
BADEN, JEREMIAH S.				3158
STATE	UNIT DESIGNATION(S):			FLA. RESIDENT SINCE:
GEORGIA	Co. E, 47TH GEORGIA			NOT GIVEN
ENLISTMENT DATE:	PLACE OF ENLISTMENT:		APPLICATION FILED:	CITY AND/OR COUNTY OF RESIDENCE:
MARCH 1862	NOT GIVEN			NONE FILED
DISCHARGE DATE:	PLACE OF DISCHARGE:		APPLICATION FILED:	CITY AND/OR COUNTY OF RESIDENCE:
CLOSE OF WAR	NOT GIVEN			
DATE OF BIRTH:	PLACE OF BIRTH:		APPLICATION FILED:	CITY AND/OR COUNTY OF RESIDENCE
NOT GIVEN	NOT GIVEN			
DATE OF DEATH:	PLACE OF DEATH:		APPLICATION FILED:	CITY AND/OR COUNTY OF RESIDENCE
3-30-1903	SUWANNEE COUNTY, FLORIDA			
WIDOW'S NAME (FIRST, MIDDLE, LAST):			APPLICATION FILED:	CITY AND/OR COUNTY OF RESIDENCE:
ANGELINA LYDIA BADEN			8-4-1903	COOPER (SUWANNEE Co.)
DATE OF MARRIAGE:	PLACE OF MARRIAGE:		APPLICATION FILED:	CITY AND/OR COUNTY OF RESIDENCE:
2-14-1865	EDEN (BRYAN) GEORGIA		7-28-1909	PINE MOUNT (SUWANNEE Co.)
FLA. RESIDENT SINCE:	DATE OF DEATH:	AGE/YEAR (AS GIVEN ON APPLICATION)	APPLICATION FILED:	CITY AND/OR COUNTY OF RESIDENCE:
2-20-1867	BEFORE 1934	60 IN 1903		

STATE OF FLORIDA
DEPARTMENT OF STATE
Division of Archives, History and
Records Management
Form DS-AR 1 (10-74)

PAGES: 8

This abstract card is NOT an original source document. The original documents are preserved in the Archives of the State of Florida.

The Archives of the State of Florida cannot certify the accuracy of any statement made on a pension application. Certification is made only as to the accuracy of the abstracted data which appears on this form.

ARC 3-1 (21)
Ref. 104

NOTE:
The license was issued 14 Feb 1865
The marriage ceremony was performed 16 July 1865
M Fries

54

Pat 4884   Vol 10   Page 100   Order 2137589

The United States of America,

TO ALL TO WHOM THESE PRESENTS SHALL COME, GREETING:

Homestead Certificate No. 4884
Application 8802

Whereas there has been deposited in the GENERAL LAND OFFICE of the United States a CERTIFICATE of the Register of the Land Office at *Gainesville, Florida*, whereby it appears that, pursuant to the Act of Congress approved 20th May, 1862, "To secure Homesteads to actual settlers on the public domain," and the acts supplemental thereto, the claim of *Jeremiah S. Paden* has been established and duly consummated in conformity to law for the *north half of the north-east quarter, the north-east quarter of the north-west quarter and the south-west quarter of the north-east quarter of section thirty-six, in township four south, of range fourteen east, of Tallahassee Meridian in Florida, containing one hundred and sixty acres and eighteen hundredths of an acre*

according to the Official Plat of the Survey of the said Land returned to the GENERAL LAND OFFICE by the SURVEYOR GENERAL.

Now know ye, That there is therefore granted by the UNITED STATES unto the said *Jeremiah S. Paden* the tract of Land above described: TO HAVE AND TO HOLD the said tract of Land, with the appurtenances thereof, unto the said *Jeremiah S. Paden* and to his heirs and assigns forever.

In testimony whereof I, Grover Cleveland President of the United States of America, have caused these letters to be made Patent, and the Seal of the General Land Office to be hereunto affixed.

Given under my hand, at the City of Washington, the *twentieth* day of *June*, in the year of Our Lord one thousand eight hundred and *eighty five*, and of the Independence of the United States the one hundred and *ninth*.

By the President: *Grover Cleveland*

By *M. McKean* Sec'y.

S. W. Clark, Recorder of the General Land Office.

55

Jeremiah Smith Baden

&

Wife, Angeline Lydia (Barber)

Now know ye, That there is therefore granted by the UNITED STATES unto the said *Jeremiah S. Baden* the tract of Land above described: TO HAVE AND TO HOLD the said tract of Land, with the appurtenances thereof, unto the said *Jeremiah S. Baden* and to his heirs and assigns forever.

In testimony whereof I, *Grover Cleveland* President of the United States of America, have caused these letters to be made Patent, and the Seal of the General Land Office to be hereunto affixed.

Given under my hand, at the City of Washington, the *twentieth* day of *June* , in the year of Our Lord one thousand eight hundred and *eighty five* , and of the Independence of the United States the one hundred and *ninth*.

By the President: *Grover Cleveland*

By *M. Mc Kean* Sec'y.

J. W. Clark , Recorder of the General Land Office.

L. S.

57

DEATHS.

BIRTHS.

NAMES.

59

ANGELINE
BADEN
WIFE OF
J. S. BADEN
MAY 27 1843
NOV 17 1928

REGISTRATION CARD—(Men born on or after April 28, 1877 and on or before February 16, 1897)

SERIAL NUMBER	1. NAME (Print)	ORDER NUMBER
2118	MARION HAMPTON HICKS	
U	(First) (Middle) (Last)	-

2. PLACE OF RESIDENCE (Print)

BAY AVE. BUCKROE BEACH ELIZ. CO., VA
(Number and street) (Town, township, village, or city) (County) (State)

(THE PLACE OF RESIDENCE GIVEN ON THE LINE ABOVE WILL DETERMINE LOCAL BOARD
JURISDICTION; LINE 2 OF REGISTRATION CERTIFICATE WILL BE IDENTICAL)

3. MAILING ADDRESS

BUCKROE BEACH BOX 117
(Mailing address if other than place indicated on line 2. If same insert word same)

4. TELEPHONE	5. AGE IN YEARS	6. PLACE OF BIRTH
	52	LIVE OAK
		(Town or county)
	DATE OF BIRTH	
(Exchange) (Number)	NOV. 20 1889	FLORIDA
	(Mo.) (Day) (Yr.)	(State or country)

7. NAME AND ADDRESS OF PERSON WHO WILL ALWAYS KNOW YOUR ADDRESS

MARY HARRIET HICKS, BAY AVE, BUCKROE BEACH VA

8. EMPLOYER'S NAME AND ADDRESS

PERRY LOFTON JUDD, NEWPORT NEWS, VA

9. PLACE OF EMPLOYMENT OR BUSINESS

DIXIE HOSPITAL HAMPTON ELIZ. CITY VA
(Number and street or R. F. D. number) (Town) (County) (State)

I AFFIRM THAT I HAVE VERIFIED ABOVE ANSWERS AND THAT THEY ARE TRUE.

D. S. S. Form 1
(Revised 4-1-42)   (over)   16-21620-2   *Marion Hampton Hicks*
(Registrant's signature)

62

and. magh Lindsay

Limer Margaret K   R B   Shocco

Lynch May Ellen   Sidney   Judkins

Latta Mary E   J P   Norlina

Lynch Geo J   Ed   Fishing Creek

Lynch Ben J   Sidney   Judkins

Lynch Ashley   June   "

Little *Muphy Coxgll*   W G   River
~~James~~ ~~Hicks~~ ~~gright~~   ~~Ling~~   ~~~~   "
Lynch ~~Hester~~ *Lola Cromwell*   Fred *Baird*

North Carolina State Board of Health
BUREAU OF VITAL STATISTICS

Nº 145022

STANDARD CERTIFICATE OF BIRTH

1. PLACE OF BIRTH—

County .... Warren .... Registration District No. .. 93-2673 ...... Certificate No. 6

Township .... River .... or Village ....

City .... Vaughan .... No. .... St. .... Ward
(If birth occurred in a hospital or institution, give its name instead of street and number)
If child is not yet named, make supplemental report, as directed

2. FULL NAME OF CHILD .... Joseph Lindsey Land

| 3. Sex Male | If plural births | 4. Twin, triplet, or other .... | 6. Premature ..... | 7. Are parents married Yes. | 8. Date of birth .. June 25, 1918 |
| | | 5. Number in order of birth .... | Full term ..... | | (Month, day, year) |

| 9. Full name | FATHER | 18. Full maiden name | MOTHER |
| | John Thomas Land | | Lois Rebecca Brice |

10. Residence (usual place of abode) (If non-resident, give place and State) .. Vaughan
19. Residence (usual place of abode) (If non-resident, give place and State) .. Vaughan

11. Color or race .. White .. 12. Age at last birthday .. — .. (years)
20. Color or race .. White .. 21. Age at last birthday .. — .. (years)

13. Birthplace (city or place) .. S. C. .. — (State or country)
22. Birthplace (City or place) .. S. C. .. (State or country)

14. Trade, profession or particular kind of work done, as spinner, sawyer, bookkeeper, etc. .. Truck Foreman
23. Trade, profession or particular kind of work done, as housekeeper, typist, nurse, clerk, etc. .. Housewife

15. Industry or business in which work was done, as silk mill, sawmill, bank, etc.
24. Industry or business in which work was done, as own home, lawyer's office, silk mill, etc.

16. Date (month and year) last engaged in this work .. 19..
17. Total time (years) spent in this work ..
25. Date (month and year) last engaged in this work .. 19..
26. Total time (years) spent in this work ..

27. Number of children of this mother (at time of this birth and including this child) (a) Born alive and now living .... 4 (b) Born alive but now dead .... (c) Stillborn ....

CERTIFICATE OF ATTENDING PHYSICIAN OR MIDWIFE

I hereby certify that I attended the birth of this child, who was born alive at .. 5:A .... m. on the date above stated.

WHEN THERE WAS NO ATTENDING PHYSICIAN OR MIDWIFE, THEN THE FATHER, HOUSEHOLDER, ETC., SHOULD MAKE THIS RETURN.

(Signed) .. L. J. Picot .... M. D
or .... Midwife

Given name added from a supplemental report .... (Date of) ....

Address .. Littleton, North Carolina

Filed .. — .. 19.. .. J. H. Harris ....
REGISTRAR

.... REGISTRAR

THIS IS TO CERTIFY that the above is a true copy of the birth certificate

of .. Joseph Lindsey Land ....

filed in this office.

J. W. R. Norton

State Registrar.

FILE .. 725 .. PAGE .. 387

Date Issued: 11-24-1958

65

APPLICATION FOR MARRIAGE LICENSE   C. J. NO. 13503

Name J. L. Land   , Address Aberdeen, N.C.

Age 23 Color white Birthplace Vaughan, N.C.

Married before? no Divorced? --- Where? ----- Occupation S.A.L.R.R.

and

Name Vivian Hicks   Address Clearwater, Fla.

Age 28 Color white Birthplace Live Oak, Fla.

Married before? no Divorced? --- Where? ----- Occupation bookkeeper

It is expected that John C. Brown

STATE OF FLORIDA,

COUNTY OF _____

Before me, the undersigned authority, personally appeared

_____ and

_____

who being first duly sworn, depose and say that __he__ the parent__ of the said

_____

who is_____years of age, and that __he__ do__ hereby consent to the marriage of the said_____

to _____

_____

_____

Subscribed and sworn to before me this, the_____day of_____, 19____

_____

(TITLE)

FORM V.S. NO. 48

Address Clearwater, Fla.

will perform the ceremony.

STATE OF FLORIDA,

COUNTY OF Pinellas

Before me, the undersigned authority, personally appeared the persons above named, who, being first duly sworn, depose and say that the information given by each of them as above set forth is true and correct, and that neither of them is married at this time and that they are not related within the prohibited degree.

J. L. Land

Vivian Hicks

Subscribed and sworn to before me this, the

1 day of June 19 42

John C. Brown

Notary Public

(TITLE)

Marriage License

CENTRAL BUREAU OF VITAL STATISTICS

C. J. No. 13503

State of Florida, Pinellas County

To any Minister of the Gospel, or any Officer Legally Authorized to Solemnize the Rite of Matrimony:

Whereas, Application having been made to the County Judge of Pinellas County, of the State of Florida, for a license for marriage, and it appearing to the satisfaction of said County Judge that no legal impediments exist to the marriage now sought to be solemnized:

These are, therefore, To authorize you to unite in the

Holy Estate of Matrimony

J. L. Land _____ and _____ Vivian Hicks

and that you make return of the same, duly certified under your hand, to the County Judge aforesaid.

Witness my name as County Judge, and the seal of said Court, at the Courthouse in Clearwater, this ____1st____ day of ____June____, A. D. 19 42 (SEAL) ____Jack F. White____, County Judge.

CERTIFICATE OF MARRIAGE

I Certify that the within-named ____J. L. Land____ and ____Vivian Hicks____ were by me, the undersigned, duly united in the Holy Estate of Matrimony, by the authority of the within License.

Done this ____1st____ day of ____June____, A. D. 19 42 at ____Clearwater____, Florida.

Witness Mrs. Johnny Williams (SEAL) ____John C. Brown - Notary Public____
MINISTER OR LEGALLY AUTHORIZED OFFICER

Witness Johnny Williams ____Clearwater, Fla.____
ADDRESS

Returned this 1 day of ____June____ A. D. 19 42, and recorded in Marriage Book 23, page 2

____Jack F. White____, County Judge.
J.B.

67

67

FLORIDA CERTIFICATE OF DEATH

Olive   Lane

April   ,   live Oak, Florida   Pinellas   October   ,

    Dunedin

Florida   Pinellas   Dunedin   34690

Bookkeeper   Retail Department Store

Marion Hicks   Mary Harriet Baden

Library   Daughter   Florida

Dunedin   34690

Sylvan Abbey Memorial Park   Florida   Clearwater

F043034   Florida

Sylvan Abbey Funeral Home   Florida

Clearwater   7965 Sunset Pt. Rd.   34756

  / /   0846

Florida   Clearwater   1969 Sunset Point Road   Suite 15   33765

November   2008

68

41488457

68

Hospital Birth Certificate

This Certifies

That _____ROBERT BRICE LAND_____ Was Born in the

Morton F. Plant Hospital
Clearwater, Florida

at _4:00A._ m. _Saturday, June 12th_ 19_43_

In Witness Whereof the said Hospital has caused this Certificate to be signed by its duly authorized officer and its Corporate Seal to be hereunto affixed.

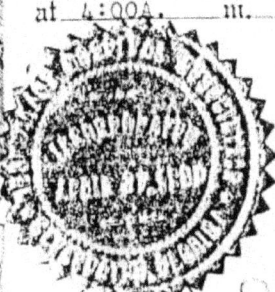

Lilly C. Foley R.N.
SUPERINTENDENT.

J. Sidley Hood M.D.
ATTENDING PHYSICIAN.

Family History

Father's full name _Joseph Lindsay Land_

Residence _Clearwater Fla._

Birthplace _Vaughan, N.C._ Date _June 25th, 1918_

Mother's maiden name _Vivian Olive Hicks_

Birthplace _Live Oak Fla._ Date _April 27th 1914_

Place of marriage of parents _Clearwater Fla._

Date of marriage of parents _June 1st, 1942_

Form B—Hollister Birth Certificate. Design © 1925, Franklin C. Hollister, Chicago

"Remember thy Creator in the days of thy youth"

69

69

Florida
State Board of Health

BUREAU OF VITAL STATISTICS
JACKSONVILLE

This is to Certify *that a* Birth Certificate *has been filed for*

Robert Brice Land _____ Sex Male

Child of: Born on_____ June 12, 1943

Mr. & Mrs. Joseph Lindsay Land
914 E. Turner St.
Clearwater, Fla.

This Record is filed in

Book No. _____ 1571

Page No. _____ 20645

Henry Hanson
State Health Officer

Edward M. L'Engle
Director Bureau of Vital Statistics

THOMAS BADEN

Thomas Baden, b. was the son of Robert Baden, Sr. and a brother to John Baden, Sr. b. 1732, Baden, Prince George's County, Maryland. Thomas Baden, married by 1761, Eleanor, daughter of John Brightwell (Maryland Marriage References – B – Maryland State Archives PG Liber T#1:70).

Liber 31, folio 707
23 Nov. 1761
BADEN, THOMAS, Prince George's Co.

To my wife, Eleanor Baden, for life, my part of The Gores & Hargrove, & for widhood, 4 negroes - Adam, Ned, Nacy, & Rachel - & on her d. or mar., the sd.
4 negroes to my 4 chldn - John, Thomas, Martha, & Lettice - & if she choose my part of The Exchange for her 1/3, my son John shall have its use during her life.

To my son John Baden, my part of The Exchange, betw. White's Br. & Rathafords Br., Sarums Forrest, in The Forrest, & negro man Ned.

To my son Thomas Baden, my part of a lease, Brookfield, on the d. of my sd. wife, the lands bequeathed her, & negro man Nacy.

To my dau. Martha Baden, negro woman Rachel, & except negro Adam., 1/3 my m. e.

To my dau. Lettice Baden, 1/3 my m. e.

My bro. John Baden is to be grdn. for my sd. 4 chldn., & he & my sd. wife my extrs.

Witn: Jonathan Oden, Vinson Oden, Ben. Baden.

23 June 1762, sworn to by all 3 witn., & the widow renounced the bequests in the will & elected what the law allows.

22 June 1762, John Baden renounced the admin. & the grdianship.   Witn: Benjn. Baden

BADEN, JOHN (of Thomas), of Prince George's County, Maryland (1805)

In the Name of God Amen. I John Baden (of Thomas) of Prince Georges County and State of Maryland being Sick and well knowing the certainty of Death and the uncertainty when it may come, do make this my last will and Testament in manner and form following –
First and principally I commit my Soul to Almighty God in hopes of a Joyful Resurrection.
Imprimis, I give to my loving Wife Margaret Baden during her life or widowhood, all my Real and personal property that I am now possessed of.
Item, I give to my son Thomas Noble Baden and his heirs for ever, part of a Tract of land called Marshams Rest lying on the South Side of the Road (leading from John Warings land to Susanna Magruders) he paying my Daughter Rebecca Dent Noble, the Sum of Three Hundred Dollars, at the end of one year after he gets possession of the Said Land.
Item, I give to my Son John Tarvin Baden and his Heirs for ever, part of a Tract of land called Marshams rest, part of a Tract called Exchange and part of a Tract called Masoonscon[?], lying on the South Side of Rutherford branch, he paying my Daughter Eleanor Baden or her Heirs the Sum of four Hundred Dollars at the end of one year after he gets possession of the Said Land.
Item, I give to my Son Clement Baden and his heirs for ever, my Grist Mill and Mill Seat on Rutherfords branch and including a small piece of land I purchased of John Baden Senr. also my

part of a Grist Mill and Mill Seat on the main branch of deep Creek – he paying my Daughter Ann Baden or her Heirs the Sum of Two Hundred Dollars, and to my Daughter Elizabeth Baden or heirs the Sum of Two hundred dollars at the end of Two years after he gets possession of the Said Mills and Mill Seats.

Item, I give to my Son Joseph Noble Baden and his Heirs for ever, the plantation whereon I now live called part of Exchange, he paying to my Daughter Margaret Baden the Sum of Three Hundred Dollars at the end of Two years after he gets possession of the said Plantation.

Item, I give to my Daughters, Eleanor, Ann, Elizabeth, and Margaret Baden, one Negroe woman named Sil and her future Increase.

Item, I give to my Daughter Ann Baden and her heirs one Negroe man named Jem.

Item, I give to my Daughter Elizabeth Baden and her heirs one Negroe Lad named Nace.

Item, I give to my Daughter Margaret Baden and her heirs one negroe boy named John.

My will and desire is that my loving wife Margaret Baden have the use and benefit of the Negroes Sil, Jem, Nace and John (which I have given to my Daughters) during her life or widowhood.

Lastly I do hereby Constitute and appoint my Sons Clement Baden and Joseph Noble Baden, Executors of this my last will and Testament. In Testimony whereof I have hereunto Set my hand and affixed my Seal this thirteenth day of May in the year of our Lord Eighteen Hundred and five.

      John Baden of Thos.

      Signed, Sealed, published, pronounced & declared to be
the last will of John Baden (of Thos.) in presence of

      Robert Baden
John Baden Junr.
John Tarvin

      Prince George's County to wit }
June 11th 1805   }
Then came Robert Baden and John Baden two of the subscribing Witnesses to the foregoing last Will and Testament and made oath on the Holy Evangely of Almighty God that they did see John Baden, of Thomas, the Testator therein named sign and seal this Will and heard him publish, pronounce and declare the same to be his last Will and Testament, that at the time of his so doing he was to the best of their apprehensions of sound and disposing mind memory and understanding and that they together with John Tarvin the other subscribing Witness respectively subscribed their names as Witnesses to this Will in presence of the Testator at his request and in the presence of each other.

      Sworn Before
Trueman Tyler Register
of Wills for Prince George's
County –

[SOURCE: Prince George's County Register of Wills (Estate Papers) John Baden (of Thomas) will, dated 13 May 1805, proven 11 Jun 1805; estate file, MSA C2119-2-4, MdHR 50,822; Maryland State Archives, Annapolis, Maryland]

JOHN ROBERT BADEN

John Robert Baden was born in 1810, died 1870. He is listed as being buried in Saint Thomas Episcopal Church Cemetery but not indicated if in an unmarked grave or on a family plantation. (Stones and Bones: Cemetery Records of Prince George's County. Maryland).

He was sheriff of Nottingham, Prince George's County, Maryland.

Session Laws, 1847

Volume 612, Page 71 View pdf image   Jump to page

1847.	LAWS OF MARYLAND.
CHAP. 86.	CHAPTER 86.
Passed Feb. 16, 1848.	An act entitled, an act to allow John Robert Baden, former Sheriff of Prince George's County, further tine to complete his collections.
Authorise to collect.	SECTION 1. Be it enacted by the General Assembly of Maryland, That John R. Baden, former sheriff of Prince George's county, by himself or any person or persons by him appointed for this purpose, is and are hereby authorised and empowered to collect the sums and balances' due him as sheriff of Prince George's county, which accrued and were due prior to the first of January, eighteen hundred and forty-three, in the same manner which the said John R. Baden could or might have done within the time limited by law.
To annex affidavit to account.	SEC. 2. And be it enacted. That it shall be the July of the said John R. Baden, before he proceeds to execute or distrain the property of any person or persons for public dues, or officers fees, by virtue of this act, to deliver to such person or persons chargeable with the same, at least thirty days previous to levying such execution or distress, an account, written in words at full length, of the public, dues for officers fees demanded of him, her or them, and that he, or either of his legally authorised deputies lor the years eighteen hundred and forty-one and forty-two, shall annex an affidavit to such account, that he hath not received any part thereof, nor anything in security or satisfaction for the same, other than the credits given, to the best of his knowledge and
Proviso.	belief; provided, that nothing in this act contained shall be so construed to affect the estate of a deceased person, except to authorise the said John R. Baden, or his deputies, to recover any claim on balance due by a deceased-person, in the same manner that claims against deceased persons are now recovered by law.
In force.	SEC. 3. And be it enacted, That this act shall be in force for twelve months from the date of its passage, and no longer.

Nottingham

St. Thomas Episcopal Church

Prince George's County, Maryland

ALEXANDER BADEN

Alexander Baden was a son of John Baden, Sr. and a brother to John Baden, Jr. He married Mary Steel 3 Jun 1797, in Prince George's County, Maryland. He is mentioned in his father's will - - ". . . all my part of two tracts of land where on my Son ALEXANDER BADEN deces. lived called Mansfield and Cullins Comfort . . .."

In the 1810 census of Prince George's County, Maryland, Alexander is listed as over 45. This would make a possible date of birth being before 1765 but not earlier than 1755.

ALEXANDER BADEN WILL

In the name of God Amen

I Alexander Baden of Prince Georges County in the State of Maryland Being sick and weak in body but of sound memory and understanding do make this my last will and testament in manner and form following, that is to say – First and principally I commit my soul into the hands of Almighty God, and my body to the Earth to be decently buried at the discretion of my Executrix herein after named. I devise and bequeath as follow.

Item. I give and bequeath to my beloved wife, Sarah F. Baden all the personal property I now posses – lastly I do hereby appoint my beloved wife Sarah F. Baden Executrix of this my last will and testament.

In testamony whereof I have hereunto affixed my hand and seal this twelvth day of January in the year of our Lord Eighteen hundred and Twenty one.

Alexander Baden (Seal)

signed sealed and delivered by Alexander Baden the
above testator in the presence of us
John Baden Jr.
John T. Baden
Josias Gibbons.

Prince Georges County to wit }

May 29th 1821   }

Then came John T. Baden & Josias Gibbons two of the subscribing Witnesses to the within Will and made oath on the Holy Evangely of Almighty God that they did see Alexander Baden the Testator therein named sign and seal this Will, that they heard him publish, pronounce and declare the same to be his last Will and Testament, that at the time of his so doing he was to the best of their apprehensions of sound and disposing mind memory and understanding and that they together with John Baden Jr. the other subscribing witness respectively subscribed their names as Witnesses to this will in Presence of the testator at his request and in the Presence of each other.

Sworn before
Trueman Tyler Regr of
Wills for PGCo.

.

THOMAS GEORGE BADEN

Thomas George Baden was the son of John Thomas Baden and Margaret Baden. He was born in 1810, Baden, Prince Georges County, Maryland. In 1853 he married Sarah Sabina b. 1811 in Prince Georges County, Maryland.

They had a son named Jeremiah Smith Baden who was left out of his grandfather's, John Baden, Jr., will.

Susanna Isabelle Rebecca Baden was a daughter of Thomas George Baden and Sarah Sabina. She married Jeremiah T. Baden who is mentioned in his grandfather's will.

Another son was named John B. Baden John Baden[9], born 7 Aug 1831, baptized 5 Apr 1832, died 17 Nov 1873 (Register of St. Paul's Church, Baden, Maryland), married 21 Jan 1857, Eleanor Ann Gantt Townshend.[10] He was murdered on the road to Washington, D.C.; interred 11 Jan 1874.

---

[9] Information from a letter written by and for the widow of JAMES THOMAS BADEN, dated Washington, D.C., 21 Nov 1913.

[10] Index of Marriage Licenses, Prince Georges County, MD, 1777-1886 by Helen Brown, 1971.

SUSANNA ISABELLA REBECCA BADEN

Susanna Isabella Rebecca Baden was a daughter of Thomas George and Sarah Sabina Baden. She married Jeremiah Thomas Baden who is mentioned in his grandfather John Baden, Jr's. will.

1.   William P. Baden, b. 4 Oct 1855, d. 4 Mar. 1937, married Ann Ellen Bean

2.   Sarah Margaret Baden, b. 26 Oct 1861, d. 2 Feb 1919, Baden, Prince George's County Maryland, married William Mortimer Baden 15 Dec 1885. They lived in Nottingham, Maryland in 1870 and in Brandywine, Maryland in 1920. The family is buried in St. Paul's Cemetery, Baden, Maryland.

3.   Ella Williams Baden, b. 11 Nov 1863, d. 24 Nov 1939.

4.   Mary Emma Baden b. 16 Feb 1865, d. 16 Jul 1942

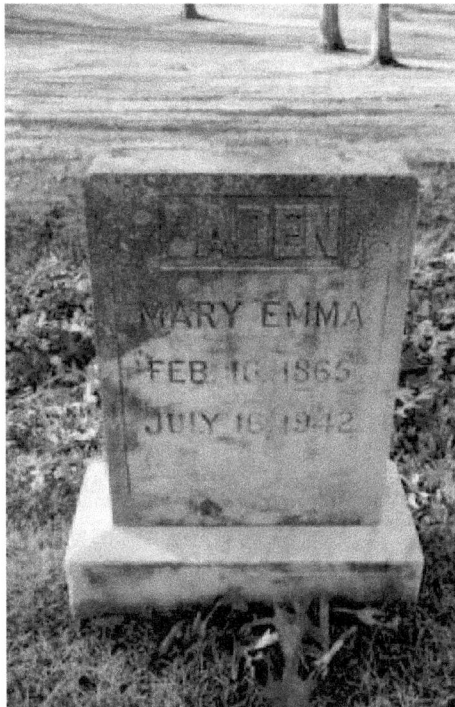

5.   John Thomas Baden, b. 18 Sep 1867, d. 4 Feb 1938

6.   Jeremiah Millard Baden b. 1861, d. 24 Jan 1893; no stone found but listed in cemetery records

ROBERT WILLIAM GOVER BADEN

Robert William Gover (probably Grover) Baden, b. 16 Jan 1815, d. 16 May, 1882, married Margaret Caroline Early.

1.   William Albert Kerr Baden, b. 22 Feb 1839, d. 21 May 1872.

2.   Margaret Marsaline Baden, b. 1845, d. 21 Nov. 1917

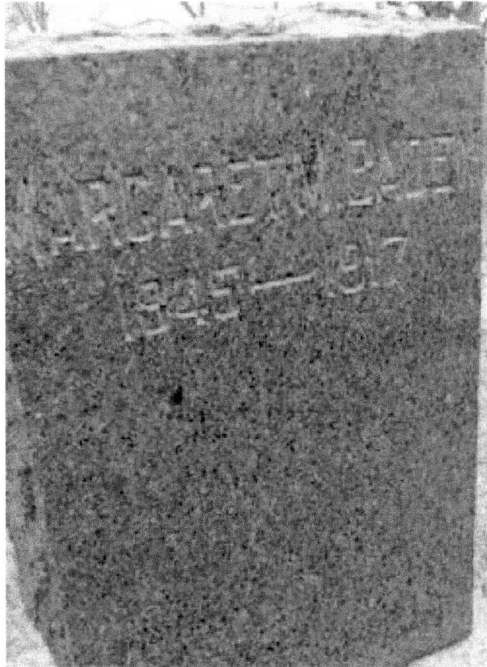

3.   James Early Baden (first wife Roberta S. Hodger; second wife, Mary Ida Monroe.

Children of James Early Baden and Roberta S. Hodger:

A. Albert Norwood Baden, Pvt. Co. F 17th Inf., Camp Meade, Maryland

B. **Clyde Hodger Baden, his wife, Edna Schaffer.** The Washington Post: On Tuesday, December 4, 1962, Clyde Hodger Baden, of Brandywine, Md. Beloved husband of the late Edna M.C. Baden, father of Col. Clyde H. Baden, Jr. USA and Charles Norwood Baden. He is also survived by a brother Grayson Baden, a sister, Mrs. Helen Pardee and four grandchildren. Friends may call at the Ritchie Bros. Funeral Home, Upper Marlboro, Md. from 2-9 p.m. Funeral services will be held in St. Paul's Episcopal Church, Baden, Md. on Friday, December 7 at 11 a.m. Interment church cemetery.

C. Robert William Gover Baden

4.   Amanda Mevina Baden
5.   Elizabeth Dorinda Baden

Robert Emmanuel Baden, b. 25 Dec 1846, d. 26 Apr 1922, married first Elizabeth Agnes Thomas; daughter Helen Frances Baden.

His second wife, Margaret Catherine Turner, b. 28 Dec 1853; d. 21 Jan 1946. Children:

A.   Jesse Ernest Baden

B.   Joseph Roy Baden, wife Agnes Brown Metcalf

C.   Bessie Wilson Baden Moss
D.   Maggie Aleine Baden, b. 27 Nov 1892, d. 27 May 1980

The Washington Post
May 28, 1980

On Tuesday, May 27, 1980, Maggie A. Baden, of Alexandria, Va., daughter of the late Robert Emanuel Baden and Margaret C. Turner Baden. Survived by Mary J. Child; six nieces and two nephews. Friends received at Huntt Funeral Home, Waldorf, Md. Wednesday evening from 7 to 9 p.m. Services at St. Paul's Episcopal Church, Baden, Md. Thursday, may 29, 11 a.m. Interment church cemtery. If desired, memorial contributions may be made to St. Paul's Episcopal Church, Baden, Md.

E.   John Turner Baden, b. 3 Mar 1880, d. 23 Jul 1965, his wife Margaret Johns Skinner Duvall, daughter of William Henry Duvall.
The Washington Post
July 25, 1965

On Friday, July 23, 1965, John Turner Baden of Brandywine, Md. Beloved husband of Margaret Duvall Baden and father of Mrs. Margaret B. Phibbons; brother of Maggie A. Baden J. Roy and Dr. R. Early Baden and Mrs. Bessie B. Moss. Also survived by one granddaughter, Margaret John Phibbons. Funeral from the Hunt Funeral Home, Waldorf, Md. on Sunday, July 25, at 2:15 p.m. Services at St. Paul's Church, Baden, Md. at 3 p.m. Interment church cemetery.

REGISTRATION CARD—(Men born on or after April 28, 1877 and on or before February 16, 1897)

SERIAL NUMBER	1 NAME (Print)			ORDER NUMBER
U 1356	JOSEPH (First)	ROY (Middle)	BADEN (Last)	

2. PLACE OF RESIDENCE (Print)

BADEN, MARYLAND

(Number and street) (Town, township, village, or city) (County) (State)

[THE PLACE OF RESIDENCE GIVEN ON THE LINE ABOVE WILL DETERMINE LOCAL BOARD JURISDICTION; LINE 2 OF REGISTRATION CERTIFICATE WILL BE IDENTICAL]

3. MAILING ADDRESS

BRANDYWINE, RFD. MARYLAND

[Mailing address if other than place indicated on line 2. If same insert word same]

4. TELEPHONE	5. AGE IN YEARS	6. PLACE OF BIRTH
2442	54	P.G Co.
BRANDYWINE (Exchange) (Number)	DATE OF BIRTH April 26, 1888 (Mo.) (Day) (Yr.)	(Town or county) Md (State or country)

7. NAME AND ADDRESS OF PERSON WHO WILL ALWAYS KNOW YOUR ADDRESS

Mrs. J. R. BADEN, BADEN, MARYLAND

8. EMPLOYER'S NAME AND ADDRESS

TREASURY DEPART. - BUREAU OF INTERNAL REV.

9. PLACE OF EMPLOYMENT OR BUSINESS

WASHINGTON, D.C.

(Number and street or R.F.D. number) (Town) (County) (State)

I AFFIRM THAT I HAVE VERIFIED ABOVE ANSWERS AND THAT THEY ARE TRUE.

D. S. S. Form 1
(Revised 4-1-42)   (over)   16—21630-8   J. Roy Baden
(Registrant's signature)

REGISTRATION CARD—(Men born on or after April 28, 1877 and on or before February 16, 1897)

SERIAL NUMBER	1 NAME (Print)			ORDER NUMBER
U 187	CLYDE (First)	HUDGINS (Middle)	BADEN (Last)	

2. PLACE OF RESIDENCE (Print)

BRANDYWINE PR. GEO. MD

(Number and street) (Town, township, village, or city) (County) (State)

[THE PLACE OF RESIDENCE GIVEN ON THE LINE ABOVE WILL DETERMINE LOCAL BOARD JURISDICTION; LINE 2 OF REGISTRATION CERTIFICATE WILL BE IDENTICAL]

SAME

[Mailing address if other than place indicated on line 2. If same insert word same]

4. TELEPHONE	5. AGE IN YEARS	6. PLACE OF BIRTH
BRANDYWINE 2543 (Exchange) (Number)	56 DATE OF BIRTH Nov 25 1885 (Mo.) (Day) (Yr.)	BALTIMORE (Town or county) MARYLAND (State or country)

7. NAME AND ADDRESS OF PERSON WHO WILL ALWAYS KNOW YOUR ADDRESS

MRS. EDNA M. BADEN, BRANDYWINE, MD.

8. EMPLOYER'S NAME AND ADDRESS

PRINCE GEO. CO. COMMISSIONERS, UPPER MARLBORO, MD

9. PLACE OF EMPLOYMENT OR BUSINESS

U   UPPER MARLBORO PR.GEO MD

(Number and street of R.F.D. number) (Town) (County) (State)

I AFFIRM THAT I HAVE VERIFIED ABOVE ANSWERS AND THAT THEY ARE TRUE.

D. S. S. Form 1
(Revised 4-1-42)   (over)   87   Clyde H Baden
(Registrant's signature)

87

REGISTRATION CARD—(Men born on or after April 28, 1877 and on or before February 16, 1897)

SERIAL NUMBER | 1. NAME (Print) | ORDER NUMBER

U 1171 | ANDREW GRAYSON BADEN |
(First) (Middle) (Last)

2. PLACE OF RESIDENCE (Print)

BRANDYWINE Pr. Geo. M.D.

(Number and street) (Town, township, village, or city) (County) (State)

[THE PLACE OF RESIDENCE GIVEN ON THE LINE ABOVE WILL DETERMINE LOCAL BOARD
JURISDICTION; LINE 2 OF REGISTRATION CERTIFICATE WILL BE IDENTICAL]

3. MAILING ADDRESS

Same

[Mailing address if other than place indicated on line 2. If same insert word same]

4. TELEPHONE | 5. AGE IN YEARS | 6. PLACE OF BIRTH
| 46 | Baden
Brandy. 2556 | DATE OF BIRTH | (Town or county)
(Exchange) (Number) | Sept 4 1895 | Md
| (Mo.) (Day) (Yr.) | (State or country)

7. NAME AND ADDRESS OF PERSON WHO WILL ALWAYS KNOW YOUR ADDRESS

MARIE B. BADEN BRANDYWINE M.D.

8. EMPLOYER'S NAME AND ADDRESS

Farmer

9. PLACE OF EMPLOYMENT OR BUSINESS

Baden Pr. Geo. Md

(Number and street or R. F. D. number) (Town) (County) (State)

I AFFIRM THAT I HAVE VERIFIED ABOVE ANSWERS AND THAT THEY ARE TRUE.

D. S. S. Form 1 | Grayson Baden
(Revised 4 1 42) (over) | 16—21630-1 | (Registrant's signature)

REGISTRATION CARD—(Men born on or after April 28, 1877 and on or before February 16, 1897)

SERIAL NUMBER | 1. NAME (Print) | ORDER NUMBER

U 181 | John Turner Baden |
(First) (Middle) (Last)

2. PLACE OF RESIDENCE (Print)

Baden Pr. Geo. Md

(Number and street) (Town, township, village, or city) (County) (State)

[THE PLACE OF RESIDENCE GIVEN ON THE LINE ABOVE WILL DETERMINE LOCAL BOARD
JURISDICTION; LINE 2 OF REGISTRATION CERTIFICATE WILL BE IDENTICAL]

3. MAILING ADDRESS

Brandywine, Pr. Geo. Co. Md.

[Mailing address if other than place indicated on line 2. If same insert word same]

4. TELEPHONE | 5. AGE IN YEARS | 6. PLACE OF BIRTH
Brandywine | 62 | Baden
2440 | DATE OF BIRTH | (Town or county)
(Exchange) (Number) | March 1, 1880 | Pr. Geo. Co. Md.
| (Mo.) (Day) (Yr.) | (State or country)

7. NAME AND ADDRESS OF PERSON WHO WILL ALWAYS KNOW YOUR ADDRESS

Mrs. Turner Baden Brandywine, Md.

8. EMPLOYER'S NAME AND ADDRESS

State Road Comm. — Baltimore, Md.

9. PLACE OF EMPLOYMENT OR BUSINESS

St. Road Comm. Baltimore, Md.

(Number and street or R. F. D. number) (Town) (County) (State)

I AFFIRM THAT I HAVE VERIFIED ABOVE ANSWERS AND THAT THEY ARE TRUE.

D. S. S. Form 1 | 86 | John Turner Baden.
(Revised 4 1 42) (over) | | (Registrant's signature)

F.   Thomas Wallace Baden, and his wife, Lillie Agusta Hyde.

Children of Thomas Wallace Baden and Lillie Agusta Hyde:

A.   Thomas Wallace Baden

B.   Roland Murphy Baden, his wife, Edna Irene Baden Baden (daughter of James A. and Myrtle M. Baden)

The Washington Post
June 3, 1957

On Saturday, June 1, 1957, Ronald M. Baden, of Brandywine, Md., beloved husband of Edna I. Baden and father of Thomas W. and Robert B. Baden. Miss Jean M. Baden, Mrs. Barbara Ann Langley, Miss Elizabeth M. and Linda Baden. He also is survived by two grandchildren. Friends may call at the Ritchie Bros. Funeral Home, Upper Marlboro, Md., after 6 p.m. on Monday, June 3, Funeral services will be held in St. Paul's Episcopal Church, Baden, Md. on Wednesday, June 5, at 11 a.m. Interment church cemetery.

Children of Roland Murphy Baden and Edna Irene Baden:

1.   James Arthur Baden

The Washington Post
February 17, 1985

On Friday, February 15, 1985, Edna I. Baden of Brandywine, Md., wife of the late Roland M. Baden; mother of Jean M. Baden, Linda B. Dixon, Thomas W. and Robert B. Baden and the late James A. and Jessie Lee Baden; sister of Elizabeth L and Minerva Baden and the late Helen B. and Ara B. McDormand; also survived by 10 grandchildren and five great-children. Funeral from the Hunt Funeral Home, Waldorf, Md., on Tuesday, February 19 at 10:30 a.m. Services will be held at St. Paul's Episcopal Church, Baden, Md. at 11 a.m. Interment church cemetery. Friends may visit at the funeral home on Monday from 2 to 4 and 7 to 9 p.m. Memorial contributions may be made in her name to St. Paul's Church Organ Fund.

2.   Jessie Lee Baden

3.Robert William Gover Baden, his wife, Evelyn Young, b. 6 Nov 1896, d. 17 Jan 1932.

    Their daughter, Lillie May.

LILLIE MAY BADEN
JULY 14, 1926
AUG. 28, 1927

D.   Gordon Milton Baden, b. 12 Feb 1899, d. 24 Mar 1964

GORDON M. BADEN
1899   1964

Children of John Henry Baden and Elizabeth Wright:
A.   James Arthur Baden, his wife, Mattie Minerva Hyde

J. A. BADEN
JULY 25, 1865
MARCH 29, 193_

MATTIE M. BADEN
MAY 22, 1870
JUNE 13, 1952

The Washington Post
June 15, 1952

On Friday, June 13, 1952, at her late residence, Baden, Md., Mattie Minerva Baden, beloved wife of the late James Arthur Baden. She is survived by four daughters, Miss Elizabeth Lederer Baden and Mrs. Roland Baden, of Baden, Md.; Mrs. Alfred McDormand of Silver Spring, Md., Miss J.O. Baden of Washington, D.C. also one brother, Edgar Hyde of Baden, Md. Friends are invited to call at her late residence, Baden, Md. after 1 p.m. Sunday, June 15. Funeral services will be held in St. Paul's Episcopal Church, Baden, Md. on Monday, June 16 at 11 a.m. Interment church cemetery.

B. George Henry Baden, his wife, Roberta Eliza Hyde; their son, Milton Leslie Baden.

C.   William Mortimer Baden, his wife, Sarah Margaret Baden Baden (daughter of Jeremiah Thomas and Susanna I. R. Baden Baden), and their daughter Grace Elizabeth Baden Rawlings.

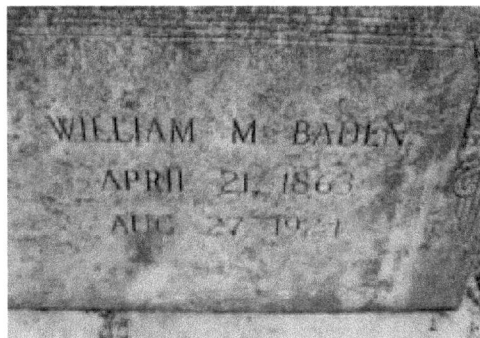

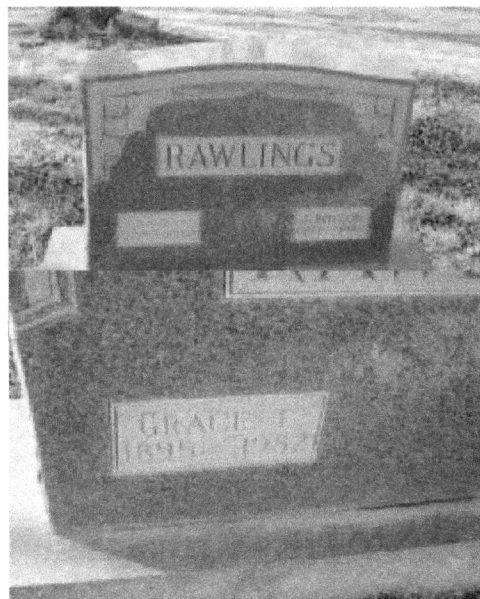

The Washington Post
August 1, 1982

On Saturday, July 31, 1982, Grace Elizabeth Rawlings of Mechanicsville, Md., beloved wife of the late Harry C. Taylor and James Wilson Rawlings; mother of Lillian B. Everson; she is also survived by four grandchildren, nine great-grandchildren and one great-great grandchild. Funeral from the Huntt Funeral Home, Waldorf, Md., on Tuesday, August 3 at 10:30 a.m. Services will be held at St. Paul's Episcopal Church, Baden, Md., at 11 a.m. Interment church cemetery. Chapel hours on Monday from 2 to 5 and 7 to 9 p.m. with prayers at 8 p.m.

Name	County	Name of Tract	Acreage	Date	Reference(s)
Baden, Robert	PG	Sarum's Forest	134	7 Feb 1757	BC8/378;BC9/403
Beane, Ebsworth	Fdk	Silent Valley	80	11 Feb 1756	BC7/358;BC9/153
Bean(e) [Been], John	Fdk	Saturday's Work	50	23 Jul 1750	74/161;BY5/593
	Fdk	Anything	50	31 Mar 1750	BY3/307;BY5/607
	StM	Bean's Thoroughfare	13	4 Aug 1743	EI6/626;LGE/177
	StM	Friends in Conjunction	250	7 Sep 1738	EI2/727;EI5/391
	Fdk	Bayne's Good Luck	120	6 Nov 1764	BC30/262;BC32/17
	Fdk	Fancy	30	5 Jun 1754	GS2/319;BC4/338
Bean, Richard	PG	Thomas's Inheritance	50	-- Jun 1734	AM1/367;EI4/240
Bean(e)s, Christopher	PG	Beans' Adventure	150	10 Nov 1703	CD4/67;DD5/87
	Cal	Beans' Hazard	200	1 Aug 1706	DD5/227;PL2/7
		Beans' Landing	137	10 Nov 1703	CD4/92;DD5/99
	PG	Enchantment	62	6 Feb 1753	YS8/719;BC1/261
Bean(e)s, Colmore	PG	Colmore's Ramble	66	28 Feb 1744	LGE/307;PT2/66
	PG	Beanes' Pasture	22	20 Oct 1755	BC7/403;BC9/143
Beans, John	Fdk	Nonsuch	150	14 Nov 1769	BC36/197;BC40/150
Beanes, Thomas	Fdk	Flag Patch	140	22 Nov 1754	BC1/356;BC2/2
Beans, William	PG	Content	20	10 Nov 1752	YS6/99;YS7/108
Brice, Anne	AA	Motherly Care	360	1719	ILA/664
Brice, James	Bal	Brice's Purchase	157	15 Jun 1742	EI6/545;LGC/277
	Bal	Brice's Purchase	253	13 Oct 1753	YS7/382;YS8/13
	Bal	Walter's Disappointment	100	31 Mar 1775	BC48/346;BC51/53
Brice, John Esq. of Cecil Co:					
	AA	Bilbury Hall	189	8 Jul 1741	LGB/321
	AA	Ferry Creek Branch	70	8 Sep 1750	BY1/586;BY2/394
	Cec	Forest Addition	13	14 Jul 1750	BY2/406
	Cec	Frisby's Neglect	71	12 Jul 1743	EI6/668;LGC/359
	Cec	Harris's Venture	20	20 Jun 1743	LGB/776;LGC/359
	Cec	Neighbours' Joke	42	14 May 1743	EI6/582;LGC/290
	Cec	Ramble	350	4 Jul 1743	LGB/629
	Cec	Three Prongs?	100	?	BY1/6
	Bal	Brice's Endeavour	200	22 Dec 1732	PL8/744;AM1/243
Brice, John Esq. of Annapolis:					
	Cec	Brice's Discovery	140	7 Feb 1764	BC23/134;BC24/247
	Cec	Brice's Purchase	25	28 Oct 1765	BC23/300;BC34/87
	AA	Brice's Security	104	12 Apr 1764	BC28/408;BC30/70
	Cec	Brice's Triangle	23	7 Feb 1763	BC23/69;BC24/254
	Fdk	Exchange	920	10 Oct 1754	BC8/6;BC9/167
	AA	Ferry Creek Branch	66	15 Aug 1753	BY4/653;GS1/249
	Fdk	Forest	2,078	30 Aug 1754	BY4/624;BC1/348

Name	County	Name of Tract	Acreage	Date	Reference(s)
	Fdk	Head's Industry Addition	840	10 Dec 1754	BC8/20;BC9/171
	Fdk	King Cole	1,970	30 Aug 1754	YS8/687;BC1/344
	Cec	Long Neglected	11	15 Apr 1765	BC25/178;BC27/127
	AA	North Crouchfield Addition	40	4 May 1762	BC25/484;BC30/113
	AA	Sure Bind Sure Find	128	16 Jun 1764	BC23/129;BC24/270
Brice, John	AA	Barron Neck	118	3 Mar 1713	DD5/733;PL3/258
	AA	Bilberry Hall	189	20 May 1705	WD/418;DD5/177
	AA	Brice's Share	900	10 Oct 1704	WD/395;DD5/141
	AA	John	478	21 Jul 1727	PL6/618
Brice, Sarah	AA	Sarah's Care for John	478	1723	ILB/237
Brice, Thomas	Bal	Ups & Downs	42	28 Oct 1774	BC48/204;BC50/31
Brice, William	Dor	Brice's Adventure	150	26 Feb 1681	24/294;28/477
	Dor	Brice's Range	100	20 Apr 1682	24/424;31/400
	Dor	Whittlewood	100	4 May 1682	24/431;31/351
Brightwell, Peter	PG	Nest Egg	30	25 Jul 1745	LGE/351;PT2/148
Brightwell, Richard	Cal	Blackwell	160	20 Sep 1683	25/19;32/31
	Cha	Brightwell's Hunting Quarter	1,086	10 Oct 1695	37/253
	Cal	Brightwell's Landing	47	1 Feb 1695	27/253
	Cal	Brightwell's Range	100	12 Sep 1688	25/429;34/100
	Cal	Spinum Land	136	5 Feb 1695	27/269
	Cal	Thatcham	123	28 Feb 1695	27/280
	PG	Padgett's Marsh	47	20 Feb 1767	BC33/74;BC34/389
	PG	Padgett's Rest	58	29 Sep 1766	BC33/73;BC34/387
	PG	Padget's Rest	78	31 Oct 1769	BC38/243;BC40/257
Maulding [Moldin], Mr. Francis:					
	Cec	Maulding's Forest	200	30 Oct 1725	PL5/821
	Cec	Mount Colleston	320	26 Apr 1758	BC8/221;BC9/531
Nailer, George	PG	Nailer's Purchase	36	1 May 1698	38/69
	PG	Nailer's Range	164	1 May 1698	38/68
Naylor, George	Cha	Stainland	27	10 Aug 1713	DD5/797;RY1/58
Naylor, George Jr	PG	Good Luck	54	17 Oct 1775	BC49/422;BC50/245

SETTLERS OF MARYLAND 1679-1783

Name	County	Name of Tract	Acreage	Date	Reference(s)
Noble, George, Deputy Surveyor for Prince George's Co.					
Noble, George & Philemon:					
	Tal	Noble's Addition	350	29 Sep 1748	TI3/327;BY1/367
Noble, Isaac	Som	Noble's Lot	73	6 Mar 1686	25/281
	Som	Winterbourne	100	10 Jul 1683	29/450
	Som	Isaac's Addition	50	10 Jun 1734	EI2/57;EI3/256
	Som	Young Timson	168	17 Apr 1752	BY3/356;YS7/337
Noble, James, gent	Som	Constantinople	100	24 Oct 1737	EI3/511;EI6/34
Noble, James	Wor	Exchange	75	19 Aug 1753	BC2/109;BC4/167
Noble, James Jr	Wor	Shockley's Beginning	50	2 Oct 1762	BC24/548;BC28/93
Noble, John	StM	Noble's Victory	50	17 Aug 1682	24/477;31/57
Noble, John of Great Britain:					
	AA	Upton Park	593	12 Aug 1760	BC13/614;BC14/457
Noble, Joseph	PG	Cold Snowy Friday	184	19 May 1765	BC22/526;BC24/293; BC30/17
	PG	Nicked Him of Deer Range	14	6 Sep 1755	BC2/95;BC4/191
Noble, Joseph Jr. of Charles Co:					
	PG	Levels Addition	100	1 Aug 1744	LGE/311;PT2/70
	PG	Joseph & Martha's Delight	200	9 Mar 1748	BT/715;TI1/425
Noble, Mark	Tal	Poor Hill	57	10 Sep 1716	FF7/86;PL4/207
Noble, Robert	Tal	Noble's Addition	150	12 Mar 1680	24/231;31/253
	Tal	Noble's Meadow	150	24 Oct 1681	24/381
	Tal	Noble Range	200	1 Jul 1679	24/218
Noble, William	Som	Cherry Garden	86	10 Nov 1695	34/63;40/216
	Som	Timber Grove	150	15 Jun 1683	25/285;33/384
	Bal	Noble's Desire	100	10 Aug 1717	EE6/322;PL4/303

St. Paul's Episcopal Church
Baden, Prince George's County, Maryland

The present church was built in 1733 but the records only go back as far as 1825. It is on the National Register of Historic Places.

St. Paul was one of the 30 parishes created in 1692 by the General Assembly into which the territory of the Province of Maryland was then divided. However, the original St. Paul's Church building had already been erected when the parish was created. Hanging over the present doorway is a sundial, installed in 1753 to serve as the community's first public time piece. This is the only sundial in the United States adorning a church edifice in such a manner.

When the mercenary soldiers hired by the British camped in the church prior to their attack on the capitol in Washington, the War of 1812, these Germans used the Baptismal Fount to water their horses. To this day the parishioners refer to "those people" as "the damn Hessians."

The Silver Service used in today's Holy Communion was give to St. Paul's by Queen Anne as was the sundial. Here then is an old town named BADEN having an old church.

Indexes of Protestant Episcopal (Anglican)
Church Registers
of

Prince George's County

Maryland
1686-1885

—Volume 2—

St. Paul's Parish at Baden
(Records Begin 1831)

and

Prince George's Parish
(Known as Rock Creek Parish, Records 1711-1798)

Helen W. Brown

These are not really indexes but an alphabetical arrangement of the vital records.

U.S.A. $20.00
B0119

ISBN 1-58549-119-5

52000>

9 781585 491193

www.HeritageBooks.com

Indexes of Protestant Episcopal
(Anglican)
Church Registers
of

Prince George's County

Maryland
1686-1885

—Volume 2—

St. Paul's Parish at Baden
(Records Begin 1831)

and

Prince George's Parish
(Known as Rock Creek Parish, Records 1711-1798)

Helen W. Brown

HISTORY

Those using the following index of records of St. Paul's Parish at Baden, Prince George's County, Maryland will be interested in the history of that parish given in the Inventory of Diocese of Washington Archives, Vol. I, p. 125 (December 1940).

"St. Paul's is one of the thirty parishes created in 1692 by the Maryland General Assembly into which the territory of the Province of Maryland was then divided. However, the original St. Paul's Church building had already been erected when the parish was created.

The present edifice was probably begun in 1733. The Vestry Minutes of 1733 specify details of a "Church to be built of brick and to be finished in 1735." The tradition in the parish is that the present church building is possibly the same site as the original one and contains some of the brick used in that structure. Over the doorway of the church is what is believed by many to be the only sundial adorning a church edifice in the United States; installed in 1735 and serving as the community's first public time piece.

About 1742, a Chapel of Ease to St. Paul's Parish was built at what is now called Croome, and named Page's Chapel (after the contractor who erected the building); it still stands and now is the parish church of St. Thomas' Parish created in 1851 from the northern section of St. Paul's Parish.

The present St. Mary's Chapel at Aquasco was organized as a parochial mission of St. Paul's, and a chapel building was erected in 1848.

The first historically conspicuous rector of the parish was Rev. John Eversfield. He was a native of Kent County, England, graduated from Oxford University February 14, 1727 and ordained priest September 24, 1727. In November of the same year he left England for America where he arrived February 28, 1728. The following May he received letters from Gov. Benedict Leonard Calvert appointing him rector of St. Paul's until about 1776. Rev. Mr. Eversfield lived a few miles from the present St. Thomas Church near Nottingham. He established a school on his plantation in 1746, conducting it until his death in 1780. Here were educated many of the youth of Southern Maryland. Among the distinguished scholars was his wife's nephew Thomas J. Claggett, who later became rector of St. Paul's Parish and First Bishop of Maryland.

It is unfortunate for research purposes that records of this parish prior to 1831 apparently do not exist. They are believed to have been burned or lost in the passage of time.

H.W.B.

Elizabeth T. m. Bennis M. Williams 7-14-1836 at Mrs. Margaret Baden's (B1, 62-63)

Frederick Ira born of John Henry & Elizabeth Baden cetas 3 months, bapt. 7-1-1870 (B2, 104)

George A. m. Martha Naylor 4-5-1832 (B1, 2); father of John Henry (B1, 22-23)

George Robert born of Jeremiah T. & Issabella Baden bapt. 10-8-1871 about 6 months old (B2, 106)

Miss Ida age 17 m. 1-27-1880 in St. Mary's Chapel James A. Goldsmith age 40, both of Prince George's County Issabella, mother of George Robert & John Thomas (B2, 106 & 101)

Capt. James funeral 12-8-1862, in the 85th year of his age (B2, 151, also 1p. 31)

James Early of Robert William & Margaret C. Baden bapt. 6-22-1856 (B2, 67)

James F. son of R. W. G. & Margaret Caroline Baden, b. 1-5-1843, bapt. Brick Church (B1, 97)

James Francis son of Mrs. Margaret Baden buried 9-20-1834 at Mrs. John Baden's (B1, 48-49)

James Thomas son of Thos. George & Sarah Sabina Baden b. 9-12-1835, bapt. 3-20-1836 (B1, 32-33)

Jeremiah Smith b. 12-8-1838, bapt. 5-26-1839, son of Thos. G. & Sabina Baden (B1, 40-41)

Jeremiah T. father of George Robert & John Thomas (B2, 106 & 101)

---- dau. of Jerry Baden and ---- bapt. 9-20-1863 (B2, 95)

Mrs. Jeremiah buried September 1881 (1p. 31) St. Paul's Churchyard)

John found dead on the road supposed to have been murdered the 17th of November 1873, buried 1-11-1874 (B2, 159)

John son of Thomas G. & Sarah Baden b. 8-7-1831 (B1, 2)

John (wife Eleanor Ann) father of Lelia Rebecca Catherine, Richard & Thomas, Josephine Isabella & John Francis (twins) (B2, 107, 155, 158, 170)

John Henry b. 2-13-1834, bapt. 3-31-1834 at Thomas Nailor's, son of George A. & Martha Baden (B1, 22-23)

John Henry father of Frederick Ira (B2, 104)

John Hollyday son of R.W.G. & Caroline M. Baden b. 2-13-1841, bapt. at Parish Church 8-29-1841 (B1, 90-91)

John Noble b. 5-9-1833, bapt. 7-26-1833, son of Joseph N. & Sarah Baden (B1, 20-21)

John Noble son of Joseph N. & Sarah Baden buried April 1, 1834 at the Baden Burying Place (B1, 48-49)

John Thomas born of Jeremiah T. & Issabella Baden cetas 6 months; bapt. 3-13-1868 (B2, 101)

John Turner son of Robert E. & Margaret Baden age 5 months, bapt. 1880 St. Paul's (1p. 16)

Joseph N. father of Joseph Noble (B1, 88-89)

Joseph Noble son of Joseph N. & ---- Baden b. prob. 1840-41 (B1, 88-87)

Joseph Noble, father of Noble Hawkins, John Noble, Mary Ann (B1, 36-37)

Joseph Noble d. 12-16-1854 aged 70, buried 12-18-1854 at his residence (B2, 48)

Josephine Isabella & John Francis (twins) of John & Eleanor Baden b. 9-23-1873, bapt. 10-7-1873 (B2, 170)

Joseph Isabella and John Francis, children of John & Eleanor Baden, burial service 11-2-1873, buried Capt. Baden's Burial Ground (R2, 158)

Lelia Rebecca Catherine born of John & Eleanor Ann Baden age 6 years, bapt. 12-1-1872 (B2, 107)

ST. PAUL'S PARISH at Baden

Margaret mother of Bessie Wilson (1p. 26)

Margaret C. mother of William Albert Kerr, Dorinda Elizabeth, James Early (B1, 42-43, B2, 7, 67)

Margaret E. m. James S. Morsell Jr. 4-30-1839 at Joseph Noble Baden's (B1, 63)

Mrs. Margaret mother of James Francis, James F. (B1, 48,49, 97)

Mrs. Margaret funeral 7-11-1870 (B2, 155)

Martha mother of John Henry (B1, 22-23)

Martha Ann dau. Thos. G. & Sarah Sabina Baden b. 2-6-1834, bapt. 6-23-1834 (B1, 22-23)

Martha Ann infant dau. John & Eleanor Ann Gantt Baden bapt. 9-22-1861 (B2, 94)

Mary Ann dau. Joseph N. & Sarah Baden buried 10-25-1834 Baden Burying Place (B1, 50-51)

Noble Hawkins son of Joseph Noble & Sarah Baden, b. 8-4-1837, bapt. 12-1837 (B1, 36-37)

Noble Hawkins (infant) buried 10-31-1839 T.M.D. Baden's Place (B1, 55)

Miss Rebecca d. 1-17-1852 age 14, buried 5-17-1853 (B1, 24)

Rebecca m. J. L. Townsend at Capt. James Baden's (B1, 62-63)

Richard age 6 days, Thomasd age 8 months born of John & Eleanor Ann Baden, funeral 7-14-1869 (B2, 155)

Robert (wife Margaret) father of Bessie Wilson (1p, 26)

Robert E. (wife Margaret) father of John Turner (1p, 16)

Robert E. (wife Elizabeth) father of Robert Early (1p, 16)

Robert Early son of Robert E. & Elizabeth Baden age 4 years, bapt. 1880 St. Paul's (1p, 16)

Robert G. buried 5-17-1882 (1p, 31)

---- of Robert Wm. & Margaret C. Baden (B2, 76)

Robert W. G. m. to Margaret C. Early (both of Prince George's County) at Capt. Early's 1-4-1838 (B1, 62-63)

Robt. W. G. father of William Albert Kerr, John Hollyday, James F., Dorinda Elizabeth (B1, 42-43, 90-91, 97, B2, 7)

Robert William father of James Early (B2, 67)

Mrs. Ruth relic of Capt. James Baden cetas 75 years, funeral 4-7-1863 (B2, 151)

Mrs. Sarah funeral at home of son Thomas M. D. Baden 8-19-1832 (B1, 8)

Sarah (wife Joseph N.) mother of Noble Hawkins, John Noble, Mary Ann (B1, 36-37, 20-21, 50-51)

Sarah M. m. 12-16-1885 at St. Paul's W. M. Baden (1p. 5)

Mrs. Sarah S. relict of Noble Baden funeral 1-5-1868 (B2, 154)

Sarah Sabina (wife of Thomas G.) mother of John, Jeremiah, Martha Ann, Susanna Isabella Rebecca, John Thomas (B1, 18-19, 40-41, 22-23, B1, 18-19, 52-53)

Sarah Susanna Victoria infant dau. Ellen Ann Gantt & John Baden, bapt. 8-4-1858 (B2, 92)

Susanna Isabella Rebecca b. 12-16-1832, bapt. 7-14-1833 at Capt. James Baden's, dau. Thos. G. & Sarah S. Baden (B1, 18-19)

Thomas George, father of John, Susanna Isabella Rebecca, Jeremiah Smith, Martha Ann, John Thomas (B1, 2, 18-19, 40-41, 22-23, 32-33)

Thomas George buried April 1842 at Capt. James Baden's Place (B1, 56)

Thomas M. D. son of Mrs. Sarah Baden (B1, 8)

Thomas N. in the 87th year of his age, funeral 6-2-1864 (B2, 152)

Miss Virginia buried 6-1---- (1p. 31)

William Albert Kerr b. 22-22-1839 bapt. 10-13-1839, son of Robt. W. G. & Margaret C. Baden (B1, 42-43)

ST. PAUL'S PARISH at Baden

W, M, m. Sarah M. Baden 12-16-1885 at St. Paul's (1p. 5)
William A. K. age 31 funeral 5-23-1872 (B2, 157)
BALL, Eliza Alice mother of James Porter, Ivy Mabel, Joseph Calvin. (B2, 105, 1p, 22 & 24)
Henry infant son of Mr. ---- Ball bapt. 1-11-1860 (B2, 41)
Ivy Mabel child of Thomas E. & Eliza A. Ball bapt. 5-30-1881 age two weeks (1p. 22)
James Porter b. of Thomas E. & Eliza A. Ball cetas 3 months bapt. 2-8-1871 (B2, 105)
Joseph Calvin child of Thomas E. & Eliza A. Ball b. 8-11-1881, bapt. 1-15-1883 (1p. 24)
Inez Mabel buried 8-5-1881 in private ground (1p. 1)
Thomas E. m. 1-13-1870 Eliza Alice Gibbons (B2, 142)
Thomas E. (wife Eliza Alice) father of James Porter, Ivy Mabel, Joseph Calvin (B2, 105, 1p. 22 & 24)
Thomas Edwin m. 3-10-1857 at Mr. Tutman's to Mary Jane Tubman (B2, 71)
Wm. to ---- Alvy at Rectory September ---. 1882 (1p. 26)
BARRON, John b. 8-12-1832, bapt. 12-2-1832 son of Samuel Barron and Rebecca his wife (B1, 12)
Rebecca mother of John (B1, 12)
Samuel father of John (B1, 12)
BATTIE, Mary Lucy born of Robert & Jane Battie, colored, bapt. 6-18-1865 (B2, 97)
BAVIN, Rachel Ann m. Henry Burroughs 4-15-1841 at Mr. Saml. Cooksie's (B1, 68)
BEALL, Aquila buried 4-29-1840 Brookefield (B1, 55)
BEALL, Brooke buried May 1843 at Brookfield by the Rector (B1, 57)
BEAN, Ann Eleanor mother of John Alexander, Eliza A. Ellen, William Noble, Thomas Leonard (B1, 3, 22-23, 40-41, 92-93, 90-91)
Ann Ellen b. of John A. & Margaret Ann Bean cetas 2 months 27 days, bapt. 10-27-1867 (B2, 101)
Anna Elizabeth b. of William N. & Henrietta Bean cetas 4 months, bapt. 9-1-1867 (B2, 100)
Dorinda Rebecca infant dau. John A. & Margaret Ann Marbury Bean bapt. 4-16-1865 (B2, 98)
Dorinda Rebecca born of John A. & Margarett A. M. Bean cetas 7 months, funeral 6-14-1865 (B2, 153)
Edward father of John Alexander, Eliza A. Ellen, William Noble, Thomas Leonard (B1, 3, 22-23, 40-41, 92-93, 90-91)
Eliza A. Ellen b. 6-15-1834, bapt. 6-15-1834 dau. of Edward & Ann Eleanor Bean (B1, 22-23)
Eliza Ellen m. Henry Snowden Wright 1-26-1854 (B2, 35)
Ella Marcelline b. of William N. & Henrietta Bean cetas 3 months. bapt. 6-6-1869 (B2, 102)
Henrietta mother of William Joseph, Ella Marcelline, Anna Elizabeth, Henry Edward (B2, 106, 102, 100, 172)
Henry Edward of William N. & Henrietta Bean b. 12-16-1871, bapt. 7-26-1874 at St. Paul's (B2, 172)
James Alexander son of John A. & Margaret A. Bean b. 4-1-1873, bapt. 6-29-1873 St. Paul's (B2, 170)
John (wife Margaret) father of John Wm. (1p, 25)
John A. father of Dorinda Rebecca, Thomas Edward, John Holiday, Ann Ellen, Mary Perry, James Alexander, Margaret Louisa (B2, 98, 153, 106, 103, 101, 186, 170, 179)

ST. PAUL'S PARISH at Baden

John Alexander b. 1-17-1872 son of Edward & Ann Eleanor Bean (B1, 3)
John Holiday b. of John A. & Margaret A. Bean cetas 19 months, bapt. 10-22-1869 (B2, 103)
John Wm. child of John & Margaret Bean b. 12-29-1883, bapt. 5-22-1884 (1p. 25)
Margaret (wife John) mother of John Wm. (1p. 25)
Margaret Ann mother of Dorinda Rebecca, Thomas Edward, John Holiday, Ann Ellen, Mary Perry, James Alexander, Margaret Louise (B3. 98, 153, 106, 103, 101, 170, 179)
Margaret Louisa child of John A. & Margaret Bean age 5 months b. 7-10-1877 (B2, 179)
Mariah dau. of Thomas Bean & Susan Hunter his concubine, buried 10-8-1834 near Woodville (B1, 50-51)
Mary Perry dau. of John A. & Margaret A. Bean bapt. 11-18-1879, age one week (B2, 196)
Thomas father of Mariah and Thomas John (B1, 50-51, 30-31)
Thomas Edward b. of John A. & Margaret A. Bean cetas 4 months, bapt. 7-16-1871 (B2, 106)
Thomas John b. 8-15-1835, bapt. 8-24-1835 at Woodville, son of Thomas Bean and Susan Hunter his concubine (B1, 30-31)
Thomas Leonard son of Edward & Anne Ellenor Bean b. 6-15-1841, bapt. 8-6-1841 (B1, 90-91)
Thomas Leonard son Ed. & Ann E. Bean b. 6-15-1840 (?) (B1, 92-93)
William Joseph b. of William N. & Henrietta cetas 4 months. bapt. 7-16-1871 (B2, 106)
William N. father of William Joseph, Ella Marcelline, Anna Elizabeth, Henry Edward (B2, 106, 102, 100, 172)
William Noble of Edward & Ann E. Bean b. 1-30-1839, bapt. 5-12-1839 (B1, 40-41)
Wm. Noble son Ed. & Ann E. Bean b. 1-30-1839 (B1, 92-93)
BEAVIN, ----- a dau. of Mrs. Beavin, funeral at St. Paul's 10-16-1853 (B2, 37)
John d. 12-30-1851 age 70, buried 12-31-1851 (B2, 11)
BEDDER, Dorinda, dau. of Catherine Bedder, funeral 10-17-1864 (B2, 152)
John Henry son of Ann Bedder bapt. 9-5-1835 Woodville (B1, 30-31)
Mrs. Polly funeral 10-17-1864 (B2, 152)
BELT, John father of Richard West (B2, 97)
Richard West b. of John & Mittie Belt, bapt. 7-15-1866 (B2, 97)
Mittie mother of Richard West (B2, 97)
BERRY, Isaac (colored) of Alfred & Chloe Ann Berry b. 4-13-1875. bapt. 2-26-1876 (B1, 176)
Matilda b. of Albert & Cloe Berry age 2 weeks, colored. bapt. 3-24-1869 (B2, 102)
BEVIN, Wm. child of John & Margaret Bevin b. 12-29-1883, bapt. 5-22-1883 (1p. 25)
BIGGER, Thomas N. child of Thomas & Ester Bigger (mother decd.) bapt. 6-20-1875, about 14 months at St. Mary's (B2, 174)
BISCOE, Ann Maria mother of Caroline Rebecca, Clarance, Emma, Edgar (B1. 7, 34-35, 42-43, 92-93)
Caroline Rebecca b. 4-26-1832 dau. Gen. George Washington & Ann Maria Biscoe. bapt. 7-31-1832 at home of Gen. G. W. Biscoe (B1, 7)
Caroline Rebecca dau. of Gen. George W. & Ann Maria Biscoe buried 2-8-1834 (B1, 46-47) Buried at Mount Airy
Clarance b. 6-20-1836, bapt. 10-8-1836 at Gen. Biscoe's child of Geo. W. & Ann Maria Biscoe

101

W. M. m. Sarah M. Baden 12-16-1885 at St. Paul's (1p. 5)
William A. K. age 31 funeral 5-23-1872 (B2. 157)
BALL, Eliza Alice mother of James Porter, Ivy Mabel, Joseph Calvin. (B2.
    105, 1p. 22 & 24)
Henry infant son of Mr. ---- Ball bapt. 1-11-1860 (B2. 91)
Ivy Mabel child of Thomas E. & Eliza A. Ball bapt. 5-30-1881 age two weeks
    (1p. 22)
James Porter b. of Thomas E. & Eliza Alice Ball cetas 3 months bapt.
    2-8-1871 (B2. 105)
Joseph Calvin child of Thomas E. & Eliza A. Ball b. 8-11-1881, bapt.
    1-15-1883 (1p. 24)
Inez Mabel buried 8-5-1881 in private ground (1p. 1)
Thomas E. m. 1-13-1870 Eliza Alice Gibbons (B2. 142)
Thomas E. (wife Eliza Alice) father of James Porter, Ivy Mabel, Joseph
    Calvin. (B2. 105, 1p. 22 & 24)
Thomas Edwin m. 3-10-1857 at Mr. Tutman's to Mary Jane Tutman (B2. 71)
Wm. to ---- Aley at Rectory September ----, 1882 (1p. 26)
BARRON, John b. 8-12-1832. bapt. 12-2-1832 son of Samuel Barron and Rebecca
    his wife (B1, 12)
Rebecca mother of John (B1, 12)
Samuel father of John (B1, 12)
BATTIE, Mary Lucy born of Robert & Jane Battie, colored, bapt. 6-18-1865
    (B2, 97)
BAVIN, Rachel Ann m. Henry Burroughs 4-15-1841 at Mr. Saml. Cooksie's (B1.
    68)
BEALL, Aquila buried 4-29-1840 Brookefield (B1. 55)
BEALL, Brooke buried May 1843 at Brookfield by the Rector (B1. 57)
BEAN, Ann Eleanor mother of John Alexander, Eliza A. Ellen, William Noble.
    Thomas Leonard (B1. 3. 22-23, 40-41, 92-93, 90-91)
Ann Ellen b. of John A. & Margaret Ann Bean cetas 2 months 27 days, bapt.
    10-27-1867 (B2. 101)
Anna Elizabeth b. of William N. & Henrietta Bean cetas 4 months, bapt.
    9-1-1867 (B2. 100)
Dorinda Rebecca infant dau. John A. & Margaret Ann Marbury Bean bapt.
    4-16-1865 (B2. 98)
Dorinda Rebecca born of John A. & Margaret A. M. Bean cetas 7 months
    funeral 6-14-1865 (B2. 153)
Edward father of John Alexander, Eliza A. Ellen, William Noble, Thomas
    Leonard (B1. 3, 22-23, 40-41, 92-93, 90-91)
Eliza A. Ellen b. 4-28-1834, bapt. 6-15-1834 dau. of Edward & Ann Eleanor
    Bean (B1. 22-23)
Eliza Ellen m. Henry Snowden Wright 1-26-1854 (B2. 35)
Ella Marcelline b. of William N. & Henrietta Bean cetas 3 months. bapt.
    6-6-1870 (B2. 102)
Henrietta mother of William Joseph, Ella Marcelline, Anna Elizabeth, Henry
    Edward (B2. 106, 102, 100, 172)
Henry Edward of William N. & Henrietta Bean b. 12-16-1873. bapt. 7-26-1874
    at St. Paul's (B2. 172)
James Alexander son of John A. & Margaret A. Bean b. 4-11-1873, bapt.
    6-29-1873 St. Paul's (B2. 170)
John (wife Margaret) father of John Wm. (1p. 25)
John A. father of Dorinda Rebecca, Thomas Edward, John Holliday, Ann. Ellen.
    Mary Perry, James Alexander, Margaret Louisa (B2. 98, 153, 106, 103.
    101, 186, 170, 179)

John Alexander b. 3-17-1832 son of Edward & Ann Eleanor Bean (B1, 3)
John Holliday b. of John A. & Margaret A. Bean cetas 19 months, bapt.
    10-24-1869 (B2, 103)
John Wm. child of John & Margaret Bean b. 12-29-1883, bapt. 5-22-1884 (1p.
    25)
Margaret (wife John) mother of John Wm. (1p. 25)
Margarett Ann mother of Dorinda Rebecca, Thomas Edward, John Holliday, Ann
    Ellen, Mary Perry, James Alexander, Margaret Louise (B2. 98, 153, 106,
    103, 101, 170, 179)
Margaret Louisa child of John A. & Margaret Bean age 5 months b. 7-16-1877
    (B2. 179)
Mariah dau. of Thomas Bean & Susan Hunter his concubine, buried 10-8-1834
    near Woodville (B1, 50-51)
Mary Perry dau. of John A. & Margaret A. Bean bapt. 11-18-1879, age one
    week (B2, 186)
Thomas father of Mariah and Thomas John (B1, 50-51, 30-31)
Thomas Edward b. of John A. & Margaret A. Bean cetas 4 months. bapt.
    7-16-1871 (B2, 106)
Thomas John b. 8-15-1835, bapt. 8-24-1835 at Woodville, son of Thomas Bean
    and Susan Hunter his concubine (B1, 30-31)
Thomas Leonard son of Edward & Anne Ellenor Bean b. 6-15-1841, bapt.
    8-6-1841 (B1, 90-91)
Thomas Leonard son of Ed. & Ann E. Bean b. 6-15-1840 (?) (B1, 92-93)
William Joseph b. of William N. & Henrietta cetas 4 months. bapt.
    7-16-1871 (B2, 106)
William N. father of William Joseph, Ella Marcelline, Anna Elizabeth,
    Henry Edward (B2, 106, 102, 100, 172)
William Noble of Edward & Ann E. Bean b. 1-30-1839, bapt. 5-12-1839 (B1.
    40-41)
Wm. Noble son Ed. & Ann E. Bean b. 1-30-1839 (B1, 92-93)
BEAVIN, ---- a dau. of Mrs. Beavin. funeral at St. Paul's 10-16-1853 (B2.
    37)
John d. 12-30-1851 age 70, buried 12-31-1851 (B2, 11)
BEDDER, Dorinda, dau. of Catherine Bedder. funeral 10-17-1864 (B2, 152)
John Henry son of Ann Bedder bapt. 9-5-1835 Woodville (B1, 30-31)
Mrs. Polly funeral 10-17-1864 (B2, 152)
BELT, John father of Richard West (B2, 97)
Mittie mother of Richard West (B2, 97)
Richard West b. of John & Mittie Belt, bapt. 7-15-1866 (B2, 97)
BERRY, Isaac (colored) of Alfred & Chloe Ann Berry b. 4-13-1875. bapt.
    2-26-1876 (B2, 97)
Matilda b. of Albert & Cloe Berry age 2 weeks, colored, bapt. 3-24-1869
    (B2, 102)
BEVIN, Wm. child of John & Margaret Bevin b. 12-29-1883. bapt. 5-22-1983
    (1p. 25)
BIGGER, Thomas N. child of Thomas & Ester Bigger (mother decd.) bapt.
    6-20-1875, about 14 months at St. Mary's (B2, 174)
BISCOE, Ann Maria mother of Caroline Rebecca, Clarance, Emma, Edgar (B1. 7.
    34-35, 42-43, 92-93)
Caroline Rebecca b. 4-26-1832 dau. Gen. George Washington & Ann Maria
    Biscoe, bapt. 7-31-1832 at home of Gen. G. W. Biscoe (B1, 7)
Caroline Rebecca dau. of Gen. George W. & Ann Maria Biscoe buried 2-8-1834
    (B1, 40-47) Buried at Mount Airy
Clarance b. 6-20-1836, bapt. 10-8-1836 at Gen. Biscoe's child of Geo. W. &
    Ann Maria Biscoe

MARYLAND MARRIAGES[11]

Prince George's County, Maryland
1777-1886

Jere (Jeremiah?) Baden	Williminia M. Moulton	12 Jan 1782
Elizabeth Baden	John Marlow	29 Oct 1791
Sarah Baden	Thomas Cater	31 Aug 1791
Alexander Baden	Mary Steel	3 Jun 1797
Thomas Baden	Sarah Dorrett	6 Feb 1797
James Baden	Susannah Gibbons	4 Dec 1799
Martha Baden	Joshua Naylor	2 Dec 1799
Elizabeth Baden	Henry Emberson	31 Dec 1800
Rebecca Badon	Richard Noble	26 Sep 1796
Elizabeth Baden	Colmore Augustus Swaine	2 Dec 1826
Elizabeth Baden	William Carr	19 Mar 1834
Elizabeth S. Baden	Zadock Robinson	18 Mar 1840
Elizabeth T. Baden	Dennis M. Williams	8 Jul 1836
George A. Baden	Martha Naylor	30 Mar 1832
George W. Baden	Rosa A. Garner	29 Dec 1873
Ida Baden	John A. Goldsmith	26 Jan 1880
James Baden	Susannah Gibbons	4 Dec 1799
James Baden	Ruth Davis	5 Feb 1811
Jeremiah T. Baden	Susanna J. Baden	5 Jul 1849
John Baden	Milley Robinson	17 Apr 1802
John Baden	Eleanor A. G. Townshend	21 Jan 1857
John Baden, Jr.	Elizabeth Naylor	24 Mar 1814
John Thomas Baden	Margaret Baden	7 Dec 1813
Joseph N. Baden	Sarah S. Hawkins	28 Nov 1826
John Baden	Willimina M. Maulden	12 Jan 1782
Lottie Baden	Guy Carlton	23 Apr 1878
Martha Baden	Samuel Mitchell	1 Jan 1816
Mary E. Baden	William N. Burch	13 Feb 1846
Martha E. Baden	James S. Morsell, Jr.	30 Apr 1839
Martha Baden	John Cooksey	18 Nov 1856
Rebecca Baden	John L. Townshend	15 May 1838
Robert Baden	Elizabeth Gover	12 May 1796
Robert Baden, Jr.	Frances Gover	10 Nov 1779
Robert E. Baden	Bessie Thomas	18 Jan 1873
Robert W. G. Baden	Margaret C. Earley	2 Jan 1838
Sarah Gover Baden	Josias Gibbons	18 Oct 1819
Sarah M. Baden	William M. Baden	15 Dec 1885
Susanna Elizabeth Baden	James Harrison	7 Oct 1823
Susanna J. Baden	Jeremiah T. Baden	5 Jul 1849
Susannah Baden	Zacheus Davis	29 Dec 1804
Thomas of Benjamin Baden	Martha Griffen	7 Jun 1811

---

[11] All Maryland Records Colonial, Revolutionary, County, and Church from Original Sources, Vol. I. Provincial Census of Prince George's County, 31 August 1776.

Prince George's was erected from Calvert and Charles counties in 1695 (Chapter 13, Acts of 1695, May Session). The County was named for Prince George of Denmark (1653-1708), who was the brother of Christian V (1646-1699), king of Denmark and Norway. Prince George was the husband of Queen Anne (1665-1714), who ruled Great Britain and Ireland from 1702 to 1714. In 1749, part of northern Prince George's County was taken to establish Frederick County. In 1777, parts of Prince George's and Frederick counties were taken to establish Montgomery County.

Baden, Benjamin of Maryland, cadet of West Point, died. Resolutions of regret by his classmates were published (Nov. 9, 1837).[12]

Baden, Clement. Lieutenant in Capt. Dyer's Co., 17th Regt.

Baden, John T. Ensign in Capt. Dyer's Co., 17th Regt.

Baden, Joseph N. Private in Capt. Haden's Co., 17th Regt.

Baden, Nehemiah [- 1836]. Assistant Deputy Commissary of Ordnance (Ag 6, 1813).

Baden, Thomas N. Private in Capt. Crawford's Co., 17th Regt.

(Maryland Settlers & Soldiers, 1700s-1800s, The British Invasion of Maryland, 1812-1815)

W. A. H. Baden, enlisted in Company E, Maryland 1st Cavalry Battalion, Mustered out 4 Oct 1864 (Index to Compiled Confederate Military Service Records; The Medical and Surgical History of the Civil War).

On the second day of February 1778, John Baden, Jr. made his Oath of Fidelity on Joshua Sander's return in Portobacco Hundred, Charles County. Each male in the state of Maryland who had celebrated his 18th birthday on or before 3 February 117, was required by law to give his oath of Fidelity and Support to the State of Maryland.

At the time of his oath, he was serving as Tobacco Inspector at Portobacco, Charles County, Maryland.

Badens in Charles County, Maryland:

Daniel Baden, d. 9 Jul 1748; probated 1749, Accts 1738-1759, p. 286

Inventories, 1748: 1735-1752, p. 374

---

[12] Maryland Gazette, 1727-1839.

Liber 27, Folio 42
Jane Baden, 1749, Charles County, Liber 27, Folio 42

John Baden, 1756, Calvert County, Liber 40, Folio 80

Robert Baden, 1760, Prince George's County, Box 19, Folder 1, Liber 52, Folio 172
Eleanor Baden, 1764, Prince George's County, Liber 52, Folio 172

Robert Baden, 1761, Prince George's County, Liber 46, Folio 402
        Liber 3, Folio 73
Ann Baden, 1761, Prince George's County, Liber 46, Folio 402

Eleanor Baden, 1764, Prince George's County, Liber 52, Folio 172

Thomas Baden, 1764, Prince George's County, Liber 4, Folio 94
            1762, Prince George's County, Liber 79, Folio 223
                            Liber 31, Folio 707

WORLD WAR REGISTRATION CARDS

REGISTRATION CARD—(Men born on or after April 28, 1877 and on or before February 16, 1897)

SERIAL NUMBER	1. NAME (Print)			ORDER NUMBER
U 1632	CLINTON (First)	Augusta (Middle)	Baden (Last)	

2. PLACE OF RESIDENCE (Print)

Piscataway   Prince George   Md
(Number and street)   (Town, township, village, or city)   (County)   (State)

[THE PLACE OF RESIDENCE GIVEN ON THE LINE ABOVE WILL DETERMINE LOCAL BOARD JURISDICTION; LINE 2 OF REGISTRATION CERTIFICATE WILL BE IDENTICAL]

3. MAILING ADDRESS

Waldorf Maryland Route 1
(Mailing address if other than place indicated on line 2. If same insert word same)

4. TELEPHONE	5. AGE IN YEARS	6. PLACE OF BIRTH
Brandywine 2755	55	Baden (Town or county)
(Exchange) (Number)	DATE OF BIRTH July 28 1891 (Mo.) (Day) (Yr.)	Maryland (State or country)

7. NAME AND ADDRESS OF PERSON WHO WILL ALWAYS KNOW YOUR ADDRESS

Mary Ruth Baden Waldorf Md. Route 1

8. EMPLOYER'S NAME AND ADDRESS

U.S. Engineer Ft. Washington Md.

9. PLACE OF EMPLOYMENT OR BUSINESS

Ft. Washington D.C.
(Number and street or R. F. D. number)   (Town)   (County)   (State)

I AFFIRM THAT I HAVE VERIFIED ABOVE ANSWERS AND THAT THEY ARE TRUE.

Clinton A Baden
(Registrant's signature)

D. M. M. Form 1
(Revised 4-1-42)   (over)   16- 21630-1

REGISTRATION CARD—(Men born on or after April 28, 1877 and on or before February 16, 1897)

SERIAL NUMBER	1. NAME (Print)			ORDER NUMBER
U 2068	HENRY (First)	DeSales (Middle)	Baden (Last)	

2. PLACE OF RESIDENCE (Print)

Piscataway   PRINCE GEORGE'S   Maryland
(Number and street)   (Town, township, village, or city)   (County)   (State)

[THE PLACE OF RESIDENCE GIVEN ON THE LINE ABOVE WILL DETERMINE LOCAL BOARD JURISDICTION; LINE 2 OF REGISTRATION CERTIFICATE WILL BE IDENTICAL]

3. MAILING ADDRESS

Piscataway Prince Georges Co. Maryland
(Mailing address if other than place indicated on line 2. If same insert word same)

4. TELEPHONE	5. AGE IN YEARS	6. PLACE OF BIRTH
Brandywine 2954	58	Baden (Town or county)
(Exchange) (Number)	DATE OF BIRTH May 10 1882 (Mo.) (Day) (Yr.)	Maryland (State or country)

7. NAME AND ADDRESS OF PERSON WHO WILL ALWAYS KNOW YOUR ADDRESS

Margaret Unkle Piscataway Md.

8. EMPLOYER'S NAME AND ADDRESS

Fred Unkle Piscataway Md.

9. PLACE OF EMPLOYMENT OR BUSINESS

Farm Piscataway Georges Md.
(Number and street or R. F. D. number)   (Town)   (County)   (State)

I AFFIRM THAT I HAVE VERIFIED ABOVE ANSWERS AND THAT THEY ARE TRUE.

Henry Baden
(Registrant's signature)

D. M. M. Form 1
(Revised 4-1-42)   (over)

REGISTRATION CARD—(Men born on or after April 28, 1877 and on or before February 16, 1897)

SERIAL NUMBER | 1. NAME (Print) | ORDER NUMBER

U 163 William Thomas Baden

(First) (Middle) (Last)

2. PLACE OF RESIDENCE (Print)

Westwood Pr. Geo's Maryland

(Number and street) (Town, township, village, or city) (County) (State)

[THE PLACE OF RESIDENCE GIVEN ON THE LINE ABOVE WILL DETERMINE LOCAL BOARD JURISDICTION; LINE 2 OF REGISTRATION CERTIFICATE WILL BE IDENTICAL]

3. MAILING ADDRESS

Brandywine, Pr. Geo's Md.

[Mailing address if other than place indicated on line 2. If same insert word same]

4. TELEPHONE | 5. AGE IN YEARS | 6. PLACE OF BIRTH

46 Townshend Pr. Geo.

(Town or county)

DATE OF BIRTH

March 11, 1896 Maryland

(Exchange) (Number) | (Mo.) (Day) (Yr.) | (State or country)

7. NAME AND ADDRESS OF PERSON WHO WILL ALWAYS KNOW YOUR ADDRESS

Mrs. Anna May Baden, Brandywine, Md.

8. EMPLOYER'S NAME AND ADDRESS

Farms for himself

9. PLACE OF EMPLOYMENT OR BUSINESS

Westwood Pr. Geo's Md.

(Number and street or R. F. D. number) (Town) (County) (State)

I AFFIRM THAT I HAVE VERIFIED ABOVE ANSWERS AND THAT THEY ARE TRUE.

D. S. S. Form 1 (Revised 4-1-42) (over) 16—21630-2 Wm T Baden

(Registrant's signature)

REGISTRATION CARD—(Men born on or after April 28, 1877 and on or before February 16, 1897)

SERIAL NUMBER | 1. NAME (Print) | ORDER NUMBER

U 711 FRANCIS HENRY BADEN

(First) (Middle) (Last)

2. PLACE OF RESIDENCE (Print)

BRANDYWINE PR. GEO. MARYLAND

(Number and street) (Town, township, village, or city) (County) (State)

[THE PLACE OF RESIDENCE GIVEN ON THE LINE ABOVE WILL DETERMINE LOCAL BOARD JURISDICTION; LINE 2 OF REGISTRATION CERTIFICATE WILL BE IDENTICAL]

3. MAILING ADDRESS

SAME

[Mailing address if other than place indicated on line 2. If same insert word same]

4. TELEPHONE | 5. AGE IN YEARS | 6. PLACE OF BIRTH

BRANDYWINE 2713 52 BRANDY WINE

(Town or county)

DATE OF BIRTH

MAY 14 1889 MARYLAND

(Exchange) (Number) | (Mo.) (Day) (Yr.) | (State or country)

7. NAME AND ADDRESS OF PERSON WHO WILL ALWAYS KNOW YOUR ADDRESS

MRS. FRANCIS HENRY BADEN

8. EMPLOYER'S NAME AND ADDRESS

CHAMBERLIN ENGINEERING Co. 30 KENNEDY DRIVE CHEVY CHASE MD.

9. PLACE OF EMPLOYMENT OR BUSINESS

ALABAMA AVE. SE. WASHINGTON D.C.

(Number and street or R. F. D. number) (Town) (County) (State)

I AFFIRM THAT I HAVE VERIFIED ABOVE ANSWERS AND THAT THEY ARE TRUE

D. S. S. Form 1 (Revised 4-1-42) (over) 98 Francis Hry Baden

(Registrant's signature)

REGISTRATION CARD—(Men born on or after April 28, 1877 and on or before February 16, 1897)

SERIAL NUMBER | 1. NAME (Print) | ORDER NUMBER
U 108. | William Thomas Baden |

2. PLACE OF RESIDENCE (Print)
Westwood Pr. Geo's Maryland
(Number and street) (Town, township, village, or city) (County) (State)
[THE PLACE OF RESIDENCE GIVEN ON THE LINE ABOVE WILL DETERMINE LOCAL BOARD JURISDICTION; LINE 2 OF REGISTRATION CERTIFICATE WILL BE IDENTICAL]

3. MAILING ADDRESS
Brandywine Pr. Geo's Md.
[Mailing address if other than place indicated on line 2. If same insert word same]

4. TELEPHONE | 5. AGE IN YEARS | 6. PLACE OF BIRTH
| 46 | Townshend Pr. Geo's
| DATE OF BIRTH | Maryland
(Exchange) (Number) | March 11, 1896 | (State or country)
| (Mo.) (Day) (Yr.) |

7. NAME AND ADDRESS OF PERSON WHO WILL ALWAYS KNOW YOUR ADDRESS
Mrs. Anna May Baden, Brandywine, Md.

8. EMPLOYER'S NAME AND ADDRESS
Farms for himself

9. PLACE OF EMPLOYMENT OR BUSINESS
Westwood Pr. Geo's Md.
(Number and street or R. F. D. number) (Town) (County) (State)

I AFFIRM THAT I HAVE VERIFIED ABOVE ANSWERS AND THAT THEY ARE TRUE.

D. S. S. Form 1
(Revised 4-1-42) (over) 16—21630-2 Wm T Baden
(Registrant's signature)

REGISTRATION CARD—(Men born on or after April 28, 1877 and on or before February 16, 1897)

SERIAL NUMBER | 1. NAME (Print) | ORDER NUMBER
U 111 | FRANCIS HENRY BADEN |

2. PLACE OF RESIDENCE (Print)
BRANDYNINE Pr. Geo. MARYLAND
(Number and street) (Town, township, village, or city) (County) (State)
[THE PLACE OF RESIDENCE GIVEN ON THE LINE ABOVE WILL DETERMINE LOCAL BOARD JURISDICTION; LINE 2 OF REGISTRATION CERTIFICATE WILL BE IDENTICAL]

3. MAILING ADDRESS
SAME
[Mailing address if other than place indicated on line 2. If same insert word same]

4. TELEPHONE | 5. AGE IN YEARS | 6. PLACE OF BIRTH
BRANDYWINE 2713 | 52 | BRANDY WINE
| DATE OF BIRTH | (Town or county)
(Exchange) (Number) | MAY 17 1889 | MARYLAND
| (Mo.) (Day) (Yr.) | (State or country)

7. NAME AND ADDRESS OF PERSON WHO WILL ALWAYS KNOW YOUR ADDRESS
MRS. FRANCIS HENRY BADEN

8. EMPLOYER'S NAME AND ADDRESS
CHAMBERLIN ENGINEERING Co. 30 KENNEDY DRIVE CHEVY CHASE MD.

9. PLACE OF EMPLOYMENT OR BUSINESS
ALABAMA AVE. SE. WASHINGTON DC
(Number and street or R. F. D. number) (Town) (County) (State)

I AFFIRM THAT I HAVE VERIFIED ABOVE ANSWERS AND THAT THEY ARE TRUE

D. S. S. Form 1
(Revised 4-1-42) (over) 98 Francis Henry Baden
(Registrant's signature)

REGISTRATION CARD—(Men born on or after April 28, 1877 and on or before February 16, 1897)

SERIAL NUMBER	1. NAME (Print)	ORDER NUMBER
U 1058	BenJAMIN CLARK BADEN	
	(First) (Middle) (Last)	

2. PLACE OF RESIDENCE (Print)

FREINLY _____ PRINCe GeORGe _____ MARYLAND
(Number no, street) (Town, township, village, or city) (County) (State)

[THE PLACE OF RESIDENCE GIVEN ON THE LINE ABOVE WILL DETERMINE LOCAL BOARD
JURISDICTION; LINE 2 OF REGISTRATION CERTIFICATE WILL BE IDENTICAL]

3. MAILING ADDRESS

ANACOSTIA Route 2
[Mailing address if other than place indicated on line 2. If same insert word same]

4. TELEPHONE	5. AGE IN YEARS	6. PLACE OF BIRTH
Van cleve STore	57	BADen (Town or county)
LOCUST 484-W-4	DATE OF BIRTH AUg. 1 1884	MARYLAND
(Exchange) (Number)	(Mo.) (Day) (Yr.)	(State or country)

7. NAME AND ADDRESS OF PERSON WHO WILL ALWAYS KNOW YOUR ADDRESS

Viola Baden Anna. Route 2

8. EMPLOYER'S NAME AND ADDRESS

Work for self

9. PLACE OF EMPLOYMENT OR BUSINESS

Freindly _____ Prince George _____ Md
(Number and street or R. F. D. number) (Town) (County) (State)

I AFFIRM THAT I HAVE VERIFIED ABOVE ANSWERS AND THAT THEY ARE TRUE.

Benjamin C. Baden

D. S. S. Form 1 (over)   16 21630 2   (Registrant's signature)
(Revised 4-1-42)

REGISTRATION CARD—(Men born on or after April 28, 1877 and on or before February 16, 1897)

SERIAL NUMBER	1. NAME (Print)	ORDER NUMBER
U 1058	Leo Levi Baden	
	(First) (Middle) (Last)	

2. PLACE OF RESIDENCE (Print)

Bowie _____ Pr. Geo., _____ Md.
(Number and street) (Town, township, village, or city) (County) (State)

[THE PLACE OF RESIDENCE GIVEN ON THE LINE ABOVE WILL DETERMINE LOCAL BOARD
JURISDICTION; LINE 2 OF REGISTRATION CERTIFICATE WILL BE IDENTICAL]

3. MAILING ADDRESS

Same
[Mailing address if other than place indicated on line 2. If same insert word same]

4. TELEPHONE	5. AGE IN YEARS	6. PLACE OF BIRTH
	48	Townshend (Town or county)
	DATE OF BIRTH Dec. 1893	Md.
(Exchange) (Number)	(Mo.) (Day) (Yr.)	(State or country)

7. NAME AND ADDRESS OF PERSON WHO WILL ALWAYS KNOW YOUR ADDRESS

Miss Mary Lou Baden, Bowie, Md.

8. EMPLOYER'S NAME AND ADDRESS

K. P. Aldrich, P.O. Dept, Wash, D.C.

9. PLACE OF EMPLOYMENT OR BUSINESS

Same
(Number and street or R. F. D. number) (Town) (County) (State)

I AFFIRM THAT I HAVE VERIFIED ABOVE ANSWERS AND THAT THEY ARE TRUE.

Leo Levi Baden

D. S. S. Form 1 (over)   16 21630 2   (Registrant's signature)
(Revised 4-1-42)

RICHARD BRIGHTWELL

1658-1758 Charles County MD Familes "The first 100 years": Wills, Court, Church, Land, Inventories & Accounts

Descendant Register, Generation No. 1

1. **Richard Brightwell** was born 1651 in England, and died 29 AUG 1698 in Prince George's County, Maryland - Probate. He married **Katherine {StepDau} Lashley** 1687 in Calvert County, Maryland, daughter of Robert Lashley and Elizabeth MNU Lashley. She was born ABT 1653 in Calvert County, Maryland, and died 1698 in Prince George's County, Maryland.

   Children of Richard Brightwell and Katherine {StepDau} Lashley are:

   + 2   i. Richard Brightwell was born 1687 in Calvert County, Maryland - now Prince George's County, Maryland, and died 29 MAR 1775 in Prince George's County, Maryland - Probate.
   + 3   ii. Peter Brightwell was born 1688 in Prince George's County, Maryland, and died 23 DEC 1747 in Prince George's County, Maryland - Probate.
   + 4   iii. Elizabeth Brightwell was born 1693 in Calvert County, Maryland - now Prince George's County, Maryland.
   + 5   iv. John Brightwell was born 1694 in Prince George's County, Maryland, and died 24 NOV 1774 in Prince George's County, Maryland - Probate.

Descendant Register, Generation No. 2

2. **Richard Brightwell** (Richard Brightwell[1]) was born 1687 in Calvert County, Maryland - now Prince George's County, Maryland, and died 29 MAR 1775 in Prince George's County, Maryland - Probate. He married **Mary Lawson** ABT 1707 in Prince George's County, Maryland. She was born ABT 1691 in Calvert County, Maryland.

   Children of Richard Brightwell and Mary Lawson are:

   6   i.   Richard Lawson Brightwell was born AFT 1707 in Prince George's County, Maryland, and died 20 MAY 1801 in Prince George's County, Maryland - Probate.
   7   ii. John Brightwell was born AFT 1708 in Prince George's County, Maryland.
   8   iii. Thomas Theodore Brightwell was born AFT 1709 in Prince George's County, Maryland.
   9   iv. Martha Brightwell was born AFT 1710 in Prince George's County, Maryland.

3. **Peter Brightwell** (Richard Brightwell[1]) was born 1688 in Prince George's County, Maryland, and died 23 DEC 1747 in Prince George's County, Maryland - Probate. He married **Anne MNU Brightwell**.

   Children of Peter Brightwell and Anne MNU Brightwell are:

   +   10   i. Elizabeth Brightwell was born ABT 1730 in Prince George's County, Maryland.
       11   ii. Catherine Brightwell.

4.   **Elizabeth Brightwell** (Richard Brightwell[1]) was born 1693 in Calvert County, Maryland - now Prince George's County, Maryland. She married **Jasper Kennick** 1718 in Prince George's County, Maryland. He was born BEF 1689, and died AFT 1764 in Charles County, Maryland.

Child of Elizabeth Brightwell and Jasper Kennick is:

    12   i. John Kennick was born in Prince George's County, Maryland, and died AFT 1792 in Charles County, Maryland.

5.   **John Brightwell** (Richard Brightwell[1]) was born 1694 in Prince George's County, Maryland, and died 24 NOV 1774 in Prince George's County, Maryland - Probate. He married **Elizabeth Coleman**, daughter of Thomas Coleman and Mary MNU Samwayes. She was born BEF 1704 in Charles County, Maryland.

Children of John Brightwell and Elizabeth Coleman are:

    13   i. John Brightwell was born 1720 in Prince George's County, Maryland, and died 1791. He married Sarah Carmack 1751 in Frederick County, Maryland, daughter of William Carmack and Jane McDaniel. She was born 2 JUL 1733 in Cecil County, Maryland, and died ABT 1791.

  + 14   ii. Catherine Brightwell was born 1722 in Prince George's County, Maryland, and died AFT 1793 in Montgomery County, Maryland.

  + 15   iii. Ursula Brightwell was born 1725 in Prince George's County, Maryland, and died AFT 1782 in Prince George's County, Maryland.

  + 16   iv. Sarah Brightwell was born 1728 in Prince George's County, Maryland, and died in Frederick County, Maryland.

    17   v. Priscilla Brightwell was born 1730 in Prince George's County, Maryland, and died AFT 1775 in Prince George's County, Maryland. She married Unknown Orme.

  + 18   vi. Eleanor Brightwell was born 1732 in Prince George's County, Maryland, and died AFT 1775 in Prince George's County, Maryland.

  + 19   vii. Martha Brightwell was born 1733 in Prince George's County, Maryland.

  + 20   viii. Thomas Coleman Brightwell was born 1735 in Prince George's County, Maryland, and died 21 DEC 1775 in Prince George's County, Maryland - Inventory.

10.   **Elizabeth Brightwell** (Peter Brightwell[2], Richard Brightwell[1]) was born ABT 1730 in Prince George's County, Maryland. She married **Joseph Cage** ABT 1746 in Charles County, Maryland, son of William Cage and Margaret Wilson. He was born 1725 in Charles County, Maryland, and died AFT 1778 in Prince George's County, Maryland.

Children of Elizabeth Brightwell and Joseph Cage are:

21   i. William Cage was born BEF 1757 in Charles County, Maryland, and died AFT 1777 in Prince George's County, Maryland. He married Mary Mayhew 18 DEC 1777 in Prince George's County, Maryland. She was born ABT 1761 in Prince George's County, Maryland, and died AFT 1777 in Prince George's County, Maryland.

22   ii. Peter Brightwell Cage was born ABT 1762 in Prince George's County, Maryland. He married Mary Parker 20 JAN 1783 in Prince George's County, Maryland. She was born BEF 1767 in Prince George's County, Maryland.

14.   **Catherine Brightwell** (John Brightwell[2], Richard Brightwell[1]) was born 1722 in Prince George's County, Maryland, and died AFT 1793 in Montgomery County, Maryland. She married **Elias Oden** in Prince George's County, Maryland, son of Francis Oden and Susannah MNU Oden. He was born in Charles County, Maryland, and died 13 AUG 1787 in Prince George's County, Maryland.

Child of Catherine Brightwell and Elias Oden is:

23   i. Elias Oden was born BEF 1773 in Prince George's County, Maryland, and died AFT 1793 in Montgomery County, Maryland.

15.   **Ursula Brightwell** (John Brightwell[2], Richard Brightwell[1]) was born 1725 in Prince George's County, Maryland, and died AFT 1782 in Prince George's County, Maryland. She married **Thomas Morton**. He was born BEF 1721, and died 22 JUN 1782 in Prince George's County, Maryland - Probate.

Children of Ursula Brightwell and Thomas Morton are:

24   i.   Joseph Morton was born BEF 1752 in Prince George's County, Maryland, and died AFT 1784 in Prince George's County, Maryland.

25   ii. George Morton was born BEF 1752 in Prince George's County, Maryland, and died AFT 1792 in Charles County, Maryland.

26   iii. John Morton was born BEF 1741 in Prince George's County, Maryland, and died AFT 1782 in Prince George's County, Maryland.

16.   **Sarah Brightwell** (John Brightwell[2], Richard Brightwell[1]) was born 1728 in Prince George's County, Maryland, and died in Frederick County, Maryland. She married **Charles Wood** 10 MAY 1748 in Prince George's County, Maryland. He was born 1720 in Virginia, and died 27 AUG 1787 in Frederick County, Maryland - Proved.

Children of Sarah Brightwell and Charles Wood are:

+ 27   i. Sarah Wood was born ABT 1748 in Frederick County, Maryland.

28   ii. <u>Benjamin Wood</u> was born ABT 1750 in Prince George's County, Maryland, and died AFT
      1815 in Mason County, Kentucky.

18.   **Eleanor Brightwell** (John Brightwell[2], Richard Brightwell[1]) was born 1732 in Prince George's
      County, Maryland, and died AFT 1775 in Prince George's County, Maryland. She married
      Thomas F. Baden AFT 1752 in Prince George's County, Maryland, son of Robert Baden and Martha
      Lawson. He was born ABT 1732, and died AFT 1775 in Prince George's County, Maryland.

      Child of Eleanor Brightwell and Thomas F. Baden is:

      + 29   i. <u>John Baden</u> was born AFT 1754 in Prince George's County, Maryland, and died
             11 JUN 1805 in Prince George's County, Maryland - Admin.

19.   **Martha Brightwell** (John Brightwell[2], Richard Brightwell[1]) was born 1733 in Prince George's County,
      Maryland. She married **Joseph Letchworth** ABT 1749 in Prince George's County, Maryland, son of
      Thomas Letchworth and Elizabeth Hutchison. He was born BEF 1718 in Prince George's County,
      Maryland, and died 8 MAY 1784 in Prince George's County, Maryland - Probate.

      Children of Martha Brightwell and Joseph Letchworth are:

      + 30   i. <u>Leonard Letchworth</u> died 10 MAR 1801 in Prince George's County, Maryland -
             Probate.
        31   ii. <u>Levi Letchworth</u>.
      + 32   iii. <u>Mary Letchworth</u> died AFT 1796 in Prince George's County, Maryland.

20.   **Thomas Coleman Brightwell** (John Brightwell[2], Richard Brightwell[1]) was born 1735 in Prince George's
      County, Maryland, and died 21 DEC 1775 in Prince George's County, Maryland - Inventory. He married
      Verlinda MNU Brightwell BEF 1766 in Prince George's County, Maryland. She was born BEF 1750,
      and died AFT 1779 in Prince George's County, Maryland.

      Children of Thomas Coleman Brightwell and Verlinda MNU Brightwell are:

        33   i. <u>Richard Brightwell</u> was born 19 AUG 1766 in Prince George's County, Maryland, and died
             AFT 1788 in Charles County, Maryland.
        34   ii. <u>Mary Brightwell</u> was born 8 FEB 1768 in Prince George's County, Maryland.
        35   iii. <u>Priscilla Brightwell</u> was born 10 JUN 1769 in Prince George's County, Maryland.
        36   iv. <u>Heneritta Brightwell</u> was born 22 FEB 1773 in Prince George's County, Maryland.

                          Descendant Register, Generation No. 4

27.   **Sarah Wood** (Sarah Brightwell[3], John Brightwell[2], Richard Brightwell[1]) was born ABT 1748 in
      Frederick County, Maryland. She married **William Lamb** ABT 1775 in Frederick County, Maryland,
      son of Edward Lamb and Eleanor MNU Lamb. He was born 9 AUG 1748 in Cecil MM, Kent County,
      Maryland.

      Children of Sarah Wood and William Lamb are:

37 i. <u>Rachel Lamb</u> was born 1781 in Frederick County, Maryland, and died 1844 in Douglas Co., Illinois. She married <u>Ephraim Minor</u> 8 MAY 1799 in Maysville, Mason Co., Kentucky. He was born 22 FEB 1778 in Lunenburg Co., Virginia, and died 1835 in Oakland, Coles County, Illinois.

38 ii. <u>Basil Lamb</u> was born 1780 in Frederick County, Maryland.

39 iii. <u>Mary Lamb</u> was born 10 SEP 1778 in Frederick County, Maryland, and died 23 JUN 1822 in Clermont County, Ohio. She married <u>John Sargent</u> 22 NOV 1796 in Maysville, Mason County, Kentucky, son of William L. Sargent and Sarah Aldridge. He was born 5 OCT 1772 in Frederick County, Maryland, and died 5 SEP 1852 in Brown County, Ohio.

29. **John Baden** (Eleanor Brightwell[3], John Brightwell[2], Richard Brightwell[1]) was born AFT 1754 in Prince George's County, Maryland, and died 11 JUN 1805 in Prince George's County, Maryland - Admin. He married **Margaret Noble** BEF 1775 in Prince George's County, Maryland, daughter of Joseph Noble and Martha Tarvin. She was born BEF 1759 in Prince George's County, Maryland, and died AFT 1813 in Prince George's County, Maryland.

Children of John Baden and Margaret Noble are:

40 i. <u>Thomas Noble Baden</u> was born BEF 1776 in Prince George's County, Maryland.

41 ii. <u>John Tarvin Baden</u> was born BEF 1778 in Prince George's County, Maryland, and died 1 JAN 1814 in Prince George's County, Maryland - Probate.

42 iii. <u>Eleanor Baden</u> was born BEF 1780 in Prince George's County, Maryland.

43 iv. <u>Clement Baden</u> was born BEF 1782 in Prince George's County, Maryland, and died AFT 1834 in Prince George's County, Maryland.

44 v. <u>Anne Baden</u> was born AFT 1789 in Prince George's County, Maryland.

45 vi. <u>Joseph Noble Baden</u> was born 1784 in Prince George's County, Maryland, and died 16 DEC 1854 in Prince George's County, Maryland.

46 vii. <u>Margaret Baden</u> was born AFT 1791 in Prince George's County, Maryland.

47 viii. <u>Elizabeth Baden</u> was born AFT 1790.

48 ix. <u>Rebecca Dent Baden</u> was born BEF 1780 in Prince George's County, Maryland, and died 3 JUN 1843 in Elizabeth Twp, Allegheny County, Pennsylvania. She married <u>Richard Noble</u> 21 OCT 1796 in Prince George's County, Maryland. He was born 1778 in Prince George's County, Maryland, and died 1826 in Elizabeth Twp, Allegheny County, Pennsylvania.

Prince George's County MD Will Book Liber T No. #1; 1803-1808;
Folio 604 JOHN BADEN, of Thomas 05/13/1805 06/11/1805 being Sick ..."
Bequeaths to:
I. Margaret Baden —wife -to have all the estate both real and personal testator is possessed of for her natural life or widowed
-to have the use of Negrocs left to whood testator's daughters for her natural life
2. Thomas Noble Baden --son -to have at widow's decease part of a tract of land called "Marshall's Rest"
lying on the south side of the road leading from John Waring's land to Susanna Magruder's land on condition

3. Rebecca Dent Noble --daughter
-as condition for the land left him, Thomas to pay her the sum of $300.00 at the end of 1 year following his possession of the land
4, John Tarvin Baden --son
-to have after widow's decease part of a tract of land called "Marshall's Rest" and part of a tract of land alled "Exchange" and part of a tract called "Masonseon" lying on the south side of Rutherford Branch --to have on condition
5. Eleanor Baden --daughter -John to pay her the sum of $300.00 within 1 years of his taking possession of the land devised to him
6. Clement Baden --son
-to have testator's grist mill on Rutherford Branch including a small piece of land
which testator purchased from John Baden, Sr. and also to have part of a grist mill
and mill seat on the main branch of Deep Creek --to have on condition
7. Ann Baden --daughter
-Clement to pay her the sum of $300.00 as condition for the mills left to him
-to have Negro man "Jim"
8. Joseph Noble Baden --son
-to have the plantation whereon testator now lives called "Part of the Exchange" on condition
-Joseph and Clement named executors of the will
9. Margaret Baden --daughter
-Joseph to pay her the sum of $300.00 within 2 years following his takirm possession of the Land
-testator's daughters to have Negro woman "Sib" and her increase to be divided among them
-to have Negro boy "John"
10. Elizabeth Baden --daughtter
-to have Negro land "Mice" Witnesses: Robert Baden
John Baden, Jr.
John Tarvin (mark)
Then came: Robert Baden and John Baden
Note the testator signed the will in his own hand
===

PRINCE GEORGE'S COUNTY, MARYLAND WILLS; Liber TT; 1813-1817; Keddie; folio 78

JOHN T. BADEN
"being weak and low in body ..." 11/16/1813; 01/01/1814 Bequeaths to:
1. Thomas N. Baden --brother
-to have all the testator's estate both personal and mixed including that parcel of land willed to the testator by his late father John Baden, of Thomas after the payment of debts and the death of testator's mother and he to keep the land at a fair valuation and such valuation reserve to himself and to pay the over balance to the testator's brothers and sisters -named executor of the will
Witnesses: Thomas John Clagett
Thomas Baden
John Duvall
Then came: John Duvall and Thomas Baden
Note: the testator signed the will in his own hand

Maryland ss

To the Honble Edmund Jenings Esqr the Lord Propr's Chief
Judge in Land affairs within this Province

The Petition of James Watson of Prince Georges County
Humbly Sheweth

That Richard and Peter Brightwell heretofore obtained out
of his Lordships Land office a Spl warrant for the Escheating the remainder
unescheated of a Certain tract of Land called Poplar Hill Originally
on the 7th Sept 1666 Granted to a Certain John Boage for the qt of
400 acres who died thereof possessed intestate and without heirs &c
by that means the Same was become Escheat to his Lop and that they
further Sat forth that before that time a Certain Wm Watson had Escheated
140a part of Said tract and forasmuch as the Remainder still undiscovered
and they being the first discoverers is also proposed thereof prayed
to be admitted to its purchase which was Granted them and In pursuance
of Said Warrant the Said Rich & Peter Brightwell caused a Resurvey
to be made on the residue unescheated as aforesd and a Certificate thereof
to be Returned into his Lordships Land office by which it appeard there was
the qt of 280 Acres aforesd Cert bearing date 27th Novr 1729 that your
your petr further Sets forth that on the 13th Aug 1731 there issued a
Proclamation intimating amongst other things that persons pretending any Right
to Lands by Certificates of Resurvey returned and Lodged in his Lops Land office
upon Escheat warrants that did not within two years from the date of
Said Proclamn Came and pay the purchase money for Such Escht Land
and Sue out patent for the Same the Land taken up by virtue of
Such warrant Sho'd Stand Subjected to the benefit of the next discoverer
that notwithstanding the Proclamation aforesd and some other proclamation
for the Same purpose since published the Said Rich & Peter Brightwell
have not complyed therewith but contrary thereto and in contempt to his
Lop have ever since holden and Occupied the Said Land without
paying any Consideration therefore by wch means your petr is advised
the Cert aforesd to become Null and void and that the remaind unescheated
of the Said tract taken up by virtue thereof Stands Subjected to the
benefit of the Next discoverer And forasmuch as your petr is the
next discoverer and desirous to take up and pay for the Same
humbly prays to be admitted to its purchase be it Such by the means
above set forth or by any other ways or means whatsoever and
a Spl warrant to Resurvey the Same with Liberty of including the
Lops Escheats if any therein Contained and of adding the Lands vacancy
and that upon return of a Cert of Such Resurvey & Complying wth
all requisites may have his Lordships Grant of Confirm issued
unto him thereon And as in duty bound he will pray &c

Let Special Warrt issue for ye purpose aforsd
By the Chief &c
Jan'y 6. 1736

James Watson

Eam: Jenings Jur

274

116

Tho County ss

George Naylor Aged fifty Seven years
or there abouts Being Sworn on the holy Evangilist
of allmighty god Deposeth as followes Viz:
this Deponant Sayeth that Peter Brightwell hath
Been in Possession of Part of a tract of Land called
Poplar Hill These one or two years, and that he
hath Occupied the said Land this Sumer in making Corn
and Tobacco, this Deponant further Sayeth that
Richard and John Brightwell are possess'd of part
of the same tract of Land, and that they have sold
Timber from off the said tract, But knows not
what Quantity, further Sayth not

Nov.r 21th 1787   Sworn Before   George
                                            W: Wilkinson

74

Chas County ss Edward Swan Aged thirty seven or there
abouts being sworn on the holy Evangelists of
allmighty god Deposeth as followes viz[t]
this Deponant sayeth that some time Last
winter having Discourse with John Brightwell
Told him he thought he and his Bro[r] had Rented
the land they live On, and that Brightwell reply'd
that they had been at Eleven hundred pounds
of tobacco Charges, and that when they went to
agree with the Agent they thought he held it
too Dear. and upon that Let it Drop, and
further sayth not

Nov[r] 21th 1737   Sworn Before   W[m] Wilkinson

274

Maryland ss.   To the Honoble Edmund Jennings Esqr the Ld Ship &c Judge in Land affairs within this Province

The petn of James Watson of Pr. Geo's County Humbly Sheweth

That a certain Peter Brightwell of Pr Geo's Co. afsd on 16th Apr. 1736 obtained a spl warrant for the Resurveying of a certain parcell of Land Called Poplar hills in order to take up the Surplus therein &c. And that in or about the year 1729 the sd John and Richd Brightwell had the Same resurv.d as escheat Land and a plat thereof ret.d into his Lops Land office but never pd any consideration for the Same nor Sued out patent and your petr upon a late discovery thereof prayd a Special warrant to take up the Same agreeable to his Lops Proclamation your petitioner therefore humbly prays that Caveat may be Entred agt the Said Peter Brightwell having a patent on any Certificate to be Returned by virtue of the warrant of Resurvey afsd as also agt the Said Peter and Richard Brightwell having a patent on the Certificate of Escheat postponed in the Office for non payment of the purchase money unt. &c your petr is heard before your Honr in relation to the premises afsd.

          And as in duty bound he'll pray &c

Let Caveat be Entred as prayd
To Tho. Clagett P.P. office   Eam: Jennigs Seer:
Febry 10. 1736

Entries: 72352   **Updated:** 2010-01-15 03:12:33 UTC (Fri)

Contact: Michael   **Home Page:** Marshall Hall

Includes early Northern Neck VA Records for counties bordering the Rappahannock & Potomac Rivers.
Please do not send Ancestry.com messages, I do not have a subscription:

- *ID:* 110981
- *Name:* **Richard Brightwell**
- *Sex:* M
- *Birth:* 1651 in England
- *Death:* 29 AUG 1698 in Prince George's County, Maryland - Probate
- *Note:*

> Brightwell, Richard, Prince George's County, 21st Aug.,
> 1698: 29th Aug., 1698.
> To Eliza: Burres, dau. of Jno. Burres, 1/12 of "Blackwell" and
> "Mattawoman. "
> to: 5 child. (unnamed), residue of estate, real and personal. In
> event of death of 2 daus. (unnamed) , their estate to pass to
> their 3 brothers (unnamed) and their hrs.
> Thos. Greenfield and Wm. Watson, exs., to hold estate in trust
> until majority of eld. son Richard.
> Test: Wm. Mills, Eliza: Mills, Geo. Mayler. MCW 6. 182.
> _____
>
> Richard Brightwell 19-1/2B.1 1 PG £52.0.5 Sep 5 1699
> (gentleman
> Appraisers; David Small, Edward Willett.
> _____
>
> Robert Kemp 14.139 A CA £13.10.0 #4192 Jun 2 1697
> Payments to: Edward Batson, Thomas Taney, Richard Keene,
> Mr. John Dent, Michael Mouring paid to Samuell Watkins.
> Executor: Capt. Richard Brightwell
> _____
>
> Charles County Circuit Court Liber S, Page 404
> 11 Nov 1694: Indenture from John Smith of Calvert County,
> planter, and Elizabeth his wife, to Jervis Windsor, planter; for
> 4,800# tobacco; a parcel called Smith's Chance on the south
> side of Mattawoman Runn; bounded by Richard Brightwell;
> located in Manor of Zachia; containing 144 acres; /s/ John
> Smith, Elizabeth Smith; wit. Sam. Peter, Edw. Potter
> _____
>
> PRINCE GEORGE'S COUNTY LAND RECORDS, Petition
> and Deed of Gift, 10 June 1693
> Between: Capt. RICHARD BRIGHTWELL and Vestry of St.

Paul.

Price: (none)

Petition: At a meeting held at Mount Calvert by the Vestry of
St. Paul, 3 June 1693, it was decided that as the lower part of
the Parish was too remote from the church, the minister would
attend every third Sabbath at the home of Capt.
BRIGHTWELL, beginning 11 June 1693. As the land near
BRIGHTWELL'S plantation was most fit for a chapel, the
Vestry re-quested that BRIGHTWELL grant land and timber
for that purpose. Confirmation was to take place at St. Pauls
Church in Charlestowne the first Saturday of July [1693].

Deed of Gift: 1 July 1693, Capt. RICHARD BRIGHTWELL
granted 2 or 3 acres of land and timber for a chapel.

Signature: THO. GREENFIELD, for the Vestry

Wit.: THO. GREENFIELD, THO. HOLLYDAY, RICH.
CHARLETT Ackn'd: (none)

Recorded: 29 September 1697, Vol. A, p. 63A

===

Prince George's Land Records 1710-1717 - Liber F -folio
402; Indenture, 23 Mar 1713

From: Richard Brightwell and Peter Brightwell, planters of
Prince George's County To: Thomas Gant, merchant of Prince
George's County

For 5,600 pounds of tobacco a tract of land in Prince George's
County called Blackwell Beginning; bounded by
Mattawoman Run; containing 160 acres

Signed: Richard Brightwell (mark & seal), Peter Brightwell
(mark & seal)

Witnessed: James Stoddert, Will Tannehill

Memo: Richard and Peter Brightwell acknowledged deed
before above witnesses

===

Prince George's Land Records 1710-1717 - Liber F -folio
404; Indenture, 23 Mar 1713

From: Elizabeth Burroughs of Charles County, spinster
To: Richard Brightwell

Richard Brightwell, Gent. late of Prince George's County by
will dated 21 Aug 1698 gave Elizabeth one moiety of the land
called Blackwell of 160 acres granted Brightwell by Charles,
Lord Baltimore; for 1,500 pounds of tobacco Elizabeth sells
her half part of that land

=== Brightwells hunting Quarter mentioned

This Indenture made this Seventeenth Day of Aprill in the
Year of our Lord God One Thousand Seven hundred and
twenty three

Between William Maria Farthing of St Marys County in the
province

of Maryland Innholder of the one part and John Bradford
of Prince Georges County in the Province abovesaid Gent of
the

other part Wittnesseth That Whereas formerly a certain
Joseph

Edloe assigned to his son Edward Edloe a certain warrant which
he had taken out for three hundred Acres of Land which was located as is hereafter expressed (Viz.t) Lying Scituate and being
in Prince Georges County then called Charles County Beginning at
a Bounded white oak by the River it being the first Bounded Tree of Capt.n Brightwells land called Brightwells hunting Quarters
and Running thence east north east Two hundred perches then North North West Two hundred and Forty perches Then West
South West Two hundred perches to Potomack River so with a Streight
Line to the first Tree containing and then laid out for three hundred
acres to be held of the Mannor of Zachiah and called Edloes Adventure
as by the certificate thereof Recorded in his Lordships land office for this Province In Lib.o C N.o 3 fol 597 and the patent
thereon grounded and the said Edward Edloe granted may appear
which said Tract of Land after the Death of the said Edward Edloe intestate and without any heirs of his body became the Right of a certain John Noble the Son of the eldest sister of the said Edward as heir at law to the said Edward which said John Noble afterwards Dying Intestate and without heirs of his body the said Land became the Right of a certain

Prince George's Land Records 1726-1730 - Liber M, Page 257
Enrolled at request of John Bradford 10 Feb 1727:
Indenture, 12 Jun 1727; Between William Maria Farthing of St. Mary's County, innholder, and John Bradford, s/o John Bradford, dec'd, Gent.; for £30; a parcel of land about 20 miles higher than the falls of the Potomac, bordering the Potomac, called Sugar Sands; bounded by Brightwells Hunting Quarter; parcel originally granted Edward Edloe of St. Mary's Co. called Edloe's Adventure containing 300 acres; devised to John Noble, of St. Mary's Co.; then to John's sister Mary Noble who died without issue and intestate; then to William Spinke of St. Mary's County, planter, being 1st cousin and heir by the father's side; from him, with consent of his wife, to Farthing; /s/ Wm. Maria Farthing; wit. John Baker, Jr., Wm. Cavenaugh; 17 Jun 1727 ack. by Wm. Maria Farthing and Anne his wife; wit. Robert Hutchins, Thomas Tolley; Thomas Aisquith and John Leigh certified as Justices of St. Mary's Co-

STAFFORD COUNTY VA DEED & WILL BOOK 1689 -
1693; THE ANTIENT PRESS

THIS INDENTURE made the Sixteenth and Seventeenth day
of Febry 1690 Betweene JOHN MATTHEWS of Stafford
County Planter of one part & Capa. GERRARD SLY of
LONDON Merchant Wittnesseth that said JOHN
MATTHEWS for ye sume of Seaventeene thousand poundes
of good Tobacco & Caske to him paid by GEORGE BRENT
of WOODSTOCKE in ye County aforesaid Genii. Atturney
and Agent for ye said GERRARD SLY for & in behalfe of the
said GERRARD SLY him ye said JOHN MATTHEWS bath
granted unto said GERRARD SLY his Exors & Assignes all
that land in Stafford County & upon GREAT HUNTING
CREEKE in the freshes of the POTOMACK RIVER (torrn) ..
beinge part of a tract of two thousand . . , Surveyed by Mr.
SAMLL ... 1672 which said Six hundred acres now in _ ..
bounded as followeth (Viz) Easterly upon GREAT
HUNTINGE CREEKE Northerly upon ye lande of Capa.
GEORGE BRENT, now in ye tenure of ROBERT
WILLIAMS Westerly by ye remaininge part of this Divident
of Two thousand six hundred sixty and six acres of land and
Southerly upon ye land of RICA. BRIGHTWELL formerly
by him purchased of EVAN JONES together wth all houses &
edifices & all whatsoever all waters and appurtenances
whatsoever to ye said Six hundred acres ye granted premises
by venue of a bargaine and sale thereof made beareinge date
ye day before & by venue of ye Statute for Transferringe uses
into possession To Have and To Hold the said Six hundred
acres of land to GERRARD SLY, In Wittness whereof ye
parties have sett their handes & wales
In presence of SAMP. DORRELL, JOHN MATTHEWS
WM. DIGGES
This above sale of lande was acknowledged in the County
Court of Stafford by SAMP. DORRELL Atturney of ye said
JOHN MATTHEWS who alsoe made oath that he did see the
said MATTHEWS signs ye same unto Capa. GEORGE
BRENT Atturney of Capt. GERRARD SLY on ye 14th day of
March 1690/1 and was then recorded
===

STAFFORD COUNTY VA DEED & WILL BOOK 1689 -
1693; THE ANTIENT PRESS
pp. 218a MARYLANDE CALVERT COUNTY, KNOW
ALL MEN by these presents that I KATHERINE
BRIGHTWELL Wife of RICHARD BRIGHTWELL of ye
County aforesaid for divers good consideracon especially
consideringe ye great distance of place between here &
Virginia to travell have appointed my Trusty and well beloved
Friend THOMAS LANDE my full & lawfull Attorney for me
to acknowledge all my right in five hundred acres of lande in
Virginia wch my husband RICHARD BRIGHTWELL bath
sold unto JOHN GREENE of ST. MARYS COUNTY of ye

123

PROVINCE aforesaid Planter and I doe confirms all my said Attorney shall doe. in Witness I have sett my hand & Seale this 9th day of November 1691
In presence of THOMAS GREENFIELD, KATHERINE BRIGHTWELL_ JAMES JEWENS
Recorded ye 13th day of November 1691

THIS INDENTURE made this thirteenth day of November 1691 Betweene RICHARD BRIGHTWELL of CALVERT COUNTY in the PROVINCE of MARYLANDE and KATHERINE his Wife of the one part and JOHN GREENE of ye said PROVINCE OF MARYLANDE & Countie of ST. MARYS of other part Wittnesseth that said RICHARD BRIGHTWELL & KATHERINE his Wife for ye summe of Eighty thousand poundes of good sounde & merchandable Tobacco & casque to them paid have sold ye said JOHN GREENE his heires a parcell of lands containinge Five hundred acres beinge in ye County of Stafford beinge part of a greater dividend bounded thus, to begin att a marked Gumme and thence to run out into ye Woods accordinge to ye Course & distances mentioned in a conveyance dated ye 10th day of March 1680/1 granted JOHN MATTHEWS the first taker up of ye said land to one EVAN JONES who married one of ye Daughters of ye said JOHN MATTHEW'S & by ye said EVAN JONES sold to ye said RICHARD BRIGHTWELL as by conveyance dated ye ninth day of March 1680/1 To Have and To Hold ye said land to him ye said JOHN GREENE in as full and ample manner as was before sold by said EVAN JONES to RICHARD BRIGHTWELL In Wittness whereof ye parties hath sett their handes Sealer
In presence of THEODORICK BLAND , RICHD. BRIGHTWELL JOHN WAUGH
This above sale of lande was acknowledged in the County Court of Stafford by RICHARD BRIGHTWELL & THOMAS LANDE Attorney of ye said KATHERINE BRIGHTWELL unto the aforesaid JOHN GREENE on the 13th day of November 1691 and was then recorded.

Stafford County Court Records, 1680: THE ANTIENT PRESS
p. 23(42) The Depo: of RICHARD BRIGHTWELL aged 29 yeares or thereabouts sworne and examined saith that about three weeks agoe being a drinking att Mr. EDWARD MASONs, yor: Deponent did heare' EVAN JONES say unto WILLM: DOWNING hee would avouch that Mare unto him, that JAMES SCOFIELD and hee ye said JONES brought upp ye Hill before them att ye ROCKS and that itt was ye Mare that bee ye said JONES had sould him.. and further saith not RICHD: BRIGHTWELL
Jar: et Recordatr: 11 Novbr: 1680

Name: mac billigins
Email: macbilligins@yahoo.ca
Note:
Vol 15 p56 Maryland State Archives - Richard Brightwell
becomes a ranger in 1675

Att a Council held att Mattapenny Sewall the third day of
Novembr in the 44th yeare of the Dominion of Cecilius &c.
Annoq Dmi 1675

Present
Charles Calvert Esqr Chiefe Governor &c
The Honble J Philipp Calvert Esqr Chancellor
Wm Calvert Esqr Princll Secretary
Jesse Wharton Esqr

Ordered that Proclamacon be forthwith made by the severall Sheriffes of each respective County That all persons that
have been att any Charge & Expences for Provision Amuni-
tion or otherwise about the late Expedicon agt the
Susquahanough Indians come to the next Provinc" Court or
deliver
their severall Accompts thereof to the respective Sheriffes of
each County who are to have the same ready to deliver to the
Governor & Council att the next Provinciall Court And that
Richard Robinson Comandr of the good Shipp the John of
Hull have notice given him by the High Sheriffe of Charles
County that he be & appeare att the next Provinciall Court to
deliver in his Acct to the Governor & Council of his Expence
& Charges about the said Expedicon.

Then Ordered that there be a party of Thirty men raised,
fifteene out of St Maryes County & fifteene out of Charles
County, to march under the Comand of Capt John Douglas,
& Capt Gerard Sly, to Range the woods about Pascattoway
& the Susquahanough ffort, to take upp all such horses as
they shall finde that were lost by the Souldiers in the late
Expedicon agt the Susquahanough Indians, whereof Jon
Burrows, Joseph Horton, Vincent Mansfield, Richard
Brightwell, Mannah Hawton the Indian & James Smallwood
are to be part.
===

Name: mac billigins
Email: macbilligins@yahoo.ca
A reference to Richard Brightwell from Maryland State
Archives. The original hand written documents are available
as .pdf files.

Assembly Proceedings, May — June 1676. Liber W H & L
An Act for payment & Assessing the Publick Charges
of this Province
Whereas there hath been two hundred Nynty Three thou-

- -

sand three hundred & two pounds of Tobacco Expended laid
out and disburst by the upper & Lower houses of this present
Generall Assembly & by severall other the good people of.
this
Prouince for the Publick good of the same And to the Intent
that the same may be satisfyed and paid to those persons to
whome the same is due Bee itt therefore Enacted by the Right
Honble the Lord Proprietary by and with the aduice and Consent of the upper & lower houses of this present Generall Assembly & the Authority of the same That the said two hundred Nynty Three thousand three hundred & three pounds of
Tobacco be paid in manner & forme as is hereafter Expressed
(that is to say)

"Richard is one of the listed"
Richard Brightwell 00600
===

Contributed by mac billigins

Note: been organizing references to Richard Brightwell
(1651-1698) found in the Maryland State Archives web site.

The page numbers are the transcribed text and the m31..... are
the hand written original documents.

Volume 2 Assembly Proceedings May-June 1676
-551, -552, -553, -554 (transcript)
m3176-0315, m3176-0316, m3176-0317, m3176-0318,
m3176-0319 (images)
m11779-0146, m11779-0147, m11779-0148, m11779-0149,
m11779-0150 (images)

Volume 8 Proceedings of the Council of Maryland
-89, -90 1687/8-89 Liber B. P.R.O.
-117 in the years 1689-90 P.R.O. Colonial Papers
-378, -379 m3154-0068 1692-94
-398 m3154-0094 1692-94
-445 m3154-0144 1692-94
-461 m3154-0155 1692-94

Volume 13 Assembly Proceedings
-259 m3184-0621 May 10-June 9, 1692
-283 m3184-0640 May 10-June 9, 1692

Volume 15 Proceedings of the Council of Maryland, 1671-
1675
-56 m3153-0506, m3153-0507

Volume 17 Proceedings of the Council of Maryland, 1681-
1685/6
-408, -409 m3153-0916, m3153-0917

Volume 19 Assembly Proceedings
-67 m3184-0783, m3184-0784 Sept. 20-Oct. 18, 1694
-227 m3184-0853, m3184-0854 Oct. 3-19, 1695
-266 m3191-1138 Oct. 3-19, 1695
-523 m3184-0949 May 26-June 11, 1697
-531 m3184-0954 May 26-June 11, 1697
-569 m3191-1238 May 26-June 11, 1697
-575 m3191-1243 May 26-June 11, 1697

Volume 20 Proceedings of the Council of Maryland
-21 m3154-0407 1693-94
-22 m3154-0408 1693-94
-28 m3154-0415, m3154-0416 1693-94
-74 m3154-0488 1694
-108 m3154-0538, m3154-0539 1694-1697
-207, -208 m3154-0634, m3154-0636 1694-1697
-379 m3154-0789 1694-1697
-396 m3154-0801 1694-1697
-423 m3154-0840 1694-1697
-452, -453 m3154-0868 1694-1697
-487 m3154-0894 1694-1697

Volume 22 Assembly Proceedings
-63 m3184-1006, m3184-1007 Mar. 8-1697/8-Apr. 4, 1698
-113 m3191-1291 Mar. 10-1697/8-Apr. 4, 1698
-165 m3184-1019 Oct. 20-Nov. 12, 1698
-168 m3184-1021, m3184-1022 Oct. 20-Nov. 12, 1698
-223 m3191-1335, m3191-1336 Oct. 20-Nov. 12, 1698

Volume 23 Proceedings of the Council of Maryland, 1696/7-
98
-75 m3154-1206
-77 m3154-1205
-91, -92 m3154-1214
-111 m3154-1002
-175, -176, -177 m3154-1236, m3154-1237, m3154-1238
-183 m3154-1277
-185 m3154-1279
-214 m3154-1291
-216 m3154-1293
-224 m3154-1059
-260 m3154-1086
-261 m3154-1087
-284 m3154-1301
-325, -326 m3154-1338
-404 m3155-0033, m3155-0034

Volume 38 Assembly Proceedings, 1694-1728
-33, -34 Public Record Office, London, C.O. 5, Vol. 731,
Maryland. From 1694-1702. Acts

Volume 67 Provincial Court Proceedings 1677/8

127

-212 Edward Ball agt Richard Brightwell
-233, -234 Feb 25 1677 Edward Ball agt Richard Brightwell,
Liber NN
-278 Ball agt Brightwell, Liber NN p. 522

Volume 202 Court Records of Prince George's County,
Maryland 1696-1699

Volume 680 Index to Maryland Provincial and General Court
Deeds, 1658-1790
-165 (Index) mentions Capt Brightwell and Brightwell's
Hunting Quarter on page 498 of Lib PL 5

Volume 717 Provincial Court Land Records, 1676*1700
pages 643, 644

Griffin Pond makes a request for his share of the Estate of the
late Mistress Mary Trueman, being held by Richard
Southerne and Richard Brightwell.

Dated 17 April 1688
Recorded 30 May 1693

Contributed by mac billigins 2009-07-25

Chancery Court (Chancery Record) 1671-1712 am748

am748 page 339 Ninian Beal & Richd Brightwell agt Henry
Hardey
ordered yt attachmt issue agt ye deft for want of answr

am748 page 353 Ninian Beal & Richd Brightwell agt Henry
Hardey
Bill attachmt to issue for want of anwr

am748 page 357 Ninian Beal & Richd Brightwell agt Henry
Hardey
ordered likewise to be dismiss't with reasonable cost to ye

deft

see ye decree for Hardey page 361

am748 pages 361-363 Decree for Henry Hardey agt Beal & Brightwell
At a Court of Chancery held at Annapolis y.e 25 day of May 1697 before y.e Hon.ble Coll Hen Jowles Chancell.r & Kenelm Chiseldyne & Edw.d Dorsey Esqrs Justices between Ninian Beal & Richd Brightwell Complts & Henr Hardey Deft

This Cause coming this day to be argued upon y.e Complts bill & y.e Defts plea & Dem.r put in thereto y.e Complts by their bill setting forth y.t y.e s.d Richard Brightwell in May 1692 being possesst of an Indian Manservant called Toby having Eight years to serve y.e s.d Richard y.e same servant agreed to sell to y.e s.d Beal for a valuable Consideration but before y.e Agreement was perfected y.e s.d Indian ran away
& as y.e plts were informed came to y.e Defts house & there was
for some time kept & harboured by y.e Deft & by him or his procurement carried out of this province into Virginia Whereupon y.e plt Brightwell being as then y.e known Master

of y.e s.d servant & obliged by y.e s.d Agreement to deliver y.e
s.d servant to y.e s.d Beal brought his action at Law against y.e Deft for sd harbouring & conveying away y.e s.d Indian servant Wherein he declared for 20000.ℓ of tob damages in
wch Issue being ioyned in a Jury who went out & whether through Ignorance partiallity or otherwise found for y.e Deft To wch verdict y.e s.d Brightwell appeared & Judgment was given against him whereby notwithstanding y.e palpable proofs y.t were then offered & y.e Confirmation of y.e same since
y.e s.d Indian Man has been taken up y.e Complts were left remediless ag.t y.e Deft & was threatened to be taken in execution
for y.e Costs & therefore they prayed y.e favourable Aid & Assistance of this Hon.ble Court & y.t process of subpena might
thereout issue ag.t y.e s.d Deft to appear in this Court & answer
y.e premisses The wch being granted & y.e s.d Deft therewith served he appeared accordingly & put in his plea & Dem.r to y.e s.d bill
& to so much of y.e s.d bill as sought to be relieved against a verdict
& Judgment obtained by y.e deft ag.t y.e s.d Brightwell upon an

Action by him brought at law ag.t y.e Deft for y.e supposed harbouring
& conveying away y.e s.d servant he saith y.t by a statute made in a parliament holden at Westminster y.e 4.th of Hen.r 4° it was ordained & enacted y.t after Judgm.t given to y.e Courts of our sov.r Lord y.e King as well in plea or as in plea personall y.e parties & their heirs should be thereof

362)

thereof in peace untill y.e Judgm.t should be undone by attarict or by
Errour And y.e Def.t averred y.t before y.e plts s.d bill of Comp.lt exhibited
y.e plt brought his s.d Action in y.e pvin.ll C.rt ag.t y.e deft & upon a Legall & fair tryall there obtained a verdict & had Judgm.t
thereupon with Costs of suit & also afterwards by virtue of a scire facias issued out of y.e s.d Court ag.t y.e s.d Brightwell y.e same
Judgm.t was affirmed as by y.e Records of y.e s.d Judgm.t provinc.ll Court may
appear wch Judgm.t y.e deft did aver was obtained before y.e s.d bill
exhibited & yet remained in full force not undone by attarict or
writt of Err.r And therefore y.e deft pleaded y.e s.d statute & Judgm.t
in bar of y.e s.d Complts bill Farther he said y.t y.e design of y.e s.d
bill was for relief in Matters properly determinable at law & y.e
Complts grounded their Comp.lts upon y.e suggestion therein y.t y.e
Complainant Brightwell did comence his action at law ag.t y.e deft
for harbouring & conveying away y.e s.d Indian serv.t wherein he
declared for 20000.ℓ tob dmgs in wch action Issue being joyned
upon y.e Countrey y.e Jury y.t went out upon y.e matter whether
through Ignorance partiallity or otherwise found for y.e deft
To wch verdict y.e then plt appeared & Judgm.t was given ag.t
him whereby (notwithstanding y.e palpable proofs y.t were then offerd
& y.e confirmation of y.e same since y.e s.d Indian Man had been
taken up y.e plt Brightwell was left remidiless ag.t y.e deft unless relieved in this Hon.ble Court To all wch y.e deft did

130

dem.r
for y.t of y.e plts own shewing there is not any sufficient Matter
in equity suggested in y.e s.d bill whereof this Court ought to take Cognizance & y.e s.d Matters were properly determinable at Comon
law for y.t in case y.e allegations of y.e plts bill were true y.t y.e
Jury went ag.t their evidence or found for y.e deft through Ignorance or partiallity y.e s.d Brightwell might have made his application to y.e s.d Court where y.e s.d action was brought
for a new tryall or moved in arrest of Judgm.t or for such other directions or Rule therein as he should think fit y.e Court being
y.e proper Judges thereof or might have brought his attarict Writt of
Errour or Appeal as y.e law of this province directs & for y.t this Court
wherefore & for many other apparent defects in y.e s.d bill this deft did
demur in law & demanded Judgm.t if he should be compelled to make
any other or farther Answer to y.e s.d bill This Court therefore upon
reading y.e s.d bill plea & dem.r & well weighing y.e Matters in y.e
same contained & hearing what could be alledged by y.e Councill &
attorneys or either side doth think fit & so order & decree y.t y.e s.d
plea & dem.r put in by y.e s.d deft be & is hereby allowed to stand
good & valid in law & y.t y.e s.d Complts bill be from henceforth
absolutely dismisst with 2298.ℓ tob costs to be paid by y.e plts
to y.e said def.t accordingly
(signed)
Hen.ry Jowles Chanc
Richard
363)

Richard Brightwell &
Ninian Beal plts Costs for allowing a Dem.r & Dismission
ag.t of y.e Complts bill
Hen.r Hardey deft

Defts Costs lbs tob
To y.e Defts entering his appearance 40
To Rule to answer 16

131

To Copie of y.e bill 128
To filing y.e plea & Dem.r 40
To oath to plea 12
To two Continuances 80
To y.e secretary for order for y.e Decree at y.e hearing 16
drawing y.e decree 7 sides 144
To Recording it 144
To Execution of y.t decree making out 144
To y.e Chancell.r signing y.e decree 480
To seal of writt of execution 162
To y.e Regist.rs Fee by order of Court 5.s or 60
To bill of Costs & Copie 32
To attorneys Fee 800
total 2298 lbs tob

Recorded by John Freeman Regist.

am748 page 386 Ninian Beal & Rich.d Brightwell ag.t Hen.r
Hardey
Philip Lynes Gentl this day made oath in open Court That he
y.e s.d Philip did serve y.e Decree upon Ninian Beal one of
y.e Compl.ts obtained by Hardey y.e Deft ag.t s.d Beal in May
last in y.e Court of Chancery And y.t he y.e s.d Lynes
demanded y.e Cost And y.t Beal refused to obey or Comply
with y.e same And therefore y.e Court ordereth y.t Attachm.t
for Contempt issue ag.st s.d Beal
=====

1642-1753 Rent Rolls Charles County MD Hundred - Port
Tobacco: Rent Roll page/Sequence: 316-107: SMITHS
CHANCE: 144 acres; Possession of - 144 Acres - Windsor,
Jarvis: Surveyed 5 May 1686 for John Smith on the South
side Mattawoman:
====

Prince George's County, Maryland - Land Owners at Time
PGCo Was Formed - 1696: Tract Name: BRIGHTWELLS
HUNTING QUARTER; Owner: Brightwell, Richard: Orig
County = C {Charles = C, Calvert = V}: Patent Date: Aug 29,
1695: Ref: Liber BB#3 f 253: Map Location: C-03
====

Prince George's County, Maryland - Land Owners at Time
PGCo Was Formed - 1696: Tract Name: BRIGHTWELL'S
LANDING - TAKEN AWAY BY SURVEY OF BROOKE
COURT: Owner: Brightwell, Richard: Orig County = V
{Charles = C, Calvert = V}: Patent Date: Feb 1, 1694 : Ref:
Liber B#23 f 253: Map Location: Not Shown
====

Prince George's County, Maryland - Land Owners at Time
PGCo Was Formed - 1696: Tract Name: BLACKWELL:
Owner: Brightwell, Richard: Orig County = V {Charles = C,
Calvert = V}: Patent Date: Sep 20, 1682: Ref: Liber 22 f 19 :
Map Location: S-18
====

Prince George's County, Maryland - Land Owners at Time PGCo Was Formed - 1696: Tract Name: SPINUM LANDS; Owner: Brightwell, Richard: Orig County = V {Charles = C, Calvert = V}; Patent Date: Feb 5, 1694 : Ref: Liber B#23 f 269: Map Location: W-20

===

Prince George's County, Maryland - Land Owners at Time PGCo Was Formed - 1696: Tract Name: THATHAM; Owner: Brightwell, Richard: Orig County = V {Charles = C, Calvert = V}; Patent Date: Feb 8, 1694 : Ref: Liber B#23 f 280: Map Location: W-20

===

Prince George's County, Maryland - Land Owners at Time PGCo Was Formed - 1696: Tract Name: BRIGHTWELL'S RANGE; Owner: Brightwell, Richard: Orig County = V {Charles = C, Calvert = V}; Patent Date: Sep 12, 1688: Ref: Liber 22 f 429 : Map Location: W-20

Marriage 1 Katherine {StepDau} Lashley b: ABT 1653 in Calvert County, Maryland

- *Married:* 1687 in Calvert County, Maryland

Children

1. Richard Brightwell b: 1687 in Calvert County, Maryland - now Prince George's County, Maryland
2. Peter Brightwell b: 1688 in Prince George's County, Maryland
3. Elizabeth Brightwell b: 1693 in Calvert County, Maryland - now Prince George's County, Maryland
4. John Brightwell b: 1694 in Prince George's County, Maryland

LAWSON FAMILY

The surname Lawson is taken from 'Law' and denotes someone who is the 'son of Law'. The most likely source of the name is either from the name Lawrence believed to have originated from a person who lived near a laurel tree of from the Old English word hlaw meaning a hill and therefore a person 'the son of one who lived on a hill or near a hill'.

Records indicates that the earliest use of the Lawson was documented in the 14th century in Upper Littondale, Yorkshire, England, an area close to the present villages of Litton and Arncliffe on the River Skirfare, a tributary of the River Wharfe. Surnames or 'add-on' names can be generally only be traced back to this time in history when they were adopted in order to distinguish individuals of the same forename. From time to time the surname was handed down from father to son and occasionally from mother to son.

It is believed that the Lawson name spread from this area to the remainder of Yorkshire and throughout several adjoining Counties in Northern England. Records also indicates that the Lawson name existed in Scotland from the 14th century where it was most commonly found in Lowland Eastern Counties. In Scotland Lawson families have links with the McLaren Clan.

It is probable that more than one original source of the name exists. The Lawson name today is found commonly in all English speaking countries. There is evidence that the Lawson name was adopted from the European (mostly Scandinavian) name Laren and similar surnames when emigration to the British Isles took place.

Lawsons of Maryland and Virginia
From *Colonial Families of the United States of America*, Volume 2, page 454, comes the earliest Lawson records in Maryland:

Edward Lloyd, the first of Wye House, born near Wye River, in Wales, circa 1600; emigrated to the Colony of Virginia, and resided there from 1637 to 1649; member of Assembly of Virginia, 1644-1845; compelled to quit Virginia on account of being a Puritan, he came to Maryland with Leonard Strong and others, settled on Greenbury Point, near Annapolis, Md. In 1650, he was appointed by Gov. Stone, Commander of Arms, Anne Arundal, County; at the river Severn, 5th July, 1652, with his associates, made a treaty with Susqwehannough Indians; 22nd, 1654, he , with Capt. Wm. Fuller, Richard Preston, Wm. Durand, Capt. John Smith, Leonard Strong, John Lawson, John Hatch, Richard Wells and Richard Ewen, took possession of the Province of Maryland in the name of the Protector, Oliver Cromwell, compelling Gov. William Stone to resign the government of the Province to them; was member of the Provincial Court, 1656, and held this position for some time.

Thomas Lawson, born ca 1672, died abt 25 Mar 1761, Prince George's County, Maryland, age 89. Thomas married in Princess Ann, Somerset County, MD Rose Thoroughgood, b. 1672, Norfolk, VA; d. bef 1761, Prince George's County, MD.

Liber 31, folio 252
30 Sept. 1756
LAWSON, THOMAS, Prince George's Co., [planter].
   To my dau. Letis Nailor, my dw. house & plntn., in Stokes Forest, & on her d. to her son John Lawson Naylor.
   To sd. dau., negro men Ben & Baker, negro girl Lucy, & the residue.
   Extr: son-in-law George Naylor.
   Witn: John Tycer, John Jaco, Mary Jaco, & Mary Williams.
   25 March 1761, sworn to by John Trycer, John Jaco, & Mary Williams.

Robert Baden, b. abt 1670, christened 13 Feb 1670, Salisbury, Wiltshire, England; father Alexander Baden, mother Elizabeth.

Robert Baden, birth date ca 1730, date of death unknown, married Martha Lawson, daughter of Thomas and Elizabeth Lawson (Maryland Marriage References – B – Maryland State Archives; PGLR BB:661; PGWB 1:413).

In 1757, Robert Baden purchased land in Maryland. The date and place of mention in land survey. The original records are contained in Land Office Registers, indexed starting on page vii of the introduction (Coldham, Peter Wilson. *Settlers of Maryland 1679-1783*. Consolidated Edition. Baltimore: Genealogical Publishing Co., Inc., 2002; original data: Filby, P. William, ed. *Passenger and Immigration Lists Index, 1500s-1900s*. Farmington Hills, MI, USA: Gale Research, 2009).

   Name: **Robert Baden,**
   Birth: AFT 1704 in Prince George's County, Maryland
   Prince George's County Land Records 1746-1749, Liber EE#1, Page 676. Deed, recorded at the request of Thomas Baden. I, Thomas Lawson of PG, for the natural love I have for my grandson, Thomas Baden, and also for 5 shillings in hand paid by Robert Baden, father of my sd grandson, I have given unto my sd grandson, all that part of a tract of land in PG called Sarum, and bounded by the eastern boundary of a tract of land called Stoke, now in possession of me, sd Thomas Lawson, containing about 119 acres.
   Signed Jul 15, 1749 -Thomas Lawson. Wit - Fs Waring*, James Russell*. This deed was ack. by sd Thomas Lawson and Elizabeth, his wife. Recorded Jul 29, 1749

PRINCE GEORGE'S COUNTY.

Larin

Acres 32

SURVEYED FOR

Thomas Lawson

2nd Nov. 1735

Returned

Ex'd. and Passed 27th March 1738

Comp. $ Pd. 27th March 1738

PATENTED TO

Thomas Lawson

4th May 1738

Rec. of Cert. E 9 M 5 Folio 577

John Lawrence Plat
& Lot of Lawrens Lott
Cont 100 acres
examined & passed by

Pr. Alexander

Patt October 16th
1732 South Carolina
4° Stork

Int: Lib: A.M: fol: 46.

Prince George County ss[?]

By Virtue of a Special Warrant of Resurvey granted out of his Lordship's Land Office to Thomas Baden of the county aforesaid bearing Date by Commencement the Thirtieth Day of November Anno Domini Seventeen Hundred and Fifty Six To Resurvey a certain Tract or Parcel of Land called Saturn Originally on the Fourth Day of May Anno Domini Seventeen Hundred and Thirty Eight Granted unto a certain Thomas Lawson (Grand Father to the said Thomas Baden) of the county aforesaid, for the Quantity of Three Hundred and Twenty Seven Acres called Stoke alias Saturn under the Rent of One Pound Five Shillings and Eight Pence three Farthings Sterling Yearly, Part Whereof the said Thomas Baden is Seized in Fee Simple under the Yearly Rent of Ten Shillings Sterling for Nineteen Acres To Resurvey the aforesaid Tract of Land to demand all Vacant and to Include the Vacant Land there Contiguous.

I Shreckford Kirby certify as Deputy Surveyor of Prince George County under His Excellency Horatio Sharpe Esqr Governor of Maryland that I have carefully Resurveyed and laid out for and in the Name of the said Thomas Baden the aforesaid Tract or Parcel of Land according to its antient Notes and Bounds as shewed to me and have laid out the said Thomas Baden's Part Resurveying to a Devisee heretofore made by Deed of Gift by the aforenamed Thomas Lawson to the said Baden, all which appears by the Plott below Beginning for the Whole Tract at a Bounded Hickory the Original Bound Tree of Stoke as mentioned in the Deed and Running thence South Fifty Perches then south ___ Degrees East One Hundred and Forty Perches then south Seventy Degrees East Sixty Perches then North Forty Eight Degrees West Eighty Perches then North Forty Perches then North Sixty Seven Degrees East One Hundred and Sixty Perches then East Three Hundred and Twenty Perches then South Twenty Four Perches then South West Forty Perches then South East Twenty Perches then East Thirty Eight Perches then North nine Degrees East Twenty Two Perches then North Twenty Eight Perches then North Eighty East One Hundred and Sixty Six Perches then south Sixty Perches then South East Eighteen Perches then North Fifteen Degrees East Fifty Four Perches then North nine Degrees East Forty Perches then East Seventy five Degrees East Twenty Eight Perches then North Forty Perches then West Fifty Two Perches then North West Twenty Six Perches then South West Twenty Eight Perches then North Eighty Degrees West Ninety Perches then South Twenty Eight Degrees West Fifty Four Perches to the third Line of Stoke then West Three Hundred and Twenty Perches, this being the River Line to the first Beginning. Containing Three Hundred ___ Acres more or less Beginning for the said Thomas Baden's

Part is a Branded Black Oak standing at the End of the East Three Hundred and Twenty Sixth Line of the aforesaid Tract and Running thence South Twenty four Perches, then South West Sixty Perches, then South East Twenty Perches then East Thirty Eight Perches then North Degrees East Twenty two Perches, then North Twenty Eight Perches then North Eighty Degrees East Six Hundred and Sixty six Perches then South Sixty Perches, then South East Eighteen Perches then North Fifteen Degrees East Fifty four Perches then North Degrees East Forty Perches then North Seventy five Degrees East Twenty Eight Perches then North Six Perches then West Fifty two Perches then North West Twenty Six Perches then South West Twenty Eight Perches then North Eighty Degrees West Ninety Twelve then South Thirty Eight Degrees West Fifty Four Perches then by a Straight line to the first Beginning containing Two Hundred and Twenty Acres.

I Also Certify that I have added to the said Thomas Baden's Part the Quantity of Sixty five Acres and half an Acre of Vacant and have Reduced the said East other of Elliss Surveys into one entire Tract Described as follows that Lying in Prince Georges County on the West side of Patuxent River Beginning at a Branded Black Oak standing at the End of the East Three Hundred and Twenty Sixth Line of the Land called Stoke then Saram and Running thence West Thirty Perches, then South Twenty Degrees West Twenty Nine Perches then South Twenty four Degrees East Fifty Perches then North Twenty one Degrees East Twenty Eight Perches then North Seventy one Degrees East Twenty Perches then North Six Degrees and half Degrees East Twenty Twelve then North Sixty two Perches then South Eighty Six Degrees East One Hundred and Forty Perches then South Two Degrees West Twenty Perches then South Thirty Eight Degrees East Thirty One Perches then North East Fifty One Perches then North Twenty Six Degrees and three Quarters of a Degree West Forty Four Perches then North Fifty Eight Degrees East Fifty Six Perches then North North West Sixty Perches then North Twenty Degrees West Forty four Perches then South Nineteen Degrees East Forty Eight Perches then South Twenty Six Degrees West Eighty Perches then South Eighty Six Degrees West Twenty Seven Perches and half a Perch then by a Straight line to the first Beginning Black Oak now Surveying and now laid out for One Hundred and Thirty Four Acres and Half an Acre more or less to be held of Calverton Mannor by the name of Sarums Forrest. Resurveyed this Eighteenth Day of January Seventeen Hundred and Fifty Seven By

Wm F H Gagg Dep. Surv.
W G County

Memorandum There is on the Vacancy Four Acres of Cultivated Ground
Improvements None

The Resurvey is Distinguished from the Original By Red Lines

Thomas Baden's Part of the Original Contains — 220 Acres
Losses in Elder Surveys — 28
Vacant Land Added — 93
Sarum's Forest Contains — 134½ Acres

Acres 99½

Sarum's Forest Acres 134½

Acres 114

Platted By a Scale of Sixty Equal Parts in an Inch

at A is The Beginning Hickory of the original Tract
at E is The Beginning Black Oak of Thos Baden's Part of the Original and the Beginning for the Resurvey of Said Part
A in its Place is The First Vacancy Containing — 1911
B is the Second Vacancy Containing — 151
C is the Third Vacancy Containing — 1319½
D is the Fourth Vacancy Containing — 360
E is the Fifth Vacancy Containing — 432

140

F........ is the Sixth Vacancy Containing 96
G........ is the Seventh Vacancy Containing 137

1807 which is 42 acres 170

The Vacancies Added By the Resurvey to Thomas Barton's Svt of Survey &c

1	A	West																
2	B	S20W	2A															
3	C	S24E	31															
4	D	S79E	28															
5	E	East	21															
6	F	S40E	20															
7	G	North	12															
8	H	S86E	14															
9	I	S3W	20	First Vacancy	Second Vacancy	Third Vacancy	Fourth Vacancy	Fifth Vacancy	Sixth Vacancy	Seventh Vacancy								
10	K	S58E	31	Beginning at the Black oak &c	Beginning at the Beginning at the	Beginning at the	Beginning at the	Beginning at the	Beginning at the								
11	L	S E	31	Beginning line														
12	M	S32W	44	of the Resurvey														
13	N	S39E	36															
14	O	S.SW	46	Y Course Dist	Y Course Dist	S Course Dist	Y Course Dist	Y Course Dist	Y Course Dist	S Course Dist								
15	P	S70W	64	A West 20	C N2E 10	H S86E 26	L NE 30	N S58E 42	P N70W 22	S S86W 12								
16	Q	S19W	48	B S20W 2A	D S79E 28	I S39E 7	M N22W 20	O S.SW 14									
17	R	S76E	80	C S24E 30	E S21E 7	K S39E	17 South 7	21 East	21 East	S86E 26							
18	S	S86E	72															

Prince Georges County

The Certificate of Plat of
Saml Ferrill

Containing 134 Acres

Received for Thomas
Baden January the 18th
1757

For The Examiner General

2 February 1758
Examined & Graded

Pd 23 February 1757
[signatures]

I have received the sum of fourteen shillings and Six
Pence for the within Vacancy and Six pence for the Improvement
Patent may therefore issue with his Excys Approbation

23 Feby 1757

Edwd Lloyd

Roberts – (Morsell)

Registrants: Under the dignity of MANORIAL RIGHTS to Sewall and Green; of ancient lineage to "John of Gaunt". And the lineage of Robert Roberts of Wales, eldest son of Hugh Roberts and Jane Owen of "Evan", b. 1673, m. at Merion, Wales, in 1696 to Kath. Jones, whose son, Robert, came to Maryland in 1702. He married secondly Priscilla Johns of the "Cliffs" dau. of Elizabeth Kensey, who m. Richard Johns. Robert Roberts d. 1728, he was a Quaker; came from north of Wales, a descendant of the eight noble tribes of Hugh Roberts of Kiltalgarth, Parish of Llanfawn, of Penllyn, of Merionetshire, who m. Elizabeth Owen Williams (widow), dau. of William Owen. Had son Richard Roberts who m. Elizabeth Allen and their son m. Mary Harris, having a son also named Richard Roberts, who m. Sarah Kent; and having a son also Richard Roberts who m. Elizabeth Gantt. His son, Richard Roberts m. Henrietta Sewall Morsell, dau. of James Sewell Morsell and wife, Elleanor Baden as his second wife; and she the dau of Joseph Noble Baden and Letitia Gebbons (Gibbons). He was the son of John Baden and Marg. Noble, dau. of Joseph Noble and Martha Tarvin. He son of Joseph Noble and Mary Wheeler, dau. of Francis Wheeler and Winnifred Green, dau. of Ann and Leonard Green, a son of Thomas Green, Gov. of Maryland 1648.

5. GEORGE NOBLE, son of Rev. Gawen Noble (2), was bapt. 2 March 1685/ 6 at Cockermouth (F). He is almost certainly the George Noble, Gent., of PG Co., who gave his age as 40 in 1730, placing his date of birth as c1690 [but ages given in these depositions are not always accurate] (B). There is a chance that he is the George Noble, servant, mentioned in the will (made 11 Nov 1717) of Josiah Wilson (MWB 14:381). He m. on 27 Jan —, Charity Wheeler.

George Noble died 14 Sep (1735?) (PGKG). He died leaving a will dated 6 Sep 1735, proved 24 Nov 1735. He mentioned property in Roper Lane, White Haven, Cumberland, and he named children Thomas, George, Elizabeth, Ann, and John. All children were to be under the care of executors until they came of age (MWB 21:483).

George and Charity (Wheeler) Noble were the parents of (PGKG): (prob.) JOHN, b. 3 Sep —; ELIZABETH, b. 23 Jan 1722, d. 17 Sep 1735; ANNE, b. 16 Feb 1725/6; m. by 1756 Zachariah Wade (MDAD 19:469, 23:169; 39:80; The IGI says they were married 3 Nov 1757); THOMAS, b. 19 April 1727 (IGI says 19 April 1728); and GEORGE, b. 16 Jan 1729; m. Elizabeth (N)

6. THOMAS NOBLE, son of Rev. Gawen Noble (2), was bapt. in 1690, and may have come to MD, as a Thomas Noble wit. a deed in PG Co. in 1708 (F: cites PGLR C:224).

7. JOSEPH NOBLE, son of Joseph (4) and Catherine, was b. in Cockermouth, Cumberland, Eng., on 17 April 1689, d. 14 Dec 1749 in MD. Joseph Noble of PG Co., Gent., gave his age as c41 in 1730 (B). He came to MD, where he m. on 2 Dec 1708, Mary Wheeler, in PG Co, dau. of Francis and Winifred Wheeler (PGKG; PGLR F:110).

On 14 Oct 1718, Francis and Winifred Wheeler conveyed 90 a. Major's Choice to their daughter Mary wife of Joseph Noble (D:45). Joseph Noble, Sr., of PG Co., died by 26 May 1750 when his personal property was appraised by John Hawkins, Jr., and Luke Marbury. They set a value on the personal property of £559.13.5. John Baynes and Anne Cunning signed as creditors. Joseph Noble and Francis Noble signed as creditors. Mrs. Mary Noble, the extx., filed the inventory on 26 May 1750 (MINV 43:105).

Joseph and Mary (Wheeler) Noble were the parents of (PGKG): SARAH, b. 8 Nov 1709; m. William Hawkins on 13 May 1735 (IGI); ELIZABETH, b. 3 May 1712; m. (N) Luckett;[70] JOSEPH, b. 15 April 1715; FRANCIS, b. 27 Dec 1719; CATHERINE, b. 14 Nov 1721, died in PG Co. leaving a will dated 24 Feb 1777, proved 18 March 1777 (PG Wills T#1:109);[71] SALOME, b. 23 April 1724; m. by 1750, James Edelen (MWB 27:141, 36:583; MDAD 29:222);[72]

[70] But Elizabeth, dau. of Joseph and Mary Noble m. by 1748, Thomas Stockett (PG Admin. Accts., DD:41). (She had at least one son: Thomas Noble Stockett, mentioned in the will of his aunt Catherine Noble).

[71] In her will she named her brothers and sisters Salome Edeline, William Fraser Noble, Francis Noble, and Joseph Noble. Then she named her nephews and nieces: Elizabeth Dent [dau. of Salome], Elizabeth Harwood and her daughter Elizabeth, Joseph Noble Baynes, John Baynes, Jr., and his dau. Mary Fell Baynes, Mary Noble Stonestreet, Margaret Baden, James Hawkins, Thomas Noble Stockett, Catherine Salome Edelin, Margaret Edelin and Sarah Edelin.

[72] She is named in the will of her sister Catherine Noble, as are her children Catherine Salome Edelin, Margaret Edelin, and Sarah Edelin.

1561

PRINCE GEORGE'S COUNTY.

———•———

Nick'd Lim of Deer Range
& Meadows

Acres 314

SURVEYED FOR

Jos: Noble
1st Aug. 1755

Returned

Ex'd. and Passed 6th Sept. 1755

Comp. $ Pd. 6th Sept. 1755

PATENTED TO

Jos. Noble
6th Sept. 1755

Rec. of Cert. BC&GS No. + Folio 192

536

PRINCE GEORGE'S COUNTY.

Cold Sunny Fryday

Acres 184

SURVEYED FOR

Joseph Noble
19th Nov. 1703

Returned

Ex'd. and Passed 25th Feb 1704

Comp. $ Pd. 5th Feb 1705

PATENTED TO

Joseph Noble
19th May 1705

Rec. of Cert. B. Bol. 8 No. 2 folio 293

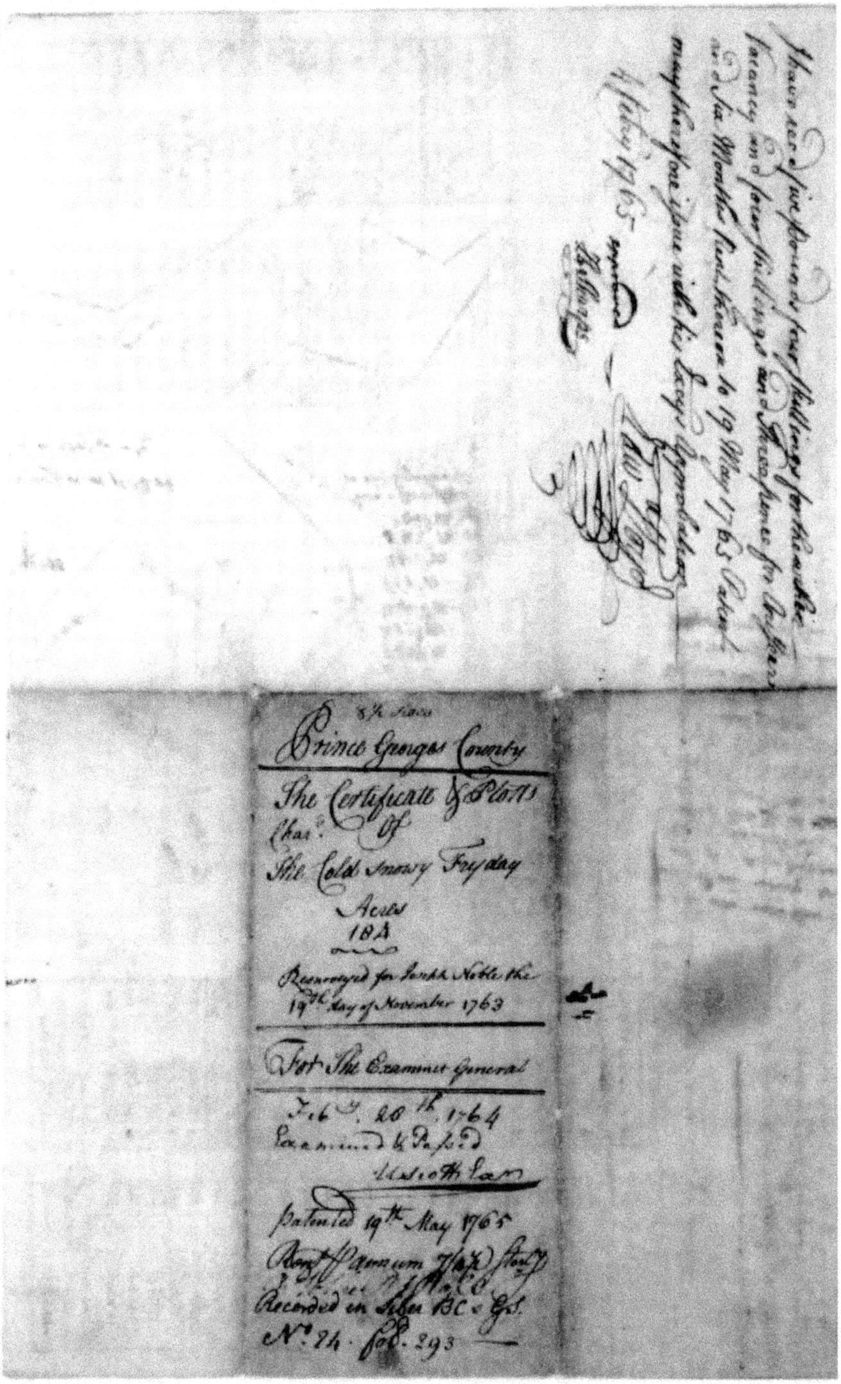

1068

PRINCE GEORGE'S COUNTY.

Hickory Ford

Acres 65

SURVEYED FOR

George Gibons

26th June 1738

Returned

Ex'd. and Passed 28th Aug. 1738

Comp. $ Pd.

PATENTED TO

George Gibons

27th Nov. 1738

Rec. of Cert. E.I. No. 5 folio 376

Prince Geo.s County ss

By Virtue of a warrant granted out of his Lordship Land office of this province bearing Date May this Nineteenth Anno Domini 1738 to Geroge Gibbons of Same Cy.t Cy.t For Sixty five acres of vacant Land in any part of this province he having paid The usual fine for the same as app.r &c

I do therefore hereby Certify and In.d Survey off the sd. Certificate he.r Twelve be.r Sam.ll Ogle Esq.r his Lordships Governor of Maryland have Carefully laid out for you the figure of here the sd. George Gibbonsall that tract or parcell of sd Land Lying in the Cy.t called Hickory ford. Beginning at a bounded red Oak standing on the Second Line of John Adams his called Birmingham twenty two feet from the Begining of said Line running thence N.o the third bounded Line North twenty four Deg.s West one hundred & twelve feet thence North one Deg.t East seventy seven feet then South Eighty eight & half Deg.t East Sixty eight feet then South one hundred & forty two feet thence by a Strait Lineto the beginning tree Containing and now Laid out for Sixty five acres of Land to be held & Surveyor the twenty Sixth day of June Anno Dom. 1738

Per Deal Dy Surv.o
of P.t Geo. County

N.o	Cours	feet
1	N.24 W	112
2	N.1 E	77
3	S.88½ E	68
4	S.	142
Then to the beginning tree

by a Scale of 100 Equal feet in an Inch

1068

Prince Georges County ss

By Virtue of a Special Warrant of Resurvey Granted out of the Lords his Land Office to Ephraim Gover of Ann Arundel County bearing Date the sixteenth day of December Anno Domini Seventeen Hundred and fifty Seven but since the Grant of the Said Warrant the said Ephraim Gover died, and on the Eighth day of June Anno Domini Seventeen Hundred & fifty Eight the said Warrant was Renewed in the Name of Ephraim Gover Junr of Prince Georges County (son to the aforesaid Ephraim Gover) Which said Warrant was to Resurvey a Certain Tract or Parcel of Land Called Deer Bought Lying & being in Prince Georges County Originally on the Sixteenth day of June Anno Domini Sixteen Hundred and Sixty four Granted unto a Certain Thomas Fredman for one hundred & fifty Acres under Old Rent To Resurvey the aforesd Tract or Parcel of Land with its Surplusage to amend all Errors & to Include the Vacant Land thereto Contiguous

I Therefore hereby Certify as Deputy Surveyor of Prince Georges County under his Excellency Horatio Sharpe Esqr Governor of Maryland that I have carefully Resurveyed and Laid out for and in the Name of him the said Ephraim Gover Junr the aforesaid Tract or Parcel of Land according to the antient marks & bounds as Shewed to me. Beginning for the Original at a Post Shewn to me to be the Post that there formerly the original Beginning Tree Stood and Running thence the Original Course West By North Three Hundred & Twenty Perches the Stood Tree being East I Stop at the corner of Distance aforesaid then (instead of South by West Twenty six Perches as marked in the Original Grant) I Run South Twenty Six degrees & a half of a degree West Ninety one Perches to a Whick Oak Claimd by the said Ephraim Gover as the Third Boundary in the Room of the thing mentioned in the Original Grant then from the said White Oak East By South five Hundred & four Perches to the Side of a branch (according to the Original Grant which claims a marked oak standing by the side of a branch) but the Oak being Lost I Stop at the side of the branch aforesaid & then Run with the branch side the following Courses Viz.t North Twenty Perches then North forty Ten Degrees West fourteen Perches then North Eighty four Degrees & a half of a degree West Sixteen Perches, then North Twenty degrees and a half of a Degree West forty Six Perches, then North Twenty Six Degrees West forty Two Perches, thence with a Straight line to the Beginning Containing Two Hundred and forty three Acres of Land ninety three acres of which is Surplus ― I also Certify that I have added to the said Tract the Quantity of forty four acres of marsh Contiguous thereto and have Reduced the Whole into one Entire Tract all which appears by the Platts below. Beginning for the Resurvey of the Whole at a Post Standing by the side of the Branch called the Eastern Branch of Potuxent River at a Landing known by the Name of the Iron Pott Landing being Point where formerly Stood the Original Beginning Tree and Running thence West By North Three Hundred and Twenty Perches then South Twenty six degrees & a half of a Degree West Ninety one Perches to a whick oak

148

then East by South, five Hundred & four Perches to a marsh side, then with a line Drawn North forty four Degrees East until it Intersect a East by South Line Drawn from the first Beginning Containing and now laid out for Two Hundred & Eighty Seven Acres of Land & marsh and now Called Dear Bought Laid off To be Held of Calverton Manor Surveyed the fourteenth day of November Anno Domini Seventeen Hundred & fifty Eight By

John T. A. Briggs Deputy Surveyor P.G. County

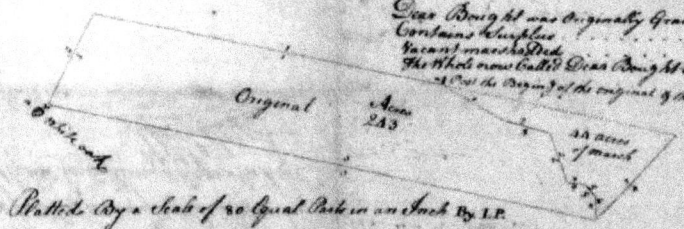

Dear Bought was Originally Granted for — 150 Acres
Contains Surplus — 93
Vacant marsh Added — 44
The Whole now Called Dear Bought Inlarg'd Cont — 287

The Courses of the Recovery

No	Courses	Per

The Courses of the original as laid out of the Recovery

No	Courses	Per

The Courses of the Vacancy

No	Courses	Per

Platted By a Scale of 80 Equal Parts in an Inch By I.P.

The Courses of Dear Bought according to the Original Grant

Lying on the west side of Patuxent River and on the west side of a branch of the said River called the Demolin Creek about a mile up the Creek. Beginning at a marked Oak by the Creek side and bounding on the North by a line Drawn West by North three Hundred & Twenty Perches to a marked Oak, bounding on the west by a line Drawn South by West Seventy five Perches to a marked Black Hickory Bounding on the South by a line Drawn East by South to a marked Oak by the side of a marsh by the Creek side on the East with the Creek. Containing and now laid out for one Hundred & fifty acres be it more or Less

---

the said Line, to the end thereof, South seventy four perches and a half of a perch, Thence with a Straight Line to the Beginning Locust first abovementioned Containing and now Laid out for One Hundred & Eighty four acres of Land more or Less, and the Whole now Called The Cold Snowy Fryday To be held of Calverton Manor Surveyed the nineteenth day of November Anno Domini Seventeen Hundred & Sixty three By

John T. A. Briggs Deputy Surveyor of P.G. County

Memorandum Part of the vacancy has been formerly Cultivated, but now no Improvements thereon of any kind

The Courses of Jos. Nobles part of the Original

No	Courses	Per

The Courses of the abovesd original Plat

No	Courses	Per

A. The Beginning of Gantts Levells.
B. The
C. The Beginning of the first vacancy.
D. The Beginning of the Second vacancy.

The Courses of the old lines of the Recovery

No	Courses	Per

By virtue of a special Warrant of Resurvey Granted out of his Lordship's Land Office to Joseph Noble of the County aforesaid bearing Date the Twenty fifth day of February Anno Domini Seventeen Hundred and Sixty three and by Assessment bearing date the 25th day of August 1760 It Resurvey Eighty above Part of a Tract or parcel of Land Called The Joseph and Martha's Delight, lying and being in the County aforesaid Originally on the ninth day of March Anno Domini Seventeen Hundred & forty Seven Granted unto the aforesaid Joseph Noble for Two Hundred acres under new Rent &c. To Resurvey the aforesaid Part of a Tract or parcel of Land to amend all Errors and to add the vacant Land thereto Contiguous &c. ——

I Hereby Certify as Deputy Surveyor of the County aforesaid under His Excellency Horatio Sharpe Esqr Governor of Maryland That I have carefully Resurveyed and laid out for and in the Name of him the said Joseph Noble his Part of the aforesaid Tract or parcel of Land called The Joseph and Martha's Delight and find the same to be bounded as follows viz: Beginning at the end of the Seventh line of a Tract or parcel of Land called Gantts Lasetts the same being the place of Beginning for the whole original Tract of Joseph and Martha's Delight and Running with the first Line of the said whole Tract North Thirty degrees West ninety four perches, then with a line Drawn North Eight degrees forty five minutes Westerly Sixty four perches & a half of a perch To the end of the Thirteenth Line of the whole Tract, the Lastmentioned Course & Distance being the Dividing Line between the said Joseph Noble and Mr John Baynes of Each of their parts of the said Tract, thence running with the four tenth Line of the said Whole Tract and the lines in Succession therefrom following Courses & distances viz: East forty Two perches, then North thirty four degrees East ninety Perches, then South fifteen degrees East ninety six Perches, then South Fifty degrees West forty perches, then South Eighty Perches, Thence with a Straight line to the Beginning Containing Eighty acres. I also Certify That I have added to the said Joseph Noble's Part aforesaid in Two surveys the Quantity of One Hundred & four acres of Contiguous vacant Land as shown to me to be vacant, and have Reduced the said Part with the vacancies added thereto Into one Entire Tract all which appears by the Plot below. Lastly Beginning for the next line of the Resurvey of the said part with the vacant Land added thereto, by virtue of the beforementioned Warrant of Resurvey, At a young Locust Tree now Planted at the end of the Seventh Line of a Tract or parcel of Land formerly surveyed for Thomas Gantt called Gantts Lasetts, being the place of beginning for the whole Tract of Joseph and Martha's delight, as also the beginning of the said Joseph Noble's Part of the said Tract and from the said Locust Running with the Lines of the said Joseph Noble's Part of the Original the Two following Courses viz: North thirty degrees West ninety four Perches, then North Eight degrees forty five minutes Westerly Sixty four Perches and a half of a perch, thence Running to Include the first corner The four following Courses viz: South forty degrees West forty Perches, then South sixty four degrees West Fifty one perches and a half of a perch, then North thirty three degrees East one Hundred and Seventy seven Perches, then South seventy degrees East Sixty nine Perches and a half of a perch to the fourth line of the said Joseph Noble's Part of the original, then with the said line to the end thereof North thirty four degrees East four Perches, then with Part of the Fifth line of the said Original Part South fifteen degrees East four Perches and a quarter of a Perch, thence running to Include the Second vacancy the four following Courses viz: South seventy degrees East Fifty Seven Perches, then South fifty five degrees East Fifty Two Perches then South Eighteen degrees forty five minutes — Westerly one Hundred and Seven Perches, then North Sixty five degrees West Seventy Six perches To the Seventh line of Joseph Noble's Part of the original, thence with

Prince Georges County ss.

By virtue of a special Warrant of Resurvey Granted out of his Lordship's Land Office to Joseph Noble of the County aforesaid bearing Date the Twenty fifth day of February Anno Domini Seventeen Hundred and Sixty three and by Assessment bearing date the 25th day of August 1760 It Resurvey Eighty above Part of a Tract or parcel of Land Called The Joseph and Martha's Delight, lying and being in the County aforesaid Originally on the ninth day of March Anno Domini Seventeen Hundred & forty Seven Granted unto the aforesaid Joseph Noble for Two Hundred acres under new Rent &c. To Resurvey the aforesaid Part of a Tract or parcel of Land to amend all Errors and to add the vacant Land thereto Contiguous &c. ——

I Hereby Certify as Deputy Surveyor of the County aforesaid under His Excellency Horatio Sharpe Esqr Governor of Maryland That I have carefully Resurveyed and laid out for and in the Name of him the said Joseph Noble his Part of the aforesaid Tract or parcel of Land called The Joseph and Martha's Delight and find the same to be bounded as follows viz: Beginning at the end of the Seventh line of a Tract or parcel of Land called Gantts Lasetts the same being the place of Beginning for the whole original Tract of Joseph and Martha's Delight and Running with the first Line of the said whole Tract North Thirty degrees West ninety four perches, then with a line Drawn North Eight degrees forty five minutes Westerly Sixty four perches & a half of a perch To the end of the Thirteenth Line of the whole Tract, the Lastmentioned Course & Distance being the Dividing Line between the said Joseph Noble and Mr John Baynes of Each of their parts of the said Tract, thence running with the four tenth Line of the said Whole Tract and the lines in Succession therefrom following Courses & distances viz: East forty Two perches, then North thirty four degrees East ninety Perches, then South fifteen degrees East ninety six Perches, then South Fifty degrees West forty perches, then South Eighty Perches, Thence with a Straight line to the Beginning Containing Eighty acres. I also Certify That I have added to the said Joseph Noble's Part aforesaid in Two surveys the Quantity of One Hundred & four acres of Contiguous vacant Land as shown to me to be vacant, and have Reduced the said Part with the vacancies added thereto Into one Entire Tract all which appears by the Plot below. Lastly Beginning for the next line of the Resurvey of the said part with the vacant Land added thereto, by virtue of the beforementioned Warrant of Resurvey, At a young Locust Tree now Planted at the end of the Seventh Line of a Tract or parcel of Land formerly surveyed for Thomas Gantt called Gantts Lasetts, being the place of beginning for the whole Tract of Joseph and Martha's delight, as also the beginning of the said Joseph Noble's Part of the said Tract and from the said Locust Running with the Lines of the said Joseph Noble's Part of the Original the Two following Courses viz: North thirty degrees West ninety four Perches, then North Eight degrees forty five minutes Westerly Sixty four Perches and a half of a perch, thence Running to Include the first corner The four following Courses viz: South forty degrees West forty Perches, then South sixty four degrees West Fifty one perches and a half of a perch, then North thirty three degrees East one Hundred and Seventy seven Perches, then South seventy degrees East Sixty nine Perches and a half of a perch to the fourth line of the said Joseph Noble's Part of the original, then with the said line to the end thereof North thirty four degrees East four Perches, then with Part of the Fifth line of the said Original Part South fifteen degrees East four Perches and a quarter of a Perch, thence running to Include the Second vacancy the four following Courses viz: South seventy degrees East Fifty Seven Perches, then South fifty five degrees East Fifty Two Perches then South Eighteen degrees forty five minutes — Westerly one Hundred and Seven Perches, then North Sixty five degrees West Seventy Six perches To the Seventh line of Joseph Noble's Part of the original, thence with

Prince George's County

The Certificate of the
north of

Dear Bought Colored
charged at Legard. & c
[illegible]

have asigned for Ephraim
[illegible] Town the 14 day
of November 1753

For the Examiner General

20th May 1759
Examined and passed

[signature]

Rec'd the 14 day of December 1730
[illegible]

[illegible lines]

[illegible] March 176[?]

4·6   No 00
24   93
1·9½   243
6·0   ·6
       3·9
44

100   46
187   5·2

PRINCE GEORGE'S COUNTY.

River Bought Enlarged

Acres 307

SURVEYED FOR

Ephraim Gover Jr.
1st Nov. 1755

Returned

Ex'd. and Passed *20th May 1757*

Comp. $ Pd.

PATENTED TO

Ephraim Gover Jr.
1st Dec. 1758

Rec. at Cert.

763

PRINCE GEORGE'S COUNTY.

Disappointment

Acres *62*

SURVEYED FOR

Christopher Beane

6th Feb. 1784

Returned

Ex'd. and Passed *July 1784*

Comp. $ _____ Pd. _____

PATENTED TO

Christopher Beane

6th Feb 1784

Rec. of Cert. *Books No. 1 folio 261*

I have received the sum of One Pound twelve shillings for the within
Vacancy Patent, may therefore issue with his Excellency's Approbation —

5 July 1754 —

Prince George's County of

By Virtue of a Warrant Granted out of his
Lordships Land Office to Christopher Browne of the said County bearing
date the fourth day of February Seventeen hundred & Fifty five for Thirty
acres of vacant Land

I hereby Certify as Deputy Surveyor of the County aforesaid under his
Excellency Horatio Sharpe Esqr that I have carefully Surveyed & Laid out for &
in the Name of him the said Christopher Browne all that Tract or piece of
Land lying in the County aforesaid in the Enlargement Beginning at a
bounded White Oak standing by the Head of a Glade that falls into a Branch called
the Beaver Dam Branch of the Eastern Branch of Patuxent River & near a
beginning Tree of a Tract of Land called Waugh's Lott & running thence North
Twenty perches thence South Eighty two degrees West two hundred & twenty
perches thence South Eight degrees East Sixty nine perches thence by a Straight
line to the beginning Tree Containing and now laid out for & Sixty two Acres of
Land to be held of Catratan Manor & Surveyed this last day of February
Anno Domini Seventeen hundred & Fifty five by

Tho Hodgkin
Dep Surveyor of P.G.C.

No	Courses	Dist
1	North	20
2	S82W	220
3	S8E	69

Then by a
Straight Line
to the first
beginning
Tree.

Plotted by a Scale of 50 Equal parts in an Inch

763

1068

PRINCE GEORGE'S COUNTY.

Hickory Ford

Acres 65

SURVEYED FOR

George Gibons

26th June 1738

Returned

Ex'd. and Passed 24th Aug. 1738

Comp. $ Pd.

PATENTED TO

George Gibons

29th Nov. 1738

Rec. of Cert. E.9. No.5 folio 376

Prince Geo County ss

By Virtue of a warrant granted out of his Lordships Land office of the province bearing Date May the Nineteenth Anno Domini 1711 To mr George Gibons of Prince Geo. For forty five acres of Vacant Land in any part of the province he having paid The usual fine for the same as appr'd Wd

I do therefore hereby Certifie and Lain of the of the most Honorable Sir Samuel Ogle Esqr his Lordships Governor of Maryland I have Carefully laid out for & in the Name of him the sd George Gibons all that tract or parcell of Land lying in the sd County called Hickory Ford Beginning at a bounded red Oak standing on the North line of John Adams land called Birmingham twenty two feet from the Beginning of sd line ...

... Containing and now laid out for forty five acres of Land to be held of ... this twenty forth Day of June Anno Domini 1738 ...

Probat D.H. Soro &
of Pr Geo County

65 A

No	Course	Per
1	N 24 W	112
2	N 72 E	77
3	S 48 E	68
4	S ---	142
	Then to the beginning 100	

by a Scale of forty equall part's to an Inch

1068

I have received Seven Pounds ten
Shillings for Gibson's Escheat, four
Shillings and three Pence for Vacancy
four Pence for Temple, and three Shillings
and three Penny for Rents to Mich.s

1772 —

Patent may therefore Issue with his
Excellency's Approbation.

Nov.r 2.d 1772   Dan.l Dulany

Approv'd
Rob Eden

				£ s d
Es	30	a 3		£7 . 10 . —
V	4	4		. . 4 . 3
		Tmp		. . 4 . —
		Rents to Mich. 1772		5 . 3
				7 . 19 . 10

1275

PRINCE GEORGE'S COUNTY.

Lawsons Lott

Acres *100*

SURVEYED FOR

John Lawson

25th Oct. 1731

Returned

Ex'd. and Passed

Comp. $ Pd.

PATENTED TO

John Lawson

16th Oct. 1732

Rec. of Cert. *A. M. No. 1 Folio 46*

John Lawson plate
Clerk of Chowan Court

Cont. 100 acres
examined expressedly

[signature]
Esqr. Ned.

patt October 16th
1738 County Court
2d Shore

Int. Lib: A. M: fol. 46.

Maryland ss. Prince Geo: County: octobr ye 25 - 1731

By Vertue of a Warr.t granted out of his Lordships Land office ye 29th day
of Aprill last unto John Lawson of the Cty afores.d for one hundred
& fifty acres of Land, I have Surveyed for the s.d John Lawson all that
tract or parcell of Land call'd Lawsons Lott lying in the s.d County
& Beginning at two bounded Oak Standing on a Gravelly Hill nigh
a Branch now call'd Taylors Branch it being likewise a Branch of
Mattabany & running thence South Seventy eight degrees East one
Hundred & twenty one perches, South Thirty degrees East forty four
perches, South eight degrees West Forty two perches, South twenty
nine degrees West forty four perches, North Seventy eight degrees
West one hundred & twenty one perches then with a Straight line
to the Beginning tree, which I now laid out for one hundred acres
of Land more or less to be held of Calverton Manor

                                              p. Geo. Noble ꝑ Dy Svy

S - 70 E - 121
S - 30 Er - 44
S - 8 W.t - 42
S - 29 W.t - 44
N - 70 W.t 121

Then with a Straight
line to the first line

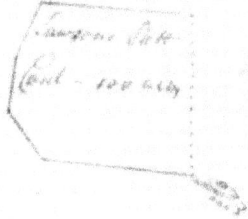

Lawsons Oak
Cont - 100 acres

Stated by order of ffice
Equal parts in an inch
                p. Geo. Noble

1275

I have received the sum of One Pound Seventeen Shillings
and Twopence farthing for the within Surplus and Two
Pounds four Shillings for the Vacancy added Patent
may therefore issue with his Excellency's Approbation———

12 March 1760

Edwd Hewes

162

954

PRINCE GEORGE'S COUNTY

Land Drains

Acres

SURVEYED FOR

George Naylor Jr

Returned

Ex'd. and Passed

Comp. $ Pd.

PATENTED TO

George Naylor Jr

Rec. of Cert.

Prince Georges County

The Certificate and Plat
of
Good Luck say'd. here

Resurveyed on the Escheat for George
Naylor Jun'r the 16th day of april 1771

For the Examiner General

Returned 20th April 1771
May 20th 1771
Examined & Pass'd
p. Rob't U Scott Esq'r

Patented 17th October 1775
Rent p. Annum 2/2 Stg.
Recorded in Liber B C & G S
N'o. 50 folio 245

all pass'd

164

ROBERT ROBERTS &

JOSEPH NOBLE

Register of Maryland's Heraldic Families

Roberts – (Morsell)

Registrants: Under the dignity of MANORIAL RIGHTS to Sewall and Green; of ancient lineage to "John of Gaunt". And the lineage of Robert Roberts of Wales, eldest son of Hugh Roberts and Jane Owen of "Evan", b. 1673, m. at Merion, Wales, in 1696 to Kath. Jones, whose son, Robert, came to Maryland in 1702. He married secondly Priscilla Johns of the "Cliffs" dau. of Elizabeth Kensey, who m. Richard Johns. Robert Roberts d. 1728, he was a Quaker; came from north of Wales, a descendant of the eight noble tribes of Hugh Roberts of Kiltalgarth, Parish of Llanfawn, of Penllyn, of Merionetshire, who m. Elizabeth Owen Williams (widow), dau. of William Owen. Had son Richard Roberts who m. Elizabeth Allen and their son m. Mary Harris, having a son also named Richard Roberts, who m. Sarah Kent; and having a son also Richard Roberts who m. Elizabeth Gantt. His son, Richard Roberts m. Henrietta Sewall Morsell, dau. of James Sewell Morsell and wife, Elleanor Baden as his second wife; and she the dau of Joseph Noble Baden and Letitia Gebbons (Gibbons). He was the son of John Baden and Marg. Noble, dau. of Joseph Noble and Martha Tarvin. He son of Joseph Noble and Mary Wheeler, dau. of Francis Wheeler and Winnifred Green, dau. of Ann and Leonard Green, a son of Thomas Green, Gov. of Maryland 1648.

PRINCE GEORGE'S COUNTY.

———•———

Joseph & Martha's
Delight (Th)

Acres 200

SURVEYED FOR

Joseph Noble
10 May 1745

Returned

Ex'd. and Passed Nov 8 1745

Comp. $ Pd.

PATENTED TO

Joseph Noble
7 Mch 1749

Rec. of Cert. L.Mo 1 fo 425

Prince Geo: County [ss?]

By Virtue of a Special Warrant of Survey Granted out of his Lordships Land Office of this Province to Joseph Noble of [ ] County for two hundred acres of Land [ ] Date the 2d Decem: 2d 1744

These therefore Certifie I a Deputy [ ] of the Right Hon: Thos. Bladen Esqr. Gov: of Maryland have laid the Survey [ ] in the name of him the said Joseph Noble All that Tract of Land Called The Joseph & Marthas Delight Begining at the end of the seventh Line of a tract of Land called [ ] by [ ] Lands called Cants Lovely & Runing thence North thirty Degrees West ninety four perches then South Sixty four Degrees [ ] thirty [ ] perches then South Eighty perches then South Sixty three Degrees West ninety two perches then South twenty Degrees West Sixty eight Perches then North forty Degrees [ ] North fifty four perches then North twenty degrees East eighty four perches then North Seventy Degrees West Eighty perches then North twenty five Deg: East thirty four perches then South twenty Degrees East one hundred perches then North twenty Deg: East Sixty four perches then North Sixty four [ ] Degrees East forty two perches then North forty Degrees East forty perches then North thirty four Degrees East thirty perches then South [ ] Degrees West forty [ ] then East Ninety Six perches then South fifty [ ] Degrees [ ] then [ ] South Eighty perches then with a [ ] Line [ ] then [ ] [ ] ing and laid out for Two Hundred Acres [ ] Surveyd the 10th ing [ ] Day of May 1745

Signd: of Order
Peter Dent Deputy Surv:

The Improvements on this Survey Consists of [ ] about Thirty Barrells of [ ] about five Acres of Cultivated Land

No	Courses	[ ]	Per.
1	N30	W	94
2	S 64	E	30
3	South		80
4	S63	W	92
5	S20	W	68
6	N40	W	54
7	N20	E	84
8	N70	W	80
9	N25	E	34
10	S20	E	100
11	N20	E	64
12	N64	E	60
13	N40	E	40
14	East		48
15	N54	E	90
16	S15	E	96
17	S53	W	40
18	South		80
	Then to the Beginning		

Platted by a Scale of 100 Equal perches in an Inch

1222

Abraham Boyd and John Smith Brookes Commissions signed by John Rogers, Chancellor of Maryland. (Ibid at 271)

The following qualified as Justices. Joshua Beall, Thomas Williams, Thomas Macgill, James Beck, Samuel Chew Hepburn, John Smith Brookes, Fielder Bowie, Frank Leeke, Thomas Boyd, David Craufurd, Henry Rozer, Alexander Howard Magruder, John Harrison, Thomas Clagett, William Berry (Ibid at 272)

Thomas Gantt, Jr, qualified as Justice before Alexander Howard Magruder, February 28, 1779 (Ibid at 278)

Rinaldo Johnson produced his power of attorney as Prosecutor for the county from Luther Martin, Attorney-General of Maryland, dated January 16, 1779. (Ibid.)

At a County Court held at Upper Marlborough Town, March 23, 1779 Present· Joshua Beall, David Craufurd, Richard Henderson, Fielder Bowie, Thomas Macgill, William Berry, Frank Leeke, Samuel Chew Hepburn, Abraham Boyd, John Smith Brookes, Gentlemen, Justices, commissioned, qualified etc (Ibid at 356)

Thos Duckett, Sheriff John Read Magruder, Clerk of the county (Ibid)

Grand Jurors. Edward Sprigg [Foreman], William Bowie the third, Zachariah Berry, Johnson Michael Riley, Charles Maddocks, Thomas Stevens, Josias Wilcoxen, Joseph Wilson, Sr, Thomas Baden, Henry Hill, Jr Nicholas Davis, John Everfield, Jr, Andrew Beall, Richard Queen, John Hamilton, Thomas Adams and William Ray (Ibid)

Abraham Boyd and John Brown qualified as Justices (Ibid at 357.)

"Richard Henderson produces to the Court here his account against the County for an allowance for Administering the Oath of Fidelity and is allowed six pounds current money in the present County Levy for that purpose." (Ibid)

Barton Lucas allowed for services as Coroner (Ibid)

At a County Court held at Upper Marlborough Town August 24, 1779 Present Joshua Beall, David Craufurd, John Harrison, Fielder Bowie, Thomas Williams, Thomas Macgill, Thomas Boyd, William Lyles, William Berry, James Mullikin, James Beck, Frank Leeke, Samuel Hepburn, John Brown, John Smith Brookes, Gen'lemen, Justices, commissioned, qualified etc (Ibid at 431.)

Thos. Duckett, Sheriff John Read Magruder, Clerk of the county (Ibid)

Grand Jurors John Addison [Foreman], John Macgill, Johnson Michael Riley, William Moore, Joseph Wilson, Thomas Harvey, John Stone, John Waring, Jacob Duckett, William Taylor, Nicholas Davis, John Baden, John Baden, Jr, William Sprigg Bowie, Richard Beall, Basil Craufurd and Thomas Beall (Ibid)

At a County Court held at Upper Marlborough Town November 23, 1779 Present. Joshua Beall, William Lock Weems, David Craufurd, John Harrison, Richard Henderson, Thomas Clagett, Alexander Howard Magruder, Fielder Bowie, Thomas Williams, Thomas Macgill, Thomas Boyd, William Lyles, William Berry, James Mullikin, James Beck, Frank Leeke, Samuel Hepburn, John Brown, Abraham Boyd, John Smith Brookes, Gentlemen, Justices, commissioned, qualified etc (Ibid at 521)

Thomas Duckett, Sheriff John Read Magruder, Clerk of the county (Ibid)

Grand Jurors· Thomas Dent [Foreman], Richard Ball, Edward Simms, John Waring, William Taylor, Edward Lanham, Basil Waring, Jr, Daniel McLish, Thomas Baden, Joseph Clarke, Edward Villers Harbin, Samuel Jones, Basil Crawford, Peter Carns, William Hall, Charles Burgess, Levin Wilcoxen, James Edmonston. (Ibid)

Josiah Hatton presented by Grand Jury for "harbouring and secreting William Whitmore a Deserter from the Southern Army" (Ibid)

Zachariah Owens, sub-sheriff of the county (Ibid at 522.)

170

uel Lusby, Cornelius Hurley, Thomas Sansbury, John Baden, Henry Hilleary, Joseph Clarke, Zachariah Berry, Thomas Ramsay Hodges, Edward Magruder, Joseph Willson, Sr, Charles Maddocks, John Wheat, John Waring, William Bowie the third, Josias Sprigg Wilson, George Moore, James Drane (Ibid.)

William Lyles referred to as Major, 1780. (Ibid at 558)

Rinaldo Johnson, Prosecutor for the county (Ibid at 569)

At a County Court held at Upper Marlborough Town August 22, 1780

Present, Joshua Beall, William Lock Weems, David Craufurd, Thomas Clagett, Alexander Howard Magruder, Fielder Bowie, Thomas Macgill, James Mullikin, James Beck, Frank Leeke, Samuel Hepburn, John Brown, Abraham Boyd, John Smith Brookes, Gentlemen, Justices, commissioned, qualified, etc. (Ibid at 629)

Thomas Williams, Sheriff. John Read Magruder, Clerk of the county (Ibid)

Grand Jurors: Thomas Dent [Foreman], Johnson Michael Riley, James Waring, Thomas Lyles, Alexander Jefferies, John Baden, Joseph Clarke Anthony Hardey, Alexander Crawford, Jacob Aldridge, Benjamin Berry, Robert Tyler, Benjamin Prather, Josias S Wilson, Jesse Duvall, Joshua Clarke, Jr, John Williams (Ibid)

Henry Nicholls appointed Drummer (Ibid at 637)

Benjamin Brookes, late Standard Keeper, ordered to deliver the standard to Robert Baden who qualified as Standard Keeper. (Ibid)

Richard Beall referred to as Captain. (Ibid at 639)

John Allen Thomas, Prosecutor for the county (Ibid at 641.)

At a County Court held at Upper Marlborough Town March 20, 1781

Present Joshua Beall, David Craufurd, John Harrison, Fielder Bowie, Thomas Boyd, James Mullikin, Frank Leeke, Samuel Hepburn, John Brown, John Smith Brookes, Gentlemen, Justices, commissioned, qualified, etc. (Ibid at 665)

Thomas Williams, Sheriff John Read Magruder, Clerk of the county (Ibid)

John Allen Thomas allowed fees as Prosecutor for the county (Ibid)

Same as to Thomas Williams, Sheriff of the county. (Ibid)

Same as to John Read Magruder, Clerk of the county (Ibid)

Same as to Henry Nicholls, Cryer of the Court (Ibid)

Same as to Samuel Tyler, Register of Wills (Ibid)

Same as to Robert Baden, Standard Keeper (Ibid)

Thomas Williams qualified as Sheriff. (Ibid at 666)

At a County Court held at Upper Marlborough Town March 27, 1781

Present Joshua Beall, David Craufurd, John Harrison, Richard Henderson, Alexander Howard Magruder, Fielder Bowie, Thomas Macgill, Thomas Boyd, James Mullikin, Henry Rozer, Frank Leeke, Samuel Hepburn, John Brown, Abraham Boyd, John Smith Brookes, Gentlemen, Justices, commissioned qualified etc. (Ibid at 667)

Thomas Williams, Sheriff John Read Magruder, Clerk of the county. (Ibid)

Grand Jurors Henry Brookes [Foreman], Tilghman Hilleary, Johnson Michael Riley, James Drane, Thomas R Hodges, Robert Whitaker, Thomas Stevens, Anthony Hardey, Charles Maddocks, Edward Lanham, Thomas Tilly, Isaac Sansbury, Jonathan Simmons, Thomas Mudd, Ignatius Fenwick, John Waring, Edward Swann, Thomas Adams, Charles R Hodges (Ibid.)

"Col Joshua Beall" produced and read in open Court Commissions as Justices of the Peace for the following Joshua Beall, Christopher Lowndes, William Lock Weems, David Craufurd, John Harrison, Richard Henderson, Thomas Gatt [Gantt], Jr, Luke Marbury, Thomas Clagett, Alexander Howard Magruder, Osborn Sprigg, Fielder Bowie, George Lee, Thomas Macgill, Thomas

Boy l, William Lyles, William Berry, James Mullikin, James Beck, Henry Rozer, Frank Leeke, Samuel Hepburn, John Brown, Abraham Boyd, John Smith Brookes Commissions signed by John Rogers, Chancellor of Maryland (Ibid at 668)

Constables appointed for the ensuing year Lingan Boteler, Mattapany hundred, Richard Brightwell, Prince Frederick; John Nevitt, Jr, King George's, Francis Wheat, Piscattaway, Walter Hilleary, Collington; Nathaniel O'Neal, Grubb, Thomas Boteler, of Charles, Mount Calvert, William Moodie, Western Branch, James Waring, New Scotland, Isaac Lansdale, Patuxtent, Richard Jameson, Rock Creek, Ralph Jones, Eastern Branch, William Hutchinson, Upper Marlborough, Charles Man (Maw?), Bladensburgh; Samuel Nicholls, Horse-pen, Nicholas Blacklock, Charlotte, George Gantt, Washington; George Upton, Hynson, James Tannihill, Jr, Oxon. (Ibid at 669)

Overseers of the Highways for ensuing year James Edmonston, New Scotland, upper part, John Robinson, same, second; Nathaniel Pope, Oxon, up-per, George Bean, same, lower, William Bowie the third, Collington, upper, Richard Lamar, same, second, Joseph Ramsay Hodges, same, third, Joseph Cross, of George, same, fourth; John Read Magruder, Mount Calvert, upper, William Newman Dorsett, same, lower, Alexis Boone, same, third; Robert Baden, Western Branch, Tilghman Hilleary, same, upper, John Burgess, same middle, John Manley, same, lower, John McKay, same, lower division, lower. Christopher Hyatt, Patuxent, upper; Elisha Green, same, fourth, Francis Bird, same, middle, George Wells, of George, same, lower; William Fergusson, Rock Creek, upper; Thomas Price, same, lower, Thomas Scissell, Eastern Branch, lower. Archibald Elson, Patuxent, Jonas Austin, Mattapany, upper, William Morton, same, middle, Thomas Smith, same, lower; Samuel Poston, same, back; Levin Covington, Prince Frederick· John Lowe, Jr, Piscattaway, upper; Robert Fish, same, middle, William Tennerly, same, fifth, Zachariah Jenkins, same, lower; Charles Jones, same, riverside, Richard Ball, Jericho precincts, John Bowling, King George's, lower, Edward Edelen, same, middle, Nathaniel New-ton, same, third; John Wynn, same, back; William Foard, same, last; John Webster, same, lower division, lower; Adam Craig, Bladensburgh (Ibid)

At a County Court held at Upper Marlborough Town August 28, 1781 Present Joshua Beall, David Craufurd, Frank Leeke, John Smith Brookes, Samuel Hepburn, William Berry, Henry Rozer, James Mullikin, Boyd [Thomas or Abraham], John Harrison, Fielder Bowie, Gentlemen, Justices, commissioned, qualified etc, (Ibid at 700)

Thomas Williams, Sheriff John Read Magruder, Clerk of the county, (Ibid)

Grand Jurors Thomas Owen Williams [Foreman], John Lowe, Jr, Sam-uel Lusby, Henry Hardey, Edward Villers Harbin, James Ray, Thomas Craw-ford, Benjamin Berry, Joshua Clarke, Charles Clagett, John Lansdale. Jr, Alex-ander Jefferies, Robert Baden, Mordecai Burgess, Thomas Baden, Thomas Duvall, Joseph Wilson, Cornelius Hurley, Thomas Ramsay Hodges (Ibid)

Thomas Atkin presented by Grand Jury on information of William Moodie and John Honnis "for harbouring and entertaining Joseph Mockbee a Deserter" (Ibid.)

Judson Coolidge referred to as Captain, August, 1781, (Ibid at 712)

At a County Court held at Upper Marlborough Town November 27, 1781 Present Joshua Beall, David Craufurd, Fielder Bowie, Thomas Boyd, William Berry, Frank Leeke, Samuel Hepburn, Abraham Boyd, Gentlemen, Justices, commissioned, qualified, etc (Ibid at 761)

Thomas Williams, Sheriff John Read Magruder, clerk of the county (Ibid)

Grand Jurors Benjamin Brookes [Foreman],John Evans, Joseph Wil-son, Thomas Mudd, Joseph White Clagett, Joseph Clarke, Alexander Jefferies,

Enlisted by Alexander Howard Magruder.   Reviewed by Jos. Sim, Col. of the 11th Battalion, Prince George's County, August 21st, 1776.

NAMES.	WHEN ENROLLED.	NAMES.	WHEN ENROLLED.
Robert Baden	July 3	Wm.T., (or F.), Greenfield, (Cadet)	July 18
Jeremiah Baden	"	William White	"
Thos. Wm. Sasser	"	William Sasser	"
Edward Mullan	4	Edwd. Stephens	"
Henry Bean	"	John White	"
John Sollers	"	Maryland Beaven	July 20
Isaac Barnett	9	John Watson	25
Randolph Marlow	10	Benjamin Rawlings	"
John Downing	"	John Rawlings	Aug. 1
Hugh Stephens	15	William Mayhew	"
John Young	18	Bryan Mayhew	5
Benj. Paggatt	"	Thomas Lane	19
Thomas Bean	"	Leonard White	"
	Put on List after viewed by the Colonel		
Peter Dayley	July 23	Joseph Bumford, (Fifer)	July 12
Charles Leech	"	Blk. Boy Gim, (Drummer)	14

Raised by Alex. Trueman, Ensign, for Capt. Magruder's Company. Passed by Jos. Sim, Prince George's County, August 21st, 1776.

NAMES.	WHEN ENROLLED.	NAMES.	WHEN ENROLLED.
Thomas Baden	July 3	Wilson Cage, (or Caye)	July 8
Elijah Rawlings	4	Nevitt Rawlings	4
Thomas Cohoe	"	William Burnes	20
John Mills	5	John West	2
Benjamin Ellis	6	Samuel Groyer	3
William Teanneclift	8	Jonathan Weeden	5
Leonard Hickey	7	John Bean	4
Richard Jones	"	George Naylor	"

ANNE ARUNDEL COUNTY.

Capt. Edward Norwood
1 Lt. Samuel Godman
2 Lt. John W. Dorsey
Ensign Richard Talbott
Capt. Edward Tillard
1 Lt. Samuel Lloyd Chew
2 Lt. John Sprigg Belt
Ensign John Gassaway, resigned and John Kilty appointed by the Convention, July 5th, 1776.

Capt. Daniel Dorsey
1 Lt. Joseph Burgess
2 Lt. John Lorah. Must be John O'Hara, who resigned and James Howard appointed by the Council of Safety, July 24th, 1776. It is printed Lorah in the Journal of the Convention, but it must be a mistake.
Ensign Michael Burgess
Capt. James Disney

173

Published from Original Returns in the Archives
of Maryland, and By Permission of The
Historical Society of Maryland.

Pages 25 to 35, Revolutionary Records of Maryland, Brumbaugh and Hodges, contain numerous references to individuals mentioned in the following "Returns" from Prince George's County, Md. and should be consulted

Revolutionary Records of Maryland, page 30

"At a County Court held at Upper Marlborough Town, March 23, 1779.

* * * * *

Richard Henderson produces to the Court here his account against the County for an allowance for Administering the Oath of Fidelity and is allowed six pounds current money in the present County Levy for that purpose " (See Return No 11)

Fielder Bowie's Return

1. ——, John
2. Baden, Robert
3. Baden, Benjª
4. Naylor, Geo. Jr.
5. Bowie, Allen, Jr.
6. Hollyday, Leoᵈ., Jr.
7. Baden, John, Senʳ
8. Baden, Jeremiah
9. Hollyday, Leonard
10. Harrison, John
11. Haye, Thomas
12. Harriss, George
13. Cox, Thomas
14. Harvey, William G.
15. Sadler, James
16. Boteler, Edward
17. Naylor, John Lawson
18. Haye, Cephas
19. Ryan, Nathaniel
20. Bowie, John Fraser
21. Haye, Sabrit
22. Orme, Richard
23. Piles, Francis
24. Hamilton, Dr. Thomas
25. Roberts, Evan
26. Earley, William, Jr.
27. Hooker, Jonas
28. Warfield, John, Jr.
29. White, Thomas T.
30. M——, Benjª.
31. Fry, James
32. Ryan, Darby
33. Freeman, Benjª.
34. Boteler, Henry
35. Boteler, Charles, Jr.
36. Boteler, Charles

303

37. Peter, Jonathan H.
38. Haye, Dorsett
39. Ryan, John of Nat.
40. Turner, Jesse
41. Earley, William, Jr.
42. Selby, Joseph
43. Orme, Hezekiah
44. Hodgken, Thomas, of Philip
45. Cramphin, Damond
46 Johns, William
47 Orme, John

48. Dorsett, William N.
49. Hodgken, Thomas
50 Harvey, James
51. Dorsett, Thomas
52. Hooper, John
53. Orme, William
54 Gray, Thomas
55. Stallions, Thomas
56 Baden, John of Thos.
57 Sadler, William
57 Sworn in before Court

The Following is what I add. to my list at March Court.

58 Larkin, Elias
59 S——, Thos.
60 Moore, Elija.
61. Clagett, Edward
62. Harvey, Thomas
63 Jackson (?), Nehemiah
64. Martin, Henry
65. Ridgway, Jonathan
66. Simpson, Gilbert
67. Sullivan, Thomas
68. ——, Nathan
69 Mullikin, Samuel
70 Ridgway, Richard
71. Dorsett, Theodore
72. Curr, John
73. Simmons, Robert
74. Higdon, Truman
75. Standage, Thomas
76. Hickey, Francis
77 Lane, John
78. Talbert, Nathaniel
79 Tannar, Ign. Nevett
80. Harris, James
81. Sollers, Sabrit
82. Campbell, James

83. Wilson, Nath.
84. Moore, John
85 Busey, William
86. McDonald, John
87. Farr, Nicholas
88. Mattingley, Clement
89 Gilpin, Edward
90. Swann, Samuel
91 Grimes, Charles
92 Long, Thomas
93. Grimes, John
94 Soper, Jonathan
95 Hale, ——
96 C——, Matthew "41"
97. Lovejoy, John
98. Gibbons, John
99 Hown, Henry
100. Gibbons, Walter
101. Michell, John
102. Sinclair, Nath.
103 Hardey, John, son of Ign.
104. Naylor, George, of Batson
105. Naylor, Batson
106. Sandsbury, Richard
    "51 add. in Court."

175

Archives of Maryland Online

Maryland State Archives | Index | Help | Search

search   this volume   for.
                                                GO

Journal and Correspondence of the Maryland Council of Safety, January 1-March 20, 1777

Volume 16, Page 356   View pdf image (33K)   Jump to page   GO   << PREVIOUS NEXT >>

356 Journal and Correspondence

C. B. That the said Treasurer pay to Capt. James Cox fifty pounds
on Account and to be charged to the marching Regiment from
Baltimore County.
That the said Treasurer pay to William Lux and Bowley
one Thousand pounds on Account.
That the said Treasurer pay to Col. Marbury four hundred
pounds on Account of his Battalion.
That the said Treasurer pay to William Lux six hundred
Dollars and that he charge it to Isaac Griest Quarter Master
of the Marching Militia on Account for so much Money
advanced to him by Mr Lux.
Commissions Issued to Luke Marbury Col. Truman Skinner
Lieut. Col. William Lyles Junr Major. Thomas Dent Capt.
John Simpson first Lieut. Henry Hill jun^r Capt. Henry Evans
second Lieut of Capt. Wheelers Company William Molton
second Lieut of Capt. Hellens Comp^y Samuel Hawkins Bayne
Capt. Richard Stonestreet second Lieut. William Wilkenson
Capt. Benjamin Wales second Lieut. John Smith Brooke first
Lieut John Magruder Burgess Ensign of Capt Belts Comp^y
Robert Bowie Capt Robert Baden second Lieut. belonging to
the Lower Battalion of Militia in Prince Georges County
The Schooner Boat Liberty. Thomas Place Master navigated with four men having proceeded on her Voyage before
and returned back to this Port on the Arrival of the Enemy's
Fleet is hereby permitted to depart this Harbour and State on
her intended Voyage but she is not to cary Muskets in her.
Amos Davis is appointed assistant to the Quarter Master
of the Marching Militia

C. C. [Council to Col. Robosson.]

155 In Council 1st Septr 1777.
Sir
We are informed that several of the Militia of Capt John
Hammonds who are of the first Class & to march in Capt
Owens's Company. have not only refused to join the Company
to march. but have entered into a Confederacy to oppose by
Force any compulsory Measures which may be made use of to
compel them to do their Duty. We shall reluctantly and only
from Necessity exert the Authority entrusted to us to the
extent of it. but shall certainly not suffer such a Conduct. if
persisted in. to go unpunished. We therefore wish you to
endeavour to convince these Men of their Error. and to let
them know that if necessary, we shall set in Motion an ample
Force to compel them to obey the Law and defend their
Country; but if Persuasion has not the desired Effect, you are
hereby authorized to make use of Force and for this Purpose

62 Journal and Correspondence

C. B. Ordered That John Smith Brooks purchaser of Provisions

under the Continental Commissary receive of Thomas Duckett
the twenty bushels Salt sent to Queen Anne in February last,
to be charged to the Continent if not when delivered
Commission of Letter of Marque and Reprisal issued to
Alexander Murray Master of the Brig Saratoga mounting 12
Carriage Guns and 8 Swivels navigated by 20 Men belonging
to Samuel & Robert Purviance and others of Baltimore and
Dated 20th October 1777 also to David Porter master of the
Sloop Delight mounting 6 Carnage Guns & 6 Carbins navi-
gated by 8 Men belonging to Hugh Young and others of
Baltimore
Outerbridge Horsey, James Leach & William Landon having
been brought before this Board and they being charged by
Daniel Bryan, John Fanning Levin Langrell, Hampton Round
William Bishop and David Sprung with inimical Conduct to
this State; And it Appearing to this Board that their going at
Large may be dangerous, It is Ordered that Capt. Campbell
take the said Horsey Leach & Landon into his Custody in
order that due inquiry may be made therein
Commissions issued to Truman Skinner appd Lieut. Col.
John Perry Capt Benjamin Wales first Lieut. James Burnes
second Lieut Moses Orme Ensign Alexr Howard Magruder
Capt. Benjamin Contee first Lieut, Geo.Gantt Junr second Lieut,
Thomas Baden Ens. Robert Bowie Capt. Robert Baden first
Lieut, Thomas Hoge second Lieut, Alextious Boone Ens.
Jesse Hellen Capt. Leonard Waring first Lieut, William Morton
second Lieut, Walter Truman Greenfield Ensign, Henry Hill
Capt, John Nailer first Lieut, Nicholas Miles Ensign. Hezekiah
Wheeler Capt, James Hawkins first Lieut, Henry Eavens
second Lieut John Dyer Ensign. Thomas Dent Capt John
Simpson first Lieut, Thomas Dyer second Lieut, Francis Dyer
Ensign, Richard Stonestreet Capt, Giles Dyer first Lieut
George Dyer second Lieut. John Stonestreet Ens" Belonging
to the Lower Battalion of Militia in Prince Georges County
John Weight Capt Edward Vellis Harbin first Lieut David
Burnes second Lieut, Joseph Queen Ensign, Joseph Carlton
Capt. Josiah Shaw first Lieut, William Moore second Lt
Thomas Boyde Ensign Joshua Wilson Selby Capt. William
Wilson Selby first Lieut, William Wilson second Lieut, William
Jackson Ens, Thomas Richardson Capt, Thomas Beall first
Lieut Isaac Walker second Lieut, March Mareen Duvall Capt,
Walter Bowie first Lieut, Jacob Duvall of John second Lieut,
Thomas Lyles Ens. Richard Beall Capt. James Beck first Lieut,
Isaac Sansbury second Lieut, James Edmonson Ens. Hender-
son Magruder Capt, Singleton Woolton first Lieut Benjamin
Harwood second Lieut, Basil Belt Ens. James Mullican Capt.

of the Council of Maryland, 1778-1779. 413

Monday 24 May 1779   C. B.

Present as on Saturday
Ordered that the western shore Treasurer pay to Robert
Reith Fourteen Pounds Eleven shillings and Eight Pence as
Messenger to the Governor & Council to the 23^d Inst. & also
the further Sum of Eight Pounds per Acc^t passed by the Dep^y
Aud.
That the said Treasurer pay to Jonathan Parker Eighty two
Pounds ten shillings Bal^a of Account passed by the Dep^y Aud.
That the said Treasurer pay to Lieut. John Hardman of the
2^d Regim^t Three thousand Dollars to be expended in the Re-
cruiting Service, he being appointed and having Genl Small-
woods Instructions of the 9th April for that purpose.
That the said Treasurer pay to Lieut John Hardman seventy
two Pounds for the use of William Veazey 3^d due him per
Acc^t passed by the Dep^y Aud.
That the said Treasurer pay to Thomas Johnson jun^r out of
the money sent by Congress for the purchase of Wheat &
flour, Forty thousand Pounds to be sent and charged to Samuel
Gilpin of Cecil County & to be accounted for
That the said Treasurer pay to William Merrit, Thirty
thousand Pounds to be by him delivered over to Col^o William
Henry to be expended in the Purchase of Wheat and Flour
and Accounted for
Ordered that the western shore Treasurer pay to Com^0
Thomas Grason seven hundred and seventy four Pounds
seven shillings and six pence on Account
That the said Treasurer pay to Col^o Joshua Beall Forty two
Pounds, Eleven shillings and three pence and also the further
Sum of Twenty six Pounds, Eleven shillings and three pence
due him per Accounts passed by the Dep^y Aud
That the Armourer deliver to Richard Bryan 300 lbs Lead,
& 500 Gun flints to be delivered over to Henry Hooper Lieut
of Dorchester County for the use of said County
The Militia of Col^o Weems and Col^o Robinsons Battalions
ordered to Annapolis having as represented to this Board by
their Officers, shewed such a strong Desire to be discharged
that there is too much Reason to belive that many of them
will go to their Homes without if they do not obtain Permission
some of them having already gone without Leave. This
Board think it more advisable to discharge them for the
present especially as they have no late Intelligence from
whence it may be collected that the Enemy design up the Bay
immediately if at all, And it is accordingly ordered that the
said Militia be discharged for the present and proper Signals

178

414 Journal and Correspondence

C. B.   in Case of Alarm depositing before they depart the Arms &^{ca}
delivered to them

Commissions issued Trueman Skinner app^d Lieut Col^o John
Dyer 2^d Lieut. Richd Clagett Ens.of Capt. Hezekiah Wheelers C^o
Nicholas Miles 2^d Lieut, Nicholas Brookes Ens. of Capt.
Henry Hill jun^r C^o John H. Beanes Capt, in the room of Robert
Bowie Robert Baden I Lieut, Thomas Hoye 2^d Lieut, Elex-
tious Boone Ens. Benjamin Wales Capt, in the room of John
Perry, Moses Orme I Lieut, Edward Lloyd Wailes 2^d Lieut,
William Grindle Ens. and Thomas Gautt jun^r I Lieut of Capt
Alex^r Howard McGuden C^o belonging to the Lower Batt of
Militia in Prince Georges County also to Josias Shaw Capt,
in the room of Joseph Carlton, William Moore I Lieut,
Thomas Boyd jun^r 2^d Lieut, Richard Cramphin Ens. Thomas
Beall Capt, in the room of Thos Richardson Isaac Walker
I Lieut, John Crow 2^d Lieut, Richard Walker Ens. Jacob
Duvall I Lieut, Thomas Lyles 2^d Lieut, Mordecai Jacobs
Ens. of Capt. Marsh M. Duvall's Co. Joseph Jones Capt, in
the room of Henderson Magruder, Basil Belt I Lieut, Richard
Lyles 2^d Lieut, & Josiah Belt Ens. belonging to the Upper
Batt of Militia in Prince Georges County and also to Joseph
White Clagget Captain in the room of Humphry Belt, Wil-
liam Nicholls I Lieut, Edward Lanham Capt, in the room of
John Cassey, Anthony Hardy I Lieut Richd Claxon 2 Lieut,
Nathaniel Wilson jun^r Ens and John Tinnerly 2 Lieut of Capt.
Mich^l Lower Co. in the Middle Batt of Militia in Prince Georges
County

C. C.   [Council to H. Hooper.]

In Council Annapolis 24th May 1779
Sir

We have ordered you by Mr Bryan 300^{lb} Lead & 500 Flints;
we cannot well spare any Powder from hence, having sent
away all but what may eventually be necessary, and, considering that Baltimore would be the first Object, we have sent our
Arms thither except about 600 Stand which we have kept here;
the second Object, doubtless, of the Enemy, which may secure
us against an Attack by a small Force only. We see by your
Return 13th March, you had 3 Half Barr^{ls} & 5 Quarter Casks
of good Musquet Powder & 165 good Musquets; these, with
the common Guns in the Hands of the People, we hope will
be fully sufficient against any little Parties which may land on
your Shores and we cannot think its probable that you will
have a more formidable Force to encounter

179

463)

further nor otherwise will for ever warrant and Defend And further the aforesaid
Elizabeth Bordley desires & Agrees that this her grant be taken in the most extensive view
In Witness whereof the said Elizabeth Bordley hath hereunto set her hand and
Seale the Day and Year above written
Sealed and Delivered
in presence of   Elizabeth Bordley   (seal)

Susannah Beard

    R Goldsborough Jun.[r]
                    On the back of the aforegoing Deed was thus Written (to wit)

    On the second day of November 1785 before me Robert Goldsborough Esquire one
of the Judges of the General Court in Maryland Elizabeth Bordley Party within Named
Acknowledged the within Indenture to be her act and Deed

3¼ sides   R Goldsborough Jun.[r]
    Recorded December the 17.th 1785

        Know all Men by these presents that we John Baden Son of Thomas
and Thomas Baden of Prince Georges County are held and firmly bound unto the State
of Maryland in the full and just Quantity of Forty thousand pounds of Tobacco To
which payment well and truly to be made and done we bind ourselves and every
of us our and every of our Heirs Executors and Administrators in the whole and for
the whole Jointly and severally firmly by these presents Sealed with our seals and
Dated this twenty third Day of September Anno Domini Seventeen hundred
and Eighty five

        The Condition of the above obligation is such that if the
above bound John Baden of Thomas shall and will diligently and carefully
view and examine all Tobacco brought to any public Warehouse or Warehouses where
he is appointed to be Inspector and all other Tobacco he shall be called upon to view
and Inspect and that he will not receive any Tobacco that is not in his Judgement
Sound well Conditioned Merchantable and clear of Trash nor receive pass or stamp
any Tobacco or Hogshead of Tobacco prohibited by an act of assembly entitled an act
for the regulation of the Staple of Tobacco and that he will receive pass and stamp all
Tobacco that is sound well conditioned Merchantable and clear of Trash and in all things
well and faithfully discharge his Duty in the office of an Inspector according to the best
of his Skill and Judgement and according to the directions of the said act without Fear
Favour Affection Mallice or partiality and that he will in all things well and faithfully
execute and perform the several Duties required of him by this act then the above obligation
to be Void otherwise to remain and be in full force and Virtue in Law
Signed Sealed and
Delivered in the presence of   John Baden of Tho.[s]   (seal)
  John Grahame
    Rob.[t] Baden   Tho.[s] Baden   (seal)

464)

Prince Georges County Sc.[t] September 23.rd 1785 Then came John Graham
and Robert Baden the two Subscribing Witnesses to the within Bond and
made Oath on the Holy Evangels of Almighty God that they were present when
the within John Baden and Thomas Baden Signed sealed and Delivered
the within Bond and at their request signed the same as Witnesses thereto
David Craufurd

Recorded this 21.st day of December 1785

Know all Men by these presents that we Zachariah Wade Richard
Stone Street & Charles Fendley of Prince Georges County are held and firmly bound unto
the State of Maryland in the full and just Quantity of Forty thousand Pounds of
Tobacco to which payment well and truly to be made and done we bind ourselves and
every of us our and every of our Heirs Executors and Administrators the whole
and for the whole Jointly and severally firmly by these presents Sealed with our seals
and dated this fifth day of October Anno Domini 1785

The Condition of the above obligation is such that if the above
bound Zachariah Wade shall and will diligently and carefully view and examine all
Tobacco brought to any Public Warehouse or Warehouses which he is appointed to be Inspector
and all other Tobacco he shall be called upon to view and Inspect and that he will
not receive any Tobacco that is not in his Judgment sound well conditioned Merchantable
and clear of Trash nor receive pass or stamp any Tobacco or Hogshead of
Tobacco prohibited by an act of assembly entitled an act for the regulation of the
Staple of Tobacco and that he will receive pass and Stamp all Tobacco that is sound
well conditioned Merchantable and clear of Trash and in all things well and faithfully
discharge his duty in the office of an Inspector according to the best of his
skill and Judgment and according to the directions of the said act without fear
favour affection mallace or partiality and that he will in all things well and
faithfully execute and perform the several Duties required of him by this act then
the above obligation to be void otherwise to remain and be in full force power and
Virtue in Law

Signed Sealed and   Zach.[a] Wade   (seal)
Delivered in the presence of
     Sam.[l] Hepburn   Rich.[d] Stonestreet   (seal)
     Hugh Lyon
                                            Charles Fendley   (seal)
          On the back of the aforegoing Bond was thus written Viz.[t]

Prince Georges County October the 5.th 1785 Then came Samuel
Hepburn and Hugh Lyon and made oath that they were present all the time
when Zachariah Wade Richard Stonestreet and Charles Fendley signed sealed
and acknowledged the within Bond and at their request subscribed their names
as Witness thereto
Robert Darnall

Recorded December the 21.st 1785

farther nor otherwise will for ever warrant and defend. And further the aforesaid Elizabeth Bradley desires & Agrees that this her grant be taken in the most extensive manner. In Witness whereof the said Elizabeth Bradley hath hereunto set her hand and Seal the Day and Year above written.

Sealed and Delivered
in presence of   Elizabeth Bradley (seal)

Susannah B Board

R Goldsborough Jun.   In the back of the aforegoing Deed was thus Written, towit

On the second Day of November 1785 before me Robert Goldsborough Esquire one of the Judges of the General Court in Maryland Elizabeth Bradley Party within named Acknowledged the within Indenture to be her act and Deed

Test   Recorded December the 17th 1785   R Goldsborough Jun.

Know all Men by these presents that we John Baden Son of Thomas and Thomas Baden of Prince Georges county are held and firmly bound unto the State of Maryland in the full and just Quantity of forty thousand pounds of tobacco to which payment well and truly to be made and done we bind ourselves and every of us our and every of our Heirs Executors and Administrators in the whole and for the whole jointly and severally firmly by these presents sealed with our seals and Dated this twenty third Day of September anno Domine seventeen hundred and eighty five

The condition of the above obligation is such that if the above bound John B Baden of Thomas shall and will diligently and carefully view and examine all tobacco brought to any public Warehouse or Warehouses where he is appointed to be Inspector and all other tobacco he shall be called upon to view and Inspect and that he will not receive any tobacco that is not in his judgement found well conditioned Merchantable and clear of trash nor receive prize or stamp any Tobacco or Hogshead of Tobacco prohibited by an act of assembly entitled an act for the regulation of the staple of Tobacco and that he will receive prize and stamp all Tobacco that is sound well conditioned Merchantable and clear of trash and in all things well and faithfully discharge his Duty in the office of an Inspector according to the best of his skill and judgement and according to the directions of the said act without fear favour affection Malice or partiality and that he will in all things well and faithfully execute and perform the several Duties required of him by this act then the above obligation to be Void otherwise to remain and be in full force and virtue in Law

Signed Sealed and
Delivered in the presence of   John Baden of Tho. (seal)

John Graham
Robt Baden   Thos Baden (seal)

On the back of the aforegoing Bond was thus Written Viz (Prince)

182

464 Prince Georges County Sct. September 23d 1785 Then came John Graham
and Robert Baden the two subscribing Witnesses to the within Bond and
made Oath on the Holy Evangels of Almighty God that they were present when
the within John Baden and Thomas Baden signed sealed and Delivered
the within Bond and at their request signed the same as Witnesses thereto

                                                    David Craufurd

Recorded this 21st day of December 1785

Know all Men by these presents that we Zachariah Wade & Richard
Stone Street & Charles Fendley of Prince Georges County are held and firmly bound unto
the State of Maryland in the full and just Quantity of Forty thousand Pounds of
Tobacco to which payment well and truly to be made and done we bind ourselves and
every of us our and every of our Heirs Executors and Administrators in the whole
and for the whole jointly and severally firmly by these presents sealed with our seals
and dated this fifth day of October Anno Domini 1785

                        The Condition of the above obligation is such that if the above
bound Zachariah Wade shall and will diligently and carefully view and examine all
Tobacco brought to any Public Warehouse or Warehouses which he is appointed to be Inspector
and all other Tobacco he shall be called upon to view and Inspect and that he will
not receive any Tobacco that is not in his Judgment sound well conditioned Merchantable and clear of Trash nor receive pass or stamp any Tobacco or Hogshead of
Tobacco prohibited by an act of Assembly entitled an act for the regulation of the
staple of Tobacco and that he will receive pass and stamp all Tobacco that is sound
well conditioned Merchantable and clear of Trash and in all things well and faithfully discharge his duty in the office of an Inspector according to the best of his
skill and Judgment and according to the directions of the said Act without fear
favour affection Mallace or partiality and that he will in all things well and
faithfully execute and perform the several Duties required of him by this Act then
the above obligation to be void otherwise to remain and be in full force power and
virtue in law.

Signed Sealed and   Zach Wade   {seal}
Delivered in the presence of

    Saml Hepburn   Richd Stonestreet   {seal}

    Hugh Lyon
                                           Charles Fendley   {seal}

            On the back of the aforegoing Bond was thus Writt viz.
Prince Georges County October the 5th 1785 then came Samuel
Hepburn and Hugh Lyon and made Oath that they were present at the time
when Zachariah Wade Richard Stonestreet and Charles Fendley signed sealed
and acknowledged the within Bond and at their request subscribed their names
as Witness thereto

                                           Robert Darnall

Recorded December the 21st 1785

Know all men by these Presents that, We John Baden son of Thomas & John Baden son of Thomas Baden of Prince George County, Gentlemen, are held and firmly Bound unto the State of Maryland, in the full and just Quantity of Forty thousand Pounds of Tobacco to be Paid unto the State, to the which Payment, well and truly to be made and done, We bind ourselves and every of us, me and Every of our Heirs Executors, in the whole and for the Whole Jointly and Severally firmly by these Presents Sealed with our Seals and dated this 18th day of September Anne Domini seventeen hundred and Eighty four — The Condition of the above obligation is such that if the above Bound John Baden (son of Thomas) do well and faithfully Execute the office of an Inspector at Nottingham Ware house so forsooth as Relates to an Act of Assembly, Entitled an Act to regulate the Staple of Tobacco then the above obligation to be Void and of no Effect, otherwise to be and remain in full force and virtue in Law ———

Signed Sealed and delivered in }
the Presence of   }
  Jas Clarke
 (Darby Ryan

      John Baden of Thos
      John Baden Senior
      Thomas Baden

       Inclosed in the Bond was the following Certificate viz!
I hereby Certify that James Clarke and Darby Ryan the subscribing Evidences to the within Bond, made oath, that they were Present when John Baden (of Thos) John Baden sent & Thomas Baden signed Sealed and Acknowledged the within Bond and at their Request signed the same as Witness thereto

Recorded the 21st December 1784   W Bowie

Know all men by these Presents that we Charles Clagett David Crawford and Frank Leeke of Prince George County, are held and firmly bound unto the State of Maryland in the full and just Quantity of Forty thousand Pounds of Tobacco to be paid unto the said State To which Payment, well and truly to be made and done, we bind ourselves and every of us Our and every of our heirs Executors and Administrators in the whole and for the whole Jointly and Severally firmly by these Presents Sealed with our Seals and Dated this twenty ninth day of October in the year Seventeen hundred and Eighty four

Monday 24 May 1779   C. B.

Present as on Saturday

Ordered that the western shore Treasurer pay to Robert Reith Fourteen Pounds Eleven shillings and Eight Pence as Messenger to the Governor & Council to the 23ᵈ Inst. & also the further Sum of Eight Pounds per Accᵗ passed by the Depʸ Aud.

That the said Treasurer pay to Jonathan Parker Eighty two Pounds ten shillings Balᵃ of Account passed by the Depʸ Aud.

That the said Treasurer pay to Lieut. John Hardman of the 2ᵈ Regimᵗ Three thousand Dollars to be expended in the Recruiting Service, he being appointed and having Genᵗ Smallwoods Instructions of the 9ᵗʰ April for that purpose.

That the said Treasurer pay to Lieut John Hardman seventy two Pounds for the use of William Veazey 3ᵈ due him per Accᵗ passed by the Depʸ Aud.

That the said Treasurer pay to Thomas Johnson junʳ out of the money sent by Congress for the purchase of Wheat & flour, Forty thousand Pounds to be sent and charged to Samuel Gilpin of Cecil County & to be accounted for

That the said Treasurer pay to William Merrit, Thirty thousand Pounds to be by him delivered over to Colᵒ William Henry to be expended in the Purchase of Wheat and Flour and Accounted for

Ordered that the western shore Treasurer pay to Comᵒ Thomas Grason seven hundred and seventy four Pounds seven shillings and six pence on Account

That the said Treasurer pay to Colᵒ Joshua Beall Forty two Pounds, Eleven shillings and three pence and also the further Sum of Twenty six Pounds, Eleven shillings and three pence due him per Accounts passed by the Depʸ Aud

That the Armourer deliver to Richard Bryan 300 lbs Lead, & 500 Gun flints to be delivered over to Henry Hooper Lieut of Dorchester County for the use of said County

The Militia of Colᵒ Weems and Colᵒ Robinsons Battalions ordered to Annapolis having as represented to this Board by their Officers, shewed such a strong Desire to be discharged that there is too much Reason to belive that many of them will go to their Homes without if they do not obtain Permission some of them having already gone without Leave. This Board think it more advisable to discharge them for the present especially as they have no late Intelligence from whence it may be collected that the Enemy design up the Bay immediately if at all, And it is accordingly ordered that the said Militia be discharged for the present and proper Signals fix' and agreed on for their reassembling again at Annapolis

C. B. in Case of Alarm depositing before they depart the Arms &cᶜᵃ delivered to them

Commissions issued Trueman Skinner appᵈ Lieut Col⁰ John Dyer 2ᵈ Lieut. Richᵈ Clagett Ens. of Capt. Hezekiah Wheelers C⁰ Nicholas Miles 2ᵈ Lieut, Nicholas Brookes Ens. of Capt. Henry Hill junr C⁰ John H. Beanes Capt. in the room of Robert Bowie. Robert Baden 1 Lieut. Thomas Hoye 2ᵈ Lieut, Elextious Boone Ens. Benjamin Wales Capt. in the room of John Perry, Moses Orme 1 Lieut, Edward Lloyd Wailes 2ᵈ Lieut, William Grindle Ens. and Thomas Gautt junr 1 Lieut of Capᵗ Alexr Howard McGuden C⁰ belonging to the Lower Batt of Militia in Prince Georges County also to Josias Shaw Capt. in the room of Joseph Carlton, William Moore 1 Lieut, Thomas Boyd junr 2ᵈ Lieut, Richard Cramphin Ens. Thomas Beall Capt. in the room of Thoₓ Richardson Isaac Walker 1 Lieut, John Crow 2ᵈ Lieut, Richard Walker Ens. Jacob Duvall 1 Lieut, Thomas Lyles 2ᵈ Lieut, Mordecai Jacobs Ens. of Capt. Marsh M. Duvall's Co. Joseph Jones Capt. in the room of Henderson Magruder, Basil Belt 1 Lieut, Richard Lyles 2ᵈ Lieut, & Josiah Belt Ens. belonging to the Upper Batt of Militia in Prince Georges County and also to Joseph White Clagget Captain in the room of Humphry Belt, William Nicholls 1 Lieut, Edward Lanham Capt. in the room of John Cassey, Anthony Hardy 1 Lieut Richᵈ Claxon 2 Lieut, Nathaniel Wilson junr Ens and John Tinnerly 2 Lieut of Capt. Michⁱ Lower Co. in the Middle Batt of Militia in Prince Georges County

C. C.   [Council to H. Hooper.]

In Council Annapolis 24ᵗʰ May 1779

Sir

We have ordered you by Mr Bryan 300ˡᵇ Lead & 500 Flints; we cannot well spare any Powder from hence, having sent away all but what may eventually be necessary, and, considering that Baltimore would be the first Object, we have sent our Arms thither except about 600 Stand which we have kept here; the second Object, doubtless, of the Enemy, which may secure us against an Attack by a small Force only. We see by your Return 13ᵗʰ March, you had 3 Half Barrˡˢ & 5 Quarter Casks of good Musquet Powder & 165 good Musquets; these, with the common Guns in the Hands of the People, we hope will be fully sufficient against any little Parties which may land on your Shores and we cannot think its probable that you will have a more formidable Force to encounter

We are &cᵃ

Henry Hooper Esqr   }
   Lᵗ of Dorchester County }

FAMILY RECORD.

BIRTHS.	DEATHS.
Elizabeth Baden wife of John Baden born Sept. 2 1764 died Sept 25th 1835	William B. Walls the son of George Walls and Martha Walls
Benjamin B. Wall son of Geo. Wall and martha [illegible] departed this life Sept 16 1836 [aged] 35 years and [illegible]	Departed this life January 29th aged 30 1823
	George Walls father of the above departed this life 11th of May 1831 aged 79 years and 8 days
	[illegible] Walls the son of George Walls and martha Walls departed this life January 15th 1835 aged 27

June 26, 1939.

BA-J/ady
George Walls
W.8973

Mrs. Hale Houts
44 East Concord
Kansas City, Missouri

Dear Madam:

Reference is made to your letter relative
to George Walls, a soldier of the Revolutionary
War.

The data contained herein were obtained
from the papers on file in the Revolutionary War
claim for pension, W.8973, based upon the military service of George Walls in that war.

George Walls was born February 14,1752,
place, and the names of his parents are not
designated.

While a resident of Charles County,Maryland,
George Walls enlisted July 37, 1776 and served
six months as private and sergeant under Captain
Belain Posey in the Flying Camp. He enlisted and
served as private in Captain Gaither's Company,
Colonel Smallwood's Maryland Regiment; was in the
battle of Yorktown and at the surrender of Corn-
wallis and was discharged December 10, 1781,having
served two months and five days.

He died May 11, 1831, place not given.

Soldier married March 28, 1784, in Prince
Georges County,Maryland, Martha Naylor. She was
born February 14, 1762, place, and the names of
her parents are not designated.

Soldier's widow, Martha Walls,was allowed
pension on her application executed June 31,1845,
at which time she was a resident of Prince Georges
County,Maryland.

In 1845,George N. Wall, son of soldier and
Martha,was living in Prince Georges County,Maryland.

The following names of the children of
George and Martha Walls are shown:

Margaret Baden Walls born January   30,1787,married Josiah Wilson,
                                           January 30,1817.
Jane N. Walls   "   May   23,1791.
William Batson"   "   July   3,1793,died January 29,1823.
George Naylor "   "   August   22,1796,married Sarah Club,
                                           January 30,1824.
Naylor Davis Walls" November 13,1798,died January 15,1835.
Benjamin Baden " " July   6,1801,died September 16,1836.
Elizabeth Ann Walls" November 11,1803.
Martha Ann Walls "   March   18,1807.

Said Benjamin Baden Walls married Elizabeth Harvey,
July 30, 1835. Their daughter Martha Ann Rebecca Walls,
was born June 10, 1836.

The following family data are (also) shown:

Elizabeth Baden wife of John Baden, born September
2, 1784 and died September 25, 1835.

There are no further family data.

In order to obtain the date of last payment of
pension, the name of person paid and possible the death
date of the widow, you should apply to the Comptroller
General, General Accounting Office, Records Division,
Washington, D. C., and cite the following data: "Martha
Walls, widow of George Walls, Certificate No.7142,issued
July 16, 1845,rate $27.22 per annum, commenced March 4,
1843, Acts of March 3, 1843 and June 17, 1844, Maryland
Agency".

               Very truly yours

               A. D. HILLER
               Executive Assistant
               to the Administrator

FAMILY RECORD.

BIRTHS.	BIRTHS

George Wall born 7th day 1752 —

Martha Wall wife George Wall born on the 14th day February 1762 —

Margaret Baden Walls daughter of George wall and Martha their wife born 30th Jan'y 1787 —

Jane N Walls as above born 23 May 1791 —

William Baien Walls Born as above 3rd July 1795 —

George Naylor walls Born as above 22 day August 1796 —

Naylor Davies Walls as above born the 12th November 1798 —

Benjamin Baden Walls as above born 6th July 1801

Elizabeth Ann Walls as above born on the 11th day of November 1803 —

Martha Ann Walls born on the 18th day of march 1807.

Martha Ann Rebecca Walls daughter of Benj B Walls and Polly Smith their wife born June 18 1836

JOHN BADEN

SIDE: CONFEDERATE
ROLL: M598_25
ROLL TITLE: SELECTED RECORDS
OF THE WAR DEPARTMENT RELATING
TO CONFEDERATE PRISONERS OF
WAR 1861-1865

SOURCE INFORMATION: WWW.ANCESTRY.COM DATABASE: CIVIL WAR PRISONER OF WAR RECORDS, 1861-1865

Index

Index